NATIONAL PARLIAMENTS AND THE EUROPEAN UNION

NATIONAL PARLIAMENTS AND THE EUROPEAN UNION

edited by

PHILIP NORTON

FRANK CASS ● LONDON

First published 1996 in Great Britain by
FRANK CASS AND COMPANY LIMITED
Newbury House, 900 Eastern Avenue,
London IG2 7HH, England

and in the United States of America by
FRANK CASS
c/o ISBS, 5602 N.E. Hassalo Street
Portland, Oregon 927213-3640
[half title]
Copyright © 1996 Frank Cass & Co. Ltd

British Library Cataloguing in Publication Data

National Parliaments and the European Union
I. Norton, Philip
328.3
ISBN 0-7146-4691-1

Library of Congress Cataloging-in-Publication Data

National Parliament and the European Union / edited by Philip Norton.
p.   cm.
"First appeared in a special issue of the Journal of legislative studies, vol. 1, no. 3 (autumn 1995)"—T.p. verso.
Includes bibliographical references and index.
ISBN 0-7146-4691-1 (cloth)
1. Legislative bodies—European Union countries. 2. European Union. I. Norton, Philip.
JN94.A71N37   1995
328'.094—dc20
95-24867
CIP

This group of studies first appeared in a Special Issue of
The Journal of Legislative Studies, Vol.1, No.3 (Autumn 1995),
[National Parliaments and the European Union].

Printed in Great Britain by
Antony Rowe Ltd, Chippenham, Wiltshire

Contents

Introduction: Adapting to European Integration

PHILIP NORTON

The European Union came into being on 1 November 1993. It was the product of more than 40 years of institutional development towards the political and economic integration of the countries of western Europe. That development has had profound implications for the national institutions of the Member States. This volume is devoted to studying how one institution has adapted to the moves towards European integration. That institution is the national Parliament.

The Parliament is an intrinsic part of the national law-effecting process. The assent of Parliament legitimises a measure. It renders it the law of the land. The assent of Parliament in most Member States is necessary for all or most measures if they are to have binding applicability within the State. In most cases it is not sufficient. The assent of the Head of State is also required. In some cases it is not necessary. The Executive may be vested with powers under the Constitution to issue orders that have the force of law. Such exceptions do not invalidate the statement that parliaments are an intrinsic part of the national law-effecting process. All fulfil the defining role of a legislature – the giving of assent on behalf of citizens to measures that are to have binding applicability – and a number of other tasks that derive from the fact that they are parliaments.[1] The parliaments in western Europe have had some modest impact on the content of legislation. They have generally formed what I have elsewhere categorised as policy-influencing legislatures (see Figure 1). One or two, notably the Italian and the Dutch, have formed particularly strong legislatures of this type, the former coming close to occupying the category of a policy-making legislature.[2] Some, notably the French and the Irish, have formed weak policy-influencing legislatures.[3] None, though, occupies the category of a legislature with little or no policy affect.

The parliaments also serve as important means of maintaining consent for the political system.[4] Each is elected. Election determines not only the

Philip Norton is Professor of Government at the University of Hull. For reading and commenting on an earlier draft of this paper, he is especially grateful to Mark Shephard and Martin Westlake. The papers in this volume are the product of a research project funded by a grant [SOC/100(235)] from the Nuffield Foundation. The contributors are grateful to the Foundation for its support.

FIGURE 1

TYPES OF LEGISLATURE

Policy-making legislature

Can modify or reject policy brought forward by the executive, and can formulate and substitute policy of its own

Policy-influencing legislature

Can modify or reject policy brought forward by the executive, but cannot formulate and substitute policy of its own

Legislature with little or no policy affect

Can neither modify or reject policy brought forward by the executive, nor formulate and substitute policy of its own

Source: P. Norton, 'Parliament and Policy in Britain: The House of Commons as a Policy Influencer', *Teaching Politics*, 13 (2), 1984, p. 201.

composition of the Parliament but also, wholly or (in the case of France) in part, the composition of the Government. When electors go to the polls they are, in effect, voting for the party they wish to be in government. Through their activities, such as errand running on behalf of electors, members of the Parliament may help maintain or enhance popular support for the system. Levels of popular confidence in parliaments, as in national institutions generally, can and do vary over time and from country to country – in some cases, accompanied by pressure for institutional change – but levels of participation in parliamentary elections have generally remained high.

THE EFFECT OF MEMBERSHIP

It would seem plausible to hypothesise that, given these characteristics of west European legislatures, the effect of membership of the European Community, now the European Union, would be profound. The treaties establishing the Community accorded no formal role to national parliaments. They created a law-making process that is *sui generis*.

The principal bodies created under the original treaties were, and remain, the Commission and the Council of Ministers. 'The Commission provides the initiatives for Community development and integration, whereas the Council ... ensures that the rate of progress is acceptable to the governments of the Member States.'[5] The Commission comprises full-time officials, headed by Commissioners drawn from each of the Member States but required to renounce national allegiances. The Council of Ministers comprises ministers from every member government, each meeting drawing together the ministers with responsibility for the sector involved, such as transport or agriculture.

A European Assembly was also established under the original treaties. Though from 1962 onwards it titled itself the European Parliament, its role in the law-making process was an advisory one. The Commission was principally responsible for formulating measures and the Council for approving them. The comments of the Assembly were invited but had persuasive force only. The Council could choose not to act upon them. Nor was the Assembly the only body that had to be consulted. The Economic and Social Committee, made up of representatives of employers, trade unions and consumers, had to be consulted on proposals relating to economic and social affairs.

The Assembly differed initially from national parliaments not only in terms of its formal role but also in that it was not directly elected. Members were nominated by national parliaments from among their own members. Though, in line with its treaty obligations, the Assembly first made proposals for direct elections as early as 1960, it was many years before the Council of Ministers was able to agree to common provisions, the first direct elections taking place in 1979.

The Assembly thus had very limited powers but it was nonetheless accorded some role under the original treaties. National parliaments were accorded no such role. They were not required to be consulted, let alone to give assent to measures enacted by the Community. Under the terms of membership, *regulations* were to have the immediate force of law within Member States. *Directives* were to be binding as to the result to be achieved, but with the national authorities being left to determine the form and method. Where deemed to form part of the national authorities, parliaments could play a role in determining how directives were to be implemented, but they were not empowered to negate them. Nor were the parliaments involved in legitimising the EC law-making process, other than tangentially. Ministers were the representatives of the national governments, and the national governments derived their popular legitimacy from elections to the national parliament. But the real driving body behind the formulation of EC law – the Commission – was not elected. And there was no direct link between national parliaments and the law-making process. Each national parliament could seek to influence, even determine, the stance taken by the minister in the Council of Ministers and seek, through its members in the European Assembly, to influence the content of EC measures, but each ultimately lacked any formal power to say 'aye' or 'nay' to a measure enacted by the institutions of the EC under the provisions of Community treaties.

The position of national parliaments has been further affected by a number of developments consequent to the original treaties, most notably the direct election of the European Assembly in 1979, the White Paper on the Internal Market in 1985, the implementation of the Single European Act in 1987 and the implementation of the Treaty on European Union (the Maastricht Treaty) in 1993. The purpose of this volume is to consider how national parliaments have adapted to these moves towards greater European integration. Institutional adaptation, then, constitutes the dependent variable in our study. Our hypothesis is a simple one: that the response of national parliaments to the moves towards integration has been one of institutional change.

Let us first consider the development of the European Union and the various landmarks in that development that have had particular significance for the parliaments of the Member States.

THE DEVELOPMENT OF THE UNION

The years following the end of the Second World War saw pressures for some political and economic integration of the countries of Europe.[6] In the economic sphere, the first institutional realisation of this goal came in 1951 with the signing of the Treaty of Paris. The treaty created the European Coal and Steel Community, under which iron, steel and coal production in the member countries was placed under a common authority. Six countries were a party to the treaty: France, West Germany, Italy and the three Benelux countries (Holland, Belgium and Luxembourg). The United Kingdom, fearful of the element of supranational control, declined to participate in the treaty negotiations.

The six Member States took a further major step towards integration with the signing in 1957 of the Treaty of Rome. The treaty established Euratom and the European Economic Community (the EEC). Both came into being on 1 January 1958, Euratom being designed to develop a civil nuclear industry in Europe and the EEC intended to create a 'common market' for goods within the community of Member States. Each had a Commission and a Council of Ministers; the ECSC had equivalent bodies, though with a different balance of powers between them. In 1967 a Merger Treaty, agreed in 1965, took effect and unified the executive and legislative functions of all three bodies. It then became common to refer to the European Communities in the singular – the European Community (the EC).

The EC has witnessed further development with the ratification of a

number of treaties. Some of the treaties have provided breadth (enlargement) and others depth (greater integration of Community institutions
and powers). Treaties of accession have provided for enlargement. The
United Kingdom, Ireland and Denmark became members on 1 January
1973, the UK achieving membership more than a decade after it first
applied for entry. Greece became a member on 1 January 1981 and Spain
and Portugal became members on 1 January 1986. The most recent
recruits – Austria, Sweden and Finland – became members of the European
Union on 1 January 1995. Enlargement has important implications for the
very nature of the Union but does not bear directly on the focus of our
concern. Rather, it is the treaties providing depth that have had particular
implications for the parliaments of the Member States. The changes
having greatest significance can be grouped under three heads: direct
elections to the European Parliament, the Single Market and the SEA,
and the Treaty on European Union.

Direct Elections to the European Parliament

An Act signed in 1976, though not ratified until 1978, provided the legal
base for direct elections to the European Parliament. The Act did not
increase the powers granted to the EP. It did, though, affect national
parliaments in two ways. It ended the dependence of the EP on members
of national parliaments. It also gave the EP a direct democratic legitimacy,
derived from popular election, instead of an indirect legitimacy derived
from being composed of members of elected national parliaments. This
legitimacy was soon to be reinforced by a landmark ruling of the European
Court of Justice (the Isolucose Case).[7] Members of the EP were to use this
democratic legitimacy as the basis for pushing for more powers for the
Parliament.

The Single Market and the SEA

A Commission White Paper, *Completing the Internal Market*, was published in 1985. In large part the work of British EC Commissioner Lord
Cockfield, the White Paper identified a timetable and the measures
needed in order to complete a single market by 1992. The Paper was
approved by heads of state and government at the Milan European
Council in 1985. The completion of the internal market by 1 January 1993
was then embodied in the Single European Act (the SEA). Ratification of
the SEA created the means by which that market could be realised.

Signed in 1986 and taking effect in 1987, the SEA incorporated a
number of policy areas not included in the existing EEC treaty, including
the environment, health and safety, and economic and social cohesion.[8] It
also brought into being a new legislative procedure – the co-operation

procedure. Through the introduction of this procedure, the Act effected a shift in the power relationship *between* the national institutions of the Member States and the institutions of the Community, the latter being given much greater power. It also effected a shift in the relationship *between* the institutions of the Community, with the European Parliament acquiring a somewhat greater role and, for the first time, a positive role in the legislative process.

The co-operation procedure allowed the Council of Ministers, subject to certain restrictions, to take decisions by qualified majority voting, instead of on the basis of unanimity. With votes allocated to each country on the basis of size (the largest countries having ten votes each, other countries having fewer), 54 votes out of 76 were necessary in most (but not all) cases for a measure to pass. This meant that one country alone, even one of the big four (Germany, France, Italy and the UK, each with ten votes), could not block a measure. At least three countries had to group together in order to exercise a veto.

The European Parliament was also given a more significant role in those areas that fell within the domain of the co-operation procedure. After the Council adopted a 'common position' on a measure, the EP was empowered to consider it and to amend or reject it. The Commission then had to re-examine the proposal, taking account of the Parliament's views. The Council could then adopt the resubmitted proposal by a qualified majority but could only amend it or reinstate a proposal rejected by the EP by unanimity. Other powers were also conferred on the Parliament, including that of approving – by an absolute majority of members – the accession of new members to the Community. The Parliament also had bestowed upon it the title that it had assumed for itself in 1962. The Assembly was now officially a Parliament.

The areas covered by the co-operation procedure included, most crucially of all, most of the measures 'which have as their object the establishment and functioning of the internal market'. This provided enormous scope for the use of the procedure. The 1985 White Paper had identified approximately 300 measures that were necessary in order to achieve a single market. By the end of 1988, almost half of them had been implemented. By early 1992, the figure was three-quarters. Though not all were enacted by the deadline of 31 December 1992, most were in place by then.

The effect of the White Paper and the SEA was a significant extension of the involvement of EC institutions in issues previously resolved within a national context. Furthermore, this involvement was made possible through a procedure (qualified majority voting) that limited even further the scope for indirect influence by national parliaments. If a parliament persuaded, or even mandated, a minister to take a particular position in the Council of Ministers, that position could be rejected by the Council and another position adopted, one that the minister alone would be unable to veto. By increasing the powers of the European Parliament, the SEA served also to raise – not greatly, but raise nonetheless – the visibility of the Parliament. The Act thus rendered the European Parliament less marginal in EC law making while apparently having the effect of further marginalising national parliaments.

The Treaty on European Union

The Treaty on European Union – more popularly dubbed the Maastricht Treaty – was signed at Maastricht on 7 February 1992 and came into force on 1 November 1993 (having, like the Single European Act, run into problems of ratification). The Treaty created a Union under three pillars (the European Community, foreign and security policy, and justice and home affairs), established a timetable for achieving economic and monetary union, created a new Committee of the Regions, and introduced – under Article 189b – a new co-decision procedure. The co-decision procedure (also known as the negative assent procedure) strengthened the role of the European Parliament, with the Council and the Parliament having to agree a common position before legislating. Under the procedure, the Parliament cannot force the Council to adopt a measure the Council does not wish to adopt, but it can block the measure.[9] Though not applying generally as the European Parliament would have wished, the procedure was provided for in 15 Treaty articles and its scope, significantly, included most internal market legislation.[10]

The Treaty also embodied the principle of subsidiarity, stating that in areas outside its exclusive competence the Community 'shall take action ... only if and in so far as the objectives of the proposed action cannot be sufficiently achieved by the Member States and can therefore ... be better achieved by the Community'. This provision was seen by some, notably the German *Länder* and the British Government, as a means of limiting the centralising tendencies of the Community. Others took a different view, seeing it as a legitimation of the Community extending its reach. (The principle itself has been found to be capable of 30 separate meanings.)[11] Given that it may prove to be non-justiciable,[12] its main effect may be to invite conflict between national governments and Community institutions.

However, for the first time, heads of government also agreed some reference to the role of national parliaments. One declaration annexed to the Treaty – prompted by the British Government and enjoying the support of the EP and the Commission – encouraged 'the greater involvement of national parliaments in the activities of the European Union' through the exchange of information between the EP and national parliaments and through granting reciprocal facilities. Another declaration, of which the EP took a less positive view, invited the Conference of Parliaments to meet as necessary to be consulted 'on the main features of the Union', with the presidents of the Commission and the Council reporting to it. The Conference of Parliaments (also known as the *Assises*) comprised representatives of national parliaments and the EP. It had informally come into being following prompting by President Mitterrand, during the 1989 French Presidency of the EC, as well as by Commission President Jacques Delors and had spontaneously met once – in Rome, in November 1990 – in the run-up to the Maastricht Inter-Governmental Conference (IGC).

The two declarations thus encouraged greater involvement by national parliaments, both individually and collectively, though conferring no powers on the parliaments nor on the Conference of the Parliaments.

CHALLENGES

By 1994, then, national parliaments could be said to be facing three challenges. First, there was the challenge posed by greater integration of institutions of the Community. More and more law-making was taking place at the level of the Community and more powers were vested with the institutions of the Community. This challenge had existed since the creation of the EC but was exacerbated by subsequent treaty amendments. Second, there was the challenge posed by the explicit invitation embodied in the declarations appended to the Maastricht Treaty to be more involved in the activities of the Community. Even if national parliaments had not wanted or not felt able to be more involved in the Community decision-making process, they now were faced with an invitation to be more involved, individually and collectively, even though they had no formal place in the process itself. Third, there was the creation of the two new pillars of the Union. The decision-making under both pillars was to take place at inter-governmental level. In other words, outside the context of the Community and the increasingly integrated institutional process of the Community. Thus new and different decision-making arenas were created within the new European Union structure.

These challenges posed both normative and empirical questions for national parliaments. Should they attempt to play some role within the decision-making processes of the Union? Should the role they played in national decision-making not be transferred to the European level? Or should that role be taken over instead by the European Parliament? Or should there be some shared, or co-operative, role played by national parliaments and the EP? If the national parliament should play some role within the Union, how and to what extent could it do so?

ADAPTING TO MEMBERSHIP

How have national parliaments adapted to the challenges posed by the move towards greater integration? Our hypothesis is that they will have responded to the challenges by undertaking some institutional change. Our purpose is to test this basic hypothesis and, if validated, to draw out the nature and extent of such change and to address why change has taken place and why it has taken the form it has.

Our assumption is that a number of variables are likely to have shaped the institutional response to European integration. The more significant we assume to be as follows.

Constitutions

The provisions of constitutions vary. Some establish a unitary system of government, others a federal system. There is also variation at national level between the powers granted to Parliament and the executive. We know that in France, for example, the Parliament is significantly constrained by the constitution. We know that in the United Kingdom, under the doctrine of parliamentary sovereignty, no law passed by the Parliament can be set aside by any body other than Parliament itself. Different structures created by the various constitutions of Member States thus suggest the need for different responses in adapting to membership.

Culture

Political cultures vary across, and sometimes within, the Member States. Some cultures may exhibit no dominant tendency, with some sectors of society differing in their orientations to national institutions. Some cultures may be more accommodating than others to the concept of European integration. Some, likely to be but not necessarily the same as those favouring integration, may not have a strong positive orientation toward the national legislature. Other cultures may not be so accommodating and some may be marked by a strong attachment to the Parliament. Some cultures we would thus expect to be well able to adapt to the concept of European integration and all that such integration entails in terms of national institutions, while others we would expect to be less well able to adapt.

Parties and Party Systems

The nature of the political parties and party systems also has a bearing. Parties individually may have particular views on integration. In some countries, there may be a divergence of views between parties, in others a convergence. Conflict may be exacerbated or diminished by the nature of the party system. An adversarial system, characterised usually by two main competing parties and majoritarian government, may facilitate conflict. A multi-party system with coalition government may generate some agreement between coalition partners or a displacement of the issue from the political agenda. We would therefore expect some difference in responses as a result of the differing party systems within the Member States.

Parliamentary Norms and Practices

We would expect variables specific to legislatures to shape the institutional response. Legislatures which are specialised, utilising permanent committees, and have flexible timetables would, on the face of it, seem better able to adapt to the volume of EC legislation and the variable speed of the legislative process than those that process business primarily in the chamber and have rigid timetables. Newer legislatures may also be more willing to accept closer links and integration with members of the European Parliament than is the case with older legislatures, more conscious of their status and history.

Parliamentary Workloads

We would also expect the workloads of parliaments to have a bearing. Some do not have a mass of business to transact. Others have to deal with a great amount. Members individually may also have to cope with a large volume of work, especially in the case of those elected by constituencies. Localism is a feature of constituency representation in some systems. There is also evidence in some countries of increasing demands on members of parliament from constituents. If parliaments – and parliamentarians – are already heavily burdened with work, how will they be able to fit in time to consider European business? We would expect the most heavily burdened parliaments to have the greatest difficulty in adapting.

These variables are not mutually exclusive. Nor is the list exhaustive. Other country-specific variables may help shape the parliamentary response. The purpose of each chapter in this volume is to describe the response of the legislature to the pressures for integration and to identify the reasons for that particular response. We will then be in a position to know whether there has been a consistency in response or a marked disparity. If the latter, we may then have sufficient data to suggest not only why there is a disparity but also what the relationship is between different responses and the impact of EC policy and legislation. The purpose of this volume is analytic rather than prescriptive. But it may provide the basis for debate as to what the role of the national legislature should be in decision making within the European Union and, more especially, for identifying ways in which legislatures can seek to achieve most effectively the role ascribed to them.

NOTES

 1. See P. Norton, 'Introduction', in P. Norton (ed.), *Legislatures* (Oxford: Oxford University Press, 1990), pp.1–2.
 2. See P. Furlong, 'Parliament in Italian Politics', in P. Norton (ed.), *Parliaments in Western Europe* (London: Frank Cass, 1990), pp. 52–67, and, in the same volume, K. Gladdish, 'Parliamentary Activism and Legitimacy in the Netherlands', pp.103–19.
 3. See the chapters by Frears and Arkins in Norton, *Parliaments in Western Europe*, and P. Norton, 'The Legislative Powers of Parliament', in C. Flinterman, A.W. Heringa and L. Waddington (eds.), *The Evolving Role of Parliaments in Europe* (Antwerp: MAKLU, 1994), pp.15–32.
 4. See Norton, *Parliaments in Western Europe*.
 5. D.A.C. Freestone and J.S. Davidson, *The Institutional Framework of the European Communities* (London: Croom Helm, 1988), p.55.
 6. See, for example, D.W. Urwin, *The Community of Europe*, 2nd edn. (London: Longman, 1955), chapters 1–3.
 7. See M. Westlake, *A Modern Guide to the European Parliament* (London: Pinter, 1994), pp.24–5, 252.
 8. See J. Lodge, 'The European Parliament', in J. Lodge (ed.), *The European Community and the Challenge of the Future* (London: Pinter, 1989), pp.68–9.
 9. See D. Macrae, 'Institutional and Decision-Making Changes', in D. O'Keefe and P.M. Twomey (eds.), *Legal Issues of the Maastricht Treaty* (London: Wiley Chancery Law, 1994), pp.174–6.
10. Westlake, *A Modern Guide to the European Parliament*, pp.144–6.
11. J. Steiner, 'Subsidiarity under the Maastricht Treaty', in O'Keefe and Twomey, *Legal Issues of the Maastricht Treaty*, p.49. See also p.51.
12. See K. Bradley and A. Sutton, 'European Union and the Rule of Law', in A. Duff, J. Pinder and R. Pryce, *Maastricht and Beyond* (London: Routledge, 1994), pp.234–7. See also the contributions in Part 2: Subsidiarity, in O'Keefe and Twomey, *Legal Issues of the Maastricht Treaty*, pp. 37–83.

The German Houses of Parliament and European Legislation

THOMAS SAALFELD

In recent decades, German politics has been increasingly characterised by complex bargaining processes between national, sub-national and supranational actors as well as the European Union (EU) as a transnational actor. While the process of European integration has generally benefited the Federal Republic of Germany, it has also caused problems of government efficiency and democratic legitimacy.[1] Due to the relative weakness of the European Parliament and the need to incorporate EU directives into German law, the Bundestag and Bundesrat, as the two Houses of Parliament, retain an important role as a check at least on the German Federal Government's activities in the EU. Both chambers are crucial for the legitimisation of EU policy. Indeed, as the German Federal Constitutional Court maintained in its 1993 ruling, the legitimacy of EU policy stems *primarily* from the authority it is given by the national parliaments.[2] There is widespread agreement, however, that the Bundestag's and Bundesrat's capacity to fulfil this function of legitimisation of EU policy is severely constrained.[3]

The political importance of the issue is in sharp contrast with the low degree of public awareness of its implications. While fears of loss of national sovereignty have come to the surface of public discourse during the 1980s and 1990s and resistance of certain groups (such as farmers) against EU policy has increased, policy-making in the European Union has never been a *major* issue of public controversy in Germany. Awareness of the way the Bundestag and Bundesrat scrutinise European Union policy is largely restricted to certain elite segments (interest groups, government officials, party leaders, federal-state governments and bureaucrats). This is not necessarily a specifically German feature but it contrasts with the higher degree of public awareness of the EU in Britain or Denmark, for example. One of the reasons for this lack of controversy is that the question of parliamentary sovereignty has never been of great significance. Unlike in Britain, where parliamentary sovereignty is a major pillar of constitutional theory, the German Basic Law (Article 24) explicitly permits the transfer of sovereign rights to international

Thomas Saalfeld is Lecturer in Political Sociology at the Dresden University of Technology.

organisations. Moreover, joining the European Coal and Steel Community (ECSC) and, later, the European Economic Community and Euratom was a step-by-step process for the Federal Republic, whose direction and pace could be influenced by the Federal Government. Britain, by contrast, joined the three Communities which had already been in operation for a quarter of a century. Moreover, for Germany, joining the ECSC did not imply a significant loss of sovereignty. Rather, it represented a means of regaining sovereignty over industries in which the allied occupying powers held important controlling powers. The lack of public awareness is a consequence also of a lack of any party political conflict over EU matters. Although some extreme right-wing parties have attempted to instrumentalise the issue in their attempt to build up a broader support base, and despite the fact that some mainstream political leaders have expressed concern over a European currency or suggested different degrees of integration for different countries, there is a high degree of consensus amongst the German political elite as to the desirability and inevitability of further European integration. The issue of European integration does not divide government and opposition, nor does it cause any intra-party divisions like in the British House of Commons.[4]

In this article, the nature of, and the German Parliament's responses to, the process of European integration will be identified and evaluated. The chapter will be a review of existing literature. The approach will be largely historical and descriptive.[5] The focus will be on the Bundestag and, to a lesser extent, on the Bundesrat. Federal-state parliaments (*Landtage*) will not be considered. Some other important actors such as the political parties and their attempts to link the domestic and European arenas cannot be specifically dealt with due to constraints of space.[6]

THE LEGISLATIVE PROCESS IN GERMANY

There are two national law-making bodies in the German political system: the Bundestag (Federal Diet) and the Bundesrat (Federal Council). The Bundestag is directly elected by the people and represents the principle of parliamentary government – the Federal Chancellor is chosen by, and responsible to, the Bundestag. The Bundesrat, by contrast, represents the interests of the federal-state (*Länder*) governments. The Chamber consists of delegates sent and instructed by the federal-state governments. It is concerned with the regional dimension of government, 'by which is meant not only geographical aspects but also the fact that the Laender are responsible for administering much of the body of federal legislation'.[7]

The bulk of German legislation is federal, while policy implementation is largely the responsibility of the federal states and their bureaucracies. Thus, the Federal Government 'has relatively little to do with controlling the vast bureaucratic apparatus, and relatively more to do with policy development'.[8] This is also reflected in the Bundestag's activities both on domestic and EU matters: the chamber is largely preoccupied with legislation. Scrutiny of policy implementation is less important than in other parliaments.

Both Bundestag and Bundesrat mainly work through their specialised standing committees which have a division of labour largely running parallel to that of the federal ministries. The Bundestag's departmental standing committees have a relatively large degree of autonomy from the Plenum. Their agendas may include matters within their jurisdiction that have not been specifically referred by the House as a whole (*Selbstbefassungsrecht*). This watchdog function is combined with the minute discussion of legislative drafts. The Bundesrat's operations are even more strongly dominated by committee work than the Bundestag's. Specialised examination of proposed legislation is usually carried out by officials from the federal states. 'The effect of this is to leave most scrutiny – except on politically controversial matters ... to civil servants. These Laender officials are able to bring specialist knowledge to committee sessions, since they are frequently responsible for the administration of legislation.'[9]

The Basic Law defines the legislative powers of both the Federation and the federal states. Article 31 of the Basic Law stipulates that, in principle, 'Federal law overrides federal-state law'. The Federation (that is, the Bundestag) has exclusive legislative powers in certain policy areas laid down in Article 73 of the Basic Law. The Basic Law also specifies areas of concurrent legislation (Articles 74 and 74a) where the Federation has the power to legislate under certain conditions defined in Article 72. Moreover, Article 75 of the Basic Law enumerates areas where the Federation can pass 'Framework Laws' (*Rahmengesetze*) that constrain the federal states' freedom to legislate in some areas. Finally, there are policy areas known as 'joint tasks' (*Gemeinschaftsaufgaben*) under Article 91a of the Basic Law (for example, regional economic development) where the Federation participates in federal-state legislation. The federal states, by contrast, enjoy exclusive legislative powers in the policy areas of education, culture and police affairs. Moreover, they have the power to legislate in those policy areas which are not defined under the Basic Law as (a) exclusive federal domain, (b) areas for framework legislation or (c) areas of concurrent legislation where the Federation has a right to legislate. The federal states also have the power to initiate federal legislation through the Bundesrat. However, only 3.3 per cent of all Acts of Parliament passed between 1949 and 1994 originated in the Bundesrat.[10] More important than the Bundesrat's initiatives are the Chamber's powers to veto the Federation's legislation under certain conditions. In the case of so-called 'consent laws' (*Zustimmungsgesetze*, that is, laws that require the Bundesrat's consent), the Bundesrat has an absolute veto. It has a suspensory veto over 'simple laws' (*einfache Gesetze*). A suspensory Bundesrat veto can be overturned by an absolute majority of the Bundestag. If a simple bill is rejected by the Bundesrat with a two-thirds majority, the suspensory veto can only be overturned if at least two-thirds of the Bundestag members present, and at least 50 per cent of the total number of the Bundestag members, reject the veto. The policy areas where the Bundesrat has an absolute veto are defined in the Basic Law. They include amendments to the Basic Law, all laws affecting the relationship between Federation and federal states (including federal-state finance), the relationship between the Federation's administration and federal-state administrations, declaration of the state of emergency and war as well as delegated legislation. In practice, more than one-half of all federal laws, and the vast majority of important domestic laws are consent laws. In the case of disputes between Bundestag and Bundesrat majorities, a conference committee can be appointed to resolve the disagreements. Mediation has usually been successful. Between 1949 and 1990, only 40 absolute Bundesrat vetos were upheld after mediation in the conference committee.[11]

THE EFFECT OF EC/EU MEMBERSHIP ON THE GERMAN PARLIAMENTARY DEMOCRACY

For both Houses of Parliament, EC/EU membership has meant a loss of powers. The Bundestag has lost legislative powers in areas such as economic policy, trade policy, tariff policy and agricultural policy. It has no direct or authoritative power over the transnational policy-making process under EU jurisdiction. In addition, the Federal Government's advantage in information on EU developments is even greater than its superiority in domestic legislation. The Council of Ministers meets in private. Information on the Federal Government's behaviour in the transnational bargaining processes is incomplete. 'Package deals' (log-rolling) are not uncommon. All these factors make it difficult for national parliaments to call 'their' government to account for a particular EU decision.[12] Lack of time and the general workload of the committees caused by domestic legislation have aggravated this problem. In addition, the willingness and capacity of committee specialists to *transmit* their expertise to the parent chamber, and to the general public, has been relatively low. Unlike the Bundesrat, the Bundestag has not even instituted a debate of the Federal Government's six-monthly Report on European Integration. Thus, what Walter Bagehot called the 'teaching' and 'informing' functions of parliament[13] have been neglected by the Bundestag in the context of EC/EU affairs.

As for the federal states represented by the Bundesrat, there has clearly been a marked 'shift in the Bund-Laender power balance as a result of German accession to the three European Communities'.[14] As early as 1976, the Inquiry Commission on Constitutional Reform (*Enquête-Kommission Verfassungsreform*) criticised Article 24 of the Basic Law under which the Federation has the right to transfer federal-state powers to transnational bodies by passing a simple Act of the Bundestag – without the consent of the Bundesrat.[15] The European Community treaties did not contain any provisions allowing the direct participation of the federal states in the European policy-making process. The Advisory Council of Regional and Local Bodies established in 1988 was not a formal organ of the European Community. Although it was entitled to advise the Commission on issues of regional policy, it did not have significant powers of its own.[16] Thus, in effect, there was a fundamental shift of power resulting

> from the fact that policy areas in which the Bundesrat had held legislative power were now decided on in the framework of the Council of Ministers. Only the federal government could represent German interests in that forum, with the result that it had received powers at the expense of the Laender level which had previously possessed them.[17]

The federal states experienced losses where the Basic Law grants them exclusive legislative powers, where the federal states and the Federation have concurrent legislative powers, where the federal states are required to legislate within a federal framework law (*Rahmengesetz*) or where Federation and federal states share legislative responsibilities in so-called 'joint tasks'. As Bulmer notes, the extent of the loss of power depends on the nature of EU legislation. Regulations are binding, whilst directives leave some room for federal-state participation in 'the choice of form and methods' of achieving the directive's objective. In any case, given that most EU legislation is implemented by the German federal states, it has been problematic that the federal states

> may have no say in the formulation of legislation which they must implement. This is a clear difference from the situation in a unitary state, such as Great Britain, where EC legislation is implemented

almost exclusively by central government which, of course, is represented fully in the Council of Ministers, the EC's decision-making organ.[18]

THE SCRUTINY OF EC/EU LEGISLATION, 1957–1994

Information and Participation

When the Treaty of Rome was ratified in 1957, Article 2 of the Act of Ratification passed by the Bundestag merely stipulated that the Federal Government

> shall keep the Bundestag and the Bundesrat continually informed of developments in the Council of the European Economic Community and in the Council of the European Atomic Energy Community. Insofar as a decision of a Council requires the making of a German Law or has immediate force of law in the Federal Republic of Germany, notification should be made prior to the Council making its decision.[19]

Between 1957 and 1992, the Bundestag's and Bundesrat's procedures for the scrutiny of EC proposed legislation were based on the right to information which both Houses share under the provisions of Article 2 of the Act of Ratification of the Rome Treaties and subsequent treaties.

In practice, the process of informing the two Houses commences once the German Permanent Representation in Brussels has received a copy of the Commission's proposals via the Secretariat of the Council of Ministers. The Permanent Representation transmits such proposals to the Federal Ministry of Economic Affairs whose European Division has traditionally co-ordinated routine matters of (west) German EC/EU policy. The Bundestag is formally informed by the Chancellor's Office, but, in order to allow more time for parliamentary scrutiny, the Bundestag's Secretariat is, in practice, informed directly by the Ministry of Economic Affairs – simultaneously with the Chancellor's Office. Formal notice by the Chancellor's Office is supplied about a week later.[20]

The 'timeliness' of information is a major precondition of parliamentarians' ability to extract information on Government policy and transmit it to Parliament and the general public.[21] Although it is very infrequent that the Federal Government fails to inform the two Houses before the Council of Ministers makes a decision, timeliness has been one of the major problems in the scrutiny of EC/EU proposed legislation under Article 2. About 65 per cent (167 out of 256) EU regulations and directives debated on the Bundestag's floor between 1980 and 1986 were already in force at the time of the debate.[22] As Bulmer argues, the Bundestag and Bundesrat receive notice of EC proposals once they have been presented to the Council of Ministers. At this (relatively late) stage, the scope for incorporation of Parliament's viewpoint is extremely limited. Informing Parliament in advance of firm proposals would be impractical, since specialised scrutiny of the Commission's preparatory work is meaningless in the absence of a concrete proposal. The problem is aggravated by the fact that the Council of Ministers may refer the Commission's proposal to one of the Committee of Permanent Representatives' (COREPER) specialist working groups.

> In the latter case, it may be meaningless to report in detail on the Commission proposal, since it may be modified in subsequent COREPER meetings beyond all recognition. ... Of course, the timing problem can operate in reverse, with a decision being reached more rapidly than expected, such that neither the Bundestag nor the Bundesrat have the opportunity to register a view.[23]

During the 1986 revision of the Treaties of Rome, the *federal states* gained some concessions from the Federal Government concerning their information and participation. Under Article 2 of the Act of Ratification of the Single European Act, the Federal Government had the duty to inform the Bundesrat comprehensively on all EC proposals relevant to the federal states. The Bundesrat was given the right to express its view on these matters, and the Federal Government had the duty to take the Bundesrat's view into account when formulating its own position. The Federal Government was only entitled to ignore the view of the Bundesrat majority on matters within the Federation's exclusive legislative domain and/or if imperative considerations of foreign or integration policy were at stake.[24]

Since December 1992, the Bundestag's and Bundesrat's right to information has been codified in the Basic Law. This constitutional amendment was prompted by the Treaty on European Union (Maastricht Treaty) and the constitutional reforms necessitated by German unification. The most important constitutional innovation with regard to the European Union was the complete rewriting of Article 23 of the Basic Law which is now referred to as the 'Article on European Union'. The old Article 23 had specified one of the possible avenues to German national unification, stipulating how individual states could join the Federal Republic. It had become obsolete after the German unification had been completed. Article 24, which had previously served as the constitutional foundation for the transfer of competences to European Community institutions, was thought to be insufficient to accommodate the new quality of integration resulting from the Maastricht Treaty.[25] Article 23 now codifies the rights and powers of the Bundestag and the Bundesrat in European Union affairs. Moreover, the two Houses passed two statutes specifying in greater detail how the new Article 23 is to be implemented: (a) The 'Act on Cooperation between the Federal Government and the Bundestag in European Union Matters' (henceforth called 'Cooperation Act [Bundestag]') and (b) the 'Act on Cooperation between the Federation and the Federal States in European Union Matters' (hereafter called 'Cooperation Act [Federal States]').[26]

The new Article 23 of the Basic Law and the Cooperation Act (Bundestag) have sharpened some provisions of Article 2 of the Act of Ratification of the Treaty of Rome. The Federal Government has now the *constitutional duty* to inform the Bundestag and Bundesrat '*comprehensively*' and '*as early as possible*'. This duty refers to all proposals of the European Union that may have implications for the Federal Republic of Germany. Before a proposal is decided upon in the Council of Ministers, the Federal Government must give the Bundestag an opportunity to express a view. The Federal Government is then obliged to consider this view in the negotiations. Paragraph 4 of the Cooperation Act (Bundestag) specifies the duties of the Federal Government with respect to proposed European Union directives and regulations. The Federal Government has to inform the Bundestag immediately about the negotiations in the Council of Ministers and about its own position. This is not to say that the Federal Government was formally bound by a parliamentary vote. 'Taking the Bundestag's view into account' is, indeed, a 'nebulous' phrase (Ress)[27] and can mean anything between accepting the Bundestag's view, incorporating elements of it or ignoring it altogether, but explaining to the Bundestag why the Government has decided to take a different course of action.[28]

One of the most important consequences of the amendment of Article 23 of the Basic Law is that the Federal Constitutional Court (*Bundesverfassungsgericht*) is likely to become a more active player in the EU policy process. In its ruling of 12 October 1993 the Court indicates that it is willing to assume a crucial role in the enforcement of Article 23. The Court generally emphasised the fundamental role of the *national* parliaments for the democratic legitimacy of the European Union while the European Parliament – in its present form – is granted only a 'supporting' role. According to the Court no further extension of EU powers can be legitimately achieved without the consent of the Member States' national parliaments, since the legitimacy of EU policy depends crucially on the linkage of EU institutions with the national parliaments. It made it clear that Article 23 requires the participation of the Bundestag in all important aspects of Union policy.[29] The Court could declare further moves towards European integration unconstitutional if it believes the Houses of Parliament have not been involved adequately. This may strengthen Parliament's role considerably, especially as parliamentary minority parties and individual federal states could appeal directly to the Court. Whether the new constitutional provisions will alleviate the dilemmas of timing as identified above remains to be seen.

Bundestag Committees and the Union: From Experiments to Lasting Reform

The constitutional amendments of December 1992 also included the insertion of Article 45 (new) in the Basic Law, explicitly requiring the Bundestag to appoint a Standing Committee on European Union Affairs. Until 1991, the Bundestag had failed to appoint a permanent committee comparable to the one regularly appointed by the Bundesrat or the Danish Folketing. Proposed EC/EU legislation had, therefore, been dealt with within the framework of the traditional departmental standing committees.

The issue of committee referral in EU matters is regulated by Paragraph 93 of the Bundestag's Rules of Procedure. Upon receipt of an EU proposal the Bundestag's President – after consultations with the Council of Elders (*Ältestenrat*) – refers it to the specialised committee(s) considered appropriate. In the case of a multiple referral, the Bundestag's Secretariat may also consult with the chairmen and clerks of all potentially relevant committees.[30] Where referral to several committees takes place, one is nominated as committee-in-charge (*federführender Ausschuß*). All other committees have the subsidiary status of a joint-deliberating-committee (*mitberatender Ausschuß*).

> The committee-in-charge has the task of combining all committee reports into a coherent single one. The reports are then submitted to the Plenum where some specific recommendations are made .... The Plenum generally adopts the committee recommendations without debate, thus making Community business even more committee-orientated than general Bundestag business ... [31]

From the 1960s onwards, it has been evident that the Bundestag's committees not only faced problems of insufficient expertise and timing: there has also been a problem of co-ordinating committee activities. EU policies often cut across departmental boundaries. Despite the possibility of multiple referrals, the Bundestag committees have tended to deal with proposed EC/EU measures from a strictly departmental point of view. Therefore, it was felt necessary that a body to co-ordinate EC/EU-related activities be created. Between January 1965 and May 1967 a special body known as the Council of Elders for Integration (*Integrationsältestenrat*) was to fulfil these functions. Composed of senior members of the Bundestag, it referred EC proposals to the appropriate committees. However, as a body including delegates to the European Assembly, the Council was difficult to convene and aggravated the problems of timing noted above. Therefore, a new system of referral was developed. Before the first directly elected European Parliament was constituted in 1979, the Bundestag appointed a 'Commission of the Council of Elders on Matters Concerning the Cooperation between the European Parliament and the German Bundestag'.[32] In effect, the Secretariat of the Bundestag President now settled questions of committee referral in consultation with the Council of Elders (*Ältestenrat*), the Bundestag's main procedural steering committee, and the chairmen and clerks of the appropriate standing committees. This procedure did not, however, institutionalise co-ordination and information exchange with Members of the European Assembly/Parliament.

After the first direct elections to the European Parliament and the phasing out of 'dual mandates', it was felt that a new body was required that would not only co-ordinate the activities of the departmental standing committees but also maintain links with the European Parliament. This caused some technical problems. The idea of appointing an ordinary standing committee on European affairs was not accepted because – according to the Bundestag's Rules of Procedure – standing committees must be composed of members of the Bundestag. Thus, members of the European Parliament could not be included in a regular standing committee with equal rights. In 1983, the Bundestag therefore established a Commission for European Affairs (*Europakommission*) which largely took the form of an Inquiry Commission (*Enquête-Kommission*).[33] An Inquiry Commission may be composed of members of the Bundestag and non-parliamentarians who enjoy the same rights as the parliamentarians do. Traditionally, inquiry commissions have been set up to gather evidence and report to the Bundestag on issues of fundamental political importance. Their reports have often been of considerable academic value, yet their recommendations have had only a very limited impact. Most importantly, inquiry commissions do not have any direct influence on the legislative process. The Commission on European Affairs consisted of 11 members of the Bundestag and 11 members of the European Parliament. Its main tasks were to deal with, and report to the Bundestag on, fundamental issues of European integration, institutional problems of the European Communities and questions relating to the co-operation between the Bundestag and the European Parliament. The Commission on European

Community Affairs met 35 times between 1983 and 1986. It did not strongly influence the way the Bundestag dealt with European Union legislation. It was not given the right to make specific recommendations to the Bundestag Plenum, which remained the privilege of the regular specialised standing committees of the House. The Commission's initiatives and public statements received little public attention and were largely ignored in the political and administrative sphere.[34]

The Commission was not reappointed in the 1987–90 Bundestag. The opposition Social Democratic Party now proposed the creation of a Standing Committee on European Affairs. The Bundestag majority of CDU/CSU and FDP, however, was reluctant to appoint a regular committee and decided to replace the Commission on European Affairs with a sub-committee of the Committee on Foreign Affairs. The sub-committee consisted of 13 members. In addition, 13 German members of the European Parliament were invited to attend sub-committee meetings although they were given no right to make formal proposals or to vote.[35] The sub-committee considered all EC proposals that were referred to the Committee on Foreign Affairs and prepared the committee's recommendations; also, it was to consider all EC proposals of 'fundamental importance' and to co-ordinate the Bundestag's position on EC proposals that were referred to several standing committees.[36] Nevertheless, the establishment of a sub-committee turned out to be less than successful. The problem of timeliness remained a severe problem. Traditional standing committees could not establish the necessary links with the European Commission and the European Parliament. Closer liaison with the European Parliament, however, was increasingly important as the powers of the European Parliament were expanded through the Single European Act (1987). The specialised standing committees, looking at EC proposals from a strictly departmental perspective, were incapable of formulating coherent EC policies. The Sub-Committee on European Affairs could only operate within the jurisdiction of the Standing Committee on Foreign Affairs. Its activities were confined to matters explicitly referred to it by the Foreign Affairs Committee. Since the sub-committee itself did not have the power to make recommendations to the Plenum independently, all proposed recommendations had to be agreed by the Foreign Affairs Committee. The Foreign Affairs Committee was reluctant to grant too much of its scarce time to the discussion of matters raised by the Sub-Committee on European Affairs – especially questions that transcended the Foreign Affairs Committee's own jurisdiction.[37]

In June 1991, therefore, the parliamentary parties agreed to establish a regular Standing Committee on European Community Affairs.[38] The European Affairs Committee's jurisdiction includes the co-ordination of

European Community matters and liaison with the European Parliament. The committee consists of 33 members of the Bundestag and 11 German members of the European Parliament who are granted the status of 'observers' without the right to vote.[39] In the constitutional amendment of December 1992, the Standing Committee on European Union Affairs was given constitutional rank. Like the Standing Committees on Foreign Affairs, Petitions and Defence, the European Union Committee is now explicitly mentioned in the revised Basic Law (Article 45). The most important constitutional innovation, however, is the fact that the Bundestag may empower the European Affairs Committee to represent the whole House according to Article 23 of the Basic Law *vis-à-vis* the Federal Government. Comparable powers have not been granted to any other Bundestag committee. The Bundestag may now delegate its rights to information and its powers to the Committee. It can, however, recall these powers at any time. The Federal Government is now confronted with a unified 'clearing house' on the parliamentary side. Until December 1992, the Federal Government operated as a unified actor *vis-à-vis* the Bundestag which was divided along departmental lines. Each departmental standing committee could only communicate its views with, and obtain information from 'its' department. Integrating departmental considerations into a broader European policy was difficult. With the new European Affairs Committee, the Bundestag has a body which – like the Federal Government, the Chancellor's Office and the Foreign Office – is able to deal with German policy comprehensively.[40] Moreover, the problem of timing can be reduced through delegation of some of the Plenum's powers to the Committee. Since the Standing Committee on European Union Affairs can potentially decide for the Bundestag Plenum, decisions can be taken with greater speed. While efficiency could be enhanced, the problem remains that the deliberation of European Union business largely takes place in committee rooms. Little detailed information is conveyed to the Plenum and the general public.

It remains to be seen whether the new standing committee will have a greater impact than the Commission on European Affairs of 1983–87 or the Foreign Affairs Committee's sub-committee of 1987–90. Some scepticism seems to be justified. The Committee's responsibilities are far-reaching. They include changes of European treaties, institutional matters of the European Union, co-operation with the European Parliament and deliberation of EU legislation. However, there is one constraint: the departmental standing committees remain in charge of all matters within their jurisdiction. According to Ismayr, it has already become evident that the departmental standing committees are reluctant to leave the role of a committee-in-charge to the new Standing Committee on

European Union Affairs, at least as far as important EU-related matters are concerned. Thus, in practice, the Committee on European Union Affairs must still fight to establish its powers not only *vis-à-vis* the Federal Government but also *vis-à-vis* the departmental standing committees. One of the main issues in this context is whether the Committee is automatically granted the role of a committee-in-charge in European Union matters or whether it has to be content with the role of a joint-deliberating committee. Given initial rivalries, the Council of Elders agreed, on an experimental basis, that the Committee on European Union Affairs or any other standing committee can be appointed as a 'first joint-deliberating committee' (*erster mitberatender Ausschuß*) with a right to present its own report to the Plenum (without recommendations) and recommend amendments to the recommendations made by the committee-in-charge. The other joint-deliberating committees now have to convey their views not only to the committee-in-charge but also to the first joint-deliberating committee. It remains to be seen whether these changes will help to improve co-ordination and alleviate rivalries between committees.[41]

TABLE 1

INFORMATION TRANSMISSION TO THE BUNDESTAG PLENUM, 1983–90:
GROßE ANFRAGEN AND AKTUELLE STUNDEN

Type of Debate	1983-87 (10th Bundestag)	1987-90 (11th Bundestag)
Große Anfragen total	175	145
Große Anfragen on EC business	0	9
Aktuelle Stunden total	117	126
Aktuelle Stunden on EC business	1	2

Source: Calculated from Peter Schindler, *Datenhandbuch zur Geschichte des Deutschen Bundestages 1983 bis 1991* (Baden-Baden: Nomos, 1994), pp.945–60 and 964–81.

Generating expertise through specialised standing committees is one aspect of a parliament's informational efficiency. Transmission of the information extracted by experts to the chamber and to the general public is another dimension. Here, the Bundestag has not been very successful. As noted, the number of EC/EU proposals dealt with on the floor is relatively small. Although the Bundestag's Rules of Procedure provide various possibilities to debate European affairs on the floor of the House, the House has not used these opportunities frequently. Unlike the Bundesrat, there have been no regular Bundestag debates on the Federal Government's six-monthly Report on European Integration. With regard to EC/EU matters, the Bundestag has made little use of the various means of parliamentary interpellation which are at its disposal. Each parliamentary party (or a group of at least five per cent of the Members of the House) may demand a so-called '*Aktuelle Stunde*', an hour-long adjournment debate on a topic of current interest. Under the Bundestag's rules of procedure, the parliamentary parties can also submit written questions (*Kleine Anfragen*) and written questions followed by a short debate (*Große Anfragen*). Table 1 shows that European Affairs have not figured prominently amongst the topics selected for '*Aktuelle Stunden*' and '*Große Anfragen*' in the two legislative sessions between 1983 and 1990. Thus, the transmission of information through parliamentary debate in the Plenum remains deficient.

Sifting Procedures

From the late 1960s onwards, there was a feeling in the Bundestag of being inundated with EC proposals. Figure 1 illustrates the multiplication of EC/EU proposals from 13 in the 1957–61 Bundestag to more than 2,000 in the 1987–90 and 1990–94 Bundestag terms. This increase required the Bundestag to concentrate its time on 'politically important' documents. In 1977, the Bundestag introduced some procedural changes aiming at a reduction of the 'flood of papers'. These procedural reforms were codified in paragraph 93 of the Rules of Procedure in 1980.[42]

Since 1978, the respective committee-in-charge has decided whether an EC/EU proposal is to be printed and distributed as a parliamentary paper (*Bundestagsdrucksache*). This happens only if the committee decides to recommend a formal decision of the House. In practice, the decision whether a piece of proposed EU legislation is discussed in committee or in the Plenum rests with the parliamentary parties' permanent spokespersons on EU matters who have usually been appoin-ted within each committee since 1978, or the parties' foremen (*Obleute*) on the committee. If a committee has a sub-committee for European Union affairs (like the Budget Committee), the decision is made by this sub-committee. The bulk of EU documents is simply not considered with the consent of the responsible spokespersons. The spokespersons or foremen operate as gatekeepers. They receive the EU documents and additional information as early as possible. If they decide just to 'take note' of a document, it will simply not be considered by the committee or the Plenum. Only occasionally are EU documents printed and distributed as papers of the Bundestag *before* this selection process is completed.

FIGURE 1

EC/EU LEGISLATIVE PROPOSALS (VORLAGEN), 1957–1994

Number of Proposals

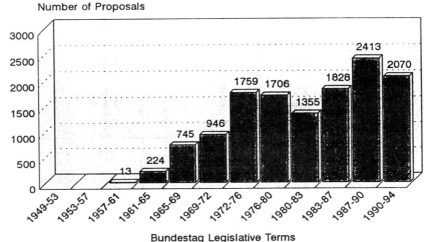

Bundestag Legislative Terms

Source: Thomas Saalfeld, 'Germany' in George Thomas Kurian and Lawrence D. Longley (eds.), *World Encyclopedia of Parliaments and Legislatures* (Washington, D.C.: Congressional Quarterly Press, 1995 [in press]), Table 3 (with further references).

Committee recommendations on EC/EU matters have been rare. In the eleventh Bundestag (1987–90), a recommendation was made in 167 out of 2,413 cases (less than seven per cent). The Bundestag Plenum routinely follows the committee recommendation. Motions to amend a committee recommendation are exceptional.[43]

The Bundesrat

Unlike the Bundestag, the Bundesrat has had a special Standing Committee on European Affairs since 1957. The Special Committee for the Common Market and Free Trade Zone established in 1957 was succeeded by a Committee for European Community Affairs in 1965. In 1988, a 'Chamber for European Community Proposals' was introduced. In 1992 a 'Chamber for European Affairs' was established, which has the power to decide for the Bundesrat (Article 52 [3a] of the Basic Law). The Bundesrat Committees for European Community Affairs have rarely carried out their own scrutiny. They have mainly combined the departmental standing committees' reports. The federal states have agreed on a functional division of their expertise. Particular federal states are given responsibility for a specific policy area with a second giving assistance. The federal state 'in charge of' a particular policy area in the EU Affairs

Committee decides whether it feels a proposal should be subject to detailed committee scrutiny. This type of sifting results in about half the EC proposals receiving scrutiny.[44] The Bundesrat's consideration of EU matters is carried out largely by senior civil servants of the federal-state governments. Federal-state ministers occasionally attend Bundesrat committee meetings, especially when major 'political' issues are considered. The Bundesrat's involvement on EU proposals 'is – as on all matters – characteristically of an administrative-technical nature. . . . That Bundesrat committees are able to make an effective specialist contribution is due to the large number of Laender civil servants whose advice may be drawn upon'.[45]

As was noted above, the federal states managed to negotiate a legally binding statement of their rights to information and participation on EC matters during the ratification process of the Single European Act. The provisions of Article 2 of the Act of Ratification of the Single European Act gave the federal states a right to participate, even if not on equal terms, in the negotiations over the Maastricht Treaty. During the Maastricht negotiations, the federal states had two major objectives: first, to increase their immediate influence on EU policy-making through (a) the establishment of a Regional Committee at the level of the European Union and (b) the right of participation of federal-state representatives in the meetings of the Council of Ministers. Second, to increase their indirect influence through a firmer commitment of the Federal Government to Bundesrat positions, in cases where the federal states' interests are affected and the Bundesrat has formulated a view. The federal states were moderately successful on both counts. The Maastricht Treaty established a Committee of the Regions representing the interests of regional and local bodies throughout the Union. Although this body has only advisory powers, it must be heard in certain policy areas. The German federal states consider the Committee of the Regions as a first step towards a Regional Chamber with significant powers. According to Article G No. 43 of the Maastricht Treaty, members of the federal-state governments will be allowed to represent the Federal Republic in the Council of Ministers, if federal-state interests are affected. From the federal states' viewpoint this is a major step forward since, until 1992, only representatives of the central governments were allowed to participate in the meetings of the Council of Ministers. Finally, the new Article 23 (1) of the Basic Law confirms the principles of federalism (in the German sense) and subsidiarity, thus protecting the powers and interests of the federal states. In the future, the Federation can only transfer legislative powers to the European Union with the consent of the Bundesrat, regardless of whether or not the federal states' interests are directly affected.[46]

The extent of the Bundesrat's power to commit the Federal Government to a certain course of action in the Council of Ministers now depends on the domestic distribution of legislative powers. This principle is codified in Article 23 and is intended to be a safeguard against any further shifts in the balance of power between the Federation and the federal states. In all policy areas where the Basic Law attributes exclusive legislative powers to the Federation, the Bundesrat's view has to be 'taken into account', if the federal states' interests are affected. However, the Bundesrat's view *does not* bind the Federal Government in these areas. The same is true for those areas of concurrent legislation and framework legislation where federal legislation is necessary and the Federation effectively has the right to legislate. If, however, EU legislative proposals fall into policy areas where the Basic Law attributes exclusive legislative powers to the federal states, or where the Basic Law does not attribute exclusive legislative powers to the Federation, the Bundesrat's vote can, in effect, bind the Federal Government. There are two restrictions, however. The right to commit the Federal Government to a certain course of action in the Council of Ministers applies only to EU proposals affecting the federal states' powers on a crucial point ('im Schwerpunkt'). Moreover, the Bundesrat's vote binds the Federal Government only in those parts of the proposed measure that affect the federal states' interests directly. The federal states' vote does not bind the Federal Government with respect to the whole measure. In the case of a dispute between the Federal Government and the Bundesrat, the Bundesrat's vote is binding for the Federation, if the Bundesrat confirms its position with a two-thirds majority.[47] If a matter falls under exclusive federal-state jurisdiction, Article 23 (6) stipulates that the right to represent the Federal Republic shall be transferred to a representative of the federal states, who is to be appointed by the Bundesrat.

The federal states' and the Bundesrat's influence over the Federation's policy in the European Union has been strengthened. Thus, the Federal Republic's policy in EU Affairs will have to be based on a broader political consensus. The Federal Government's room for manoeuvre will be much more circumscribed than prior to 1992. On the other hand, this may have negative implications for political efficiency and the scope for further moves towards European integration. Goetz and Cullen argue, for instance, that the amendment of Article 23

> eats into the Federal Government's traditional monopoly of representation of the Federal Republic on the international plane by allowing Länder government representatives to sit and speak for Germany in the Council of Ministers ... The new clause threatens to weaken the coherence of German European policy ... .[48]

Moreover, the less than precise wording of Article 23 and the Cooperation Act (Federal States) poses considerable legal problems of interpretation especially of the Bundesrat's rights of participation. According to Ress, therefore, 'these provisions are little more than a recipe for future conflicts, which the Federal Constitutional Court will have to settle.'[49]

ANALYSIS AND CONCLUSIONS

The European policy-making process is characterised by a high degree of uncertainty about the relationship between policies and outcomes. From a national Parliament's viewpoint, this uncertainty is largely due to the scope and complexity of the legislation and a high number of relevant players in the policy process. The expertise available to some of these players extends the national Parliament's expertise significantly. Since some of these players have competing interests, they tend to use their information strategically. For the national Parliament, therefore, the major challenge is to generate sufficient independent expertise to fulfil its functions of scrutiny and influence. A significant reduction of uncertainty, and sufficient knowledge on the information available to other players, is necessary for the national parliaments to make a meaningful contribution to the European policy process and hold the national Government to account for its position in the Council of Ministers, the EU's main decision-making body.

The most important attempts to improve the flow of information between the Federal Government and the two Houses of Parliament have been the 1991–92 reforms codifying both Houses' right to information in the Basic Law and establishing a new Standing Committee on European Union Affairs in the Bundestag. The Bundestag Standing Committee has been given considerable powers which may prove to be an incentive for Members of Parliament to devote more time and other resources to the scrutiny of EU legislative proposals. Its powers to act for the Bundestag may also mitigate the problem of timeliness. Under Article 2 of the Act of Ratification of the Rome Treaties (1957), the Federal Government had always had the duty to inform both Houses of Parliament on all proposals submitted to the Council of Ministers. The 1992 constitutional amendments have codified the Government's duty to inform both Houses of Parliament 'comprehensively' and 'as early as possible'. Whether this legal reform will improve and speed up the flow of information between Government and Parliament remains to be seen in the future. The constitutional codification has certainly strengthened the position of Bundestag parliamentary parties (for example, one of the opposition parties) and individual federal-state governments which now can appeal directly to the

Federal Constitutional Court, if they believe that the Houses of Parliament have not been informed and involved adequately.

The most significant gains in the 1992 reforms have been made by the Bundesrat and the federal states. The Bundesrat committees have traditionally been in a unique position to specialise at relatively low cost. There has always been a successful division of labour between the different federal states and, above all, the Bundesrat committees have been able to draw on the expertise of the federal states' civil servants. Moreover, the Bundesrat has had a Standing Committee on European Affairs since 1957. Since 1992, the Bundesrat has the power to commit the Federal Government to a particular course of action in the Council of Ministers in certain policy areas that are vital to the federal states' interests. Bundesrat appointees are entitled to participate in meetings of the Council of Ministers if a proposal falls into the domain of exclusive legislative powers of the federal states. These concessions have been secured because the Bundesrat could credibly threaten to block the ratification of the Maastricht Treaty.

The scrutiny of EC/EU proposals in the Bundestag has largely followed the traditional patterns of German parliamentarism:

> . . . parliamentarians have taken on the role of specialist analysis of the likely impact of EC proposals on the Federal Republic. The committee structure of the Bundestag is well attuned to such activity . . . . EC business has been fully integrated into the existing domestic political structures of the Bundestag.[50]

The specialised system of standing committees has allowed the Bundestag to generate a certain degree of technical expertise. However, several problems have remained. As noted, timing is one of the most crucial constraints on the Bundestag's ability to scrutinise EU legislative proposals. Frequently, the Council of Ministers has already reached a decision before a proposal is dealt with by the Bundestag's standing committees. This is partly the result of the short notice the Council of Ministers gives of legislative proposals, and partly it is due to the domestic workload the committees are faced with. Moreover, both Houses have suffered from information 'overflow'. Since the 1970s, Bundestag and Bundesrat have, therefore, increasingly resorted to sifting procedures transferring the power to decide whether or not a matter is discussed in the Plenum to a small number of party managers in the committees and the parliamentary parties' study groups. The integration into the existing Bundestag committee system followed the logic of the German parliamentary system. The main problem of this approach has been that the departmental standing committees are already overloaded with domestic business. Thus, in the meetings of the departmental standing committees and the corresponding working groups of the parliamentary parties. European issues usually play a minor role. A related problem has been the 'segmentation' of information. European matters often cut across departmental boundaries. This problem could not be solved with multiple referrals alone, which increased the transaction costs of the departmental committees that were already overloaded. The establishment of a Standing Committee on European Affairs in the Bundestag in 1991 may help alleviate this problem. As yet, there are no systematic empirical studies assessing the impact of the new committee.

Why did the Bundestag fail to establish a specialised Standing Committee on European Union Affairs prior to 1991? After all, the Bundesrat has had such a committee since 1957. The referral of EC/EU business to the departmental standing committees did not only correspond to the traditions of German parliamentarism. The Federal Government's resistance to a specialist Standing Committee on European Affairs indicates that the segmentation of information suited its interests. The government's reasoning may have been influenced by considerations of 'divide et impera'. The solution also suited the existing departmental standing committees' interests. The departmental standing committees defended their 'property rights', that is, they wanted to avoid any intrusion of a cross-cutting European Affairs Committee into their jurisdiction. The Foreign Affairs Committee especially has been reluctant to give up its right to deal with EC/EU matters.[51] The new committee may help to improve the problem of segmentation and to formulate a comprehensive and coherent Bundestag view on European matters. The constitutional right to information may also improve its chances to secure the Federal Government's co-operation. Whether the new Standing Committee on European Affairs will have an impact in competition with the departmental committees remains to be seen.

Why has the resistance been given up in 1991? Two exogeneous factors have probably contributed to increase the workload of the departmental committees to an extent that may have given them incentives to accept a specialist Standing Committee on European Affairs: the ratification process of the Maastricht Treaty plus the formidable legislative programme necessitated by German unification. The growing workload has increased the pressure on the deputies' time budgets. This may have served as an inducement to consider further specialisation and delegate special powers of the Chamber to that committee.

One of the most serious problems even after the reforms of 1992 remains the problem of information transmission: the expertise that specialist committees may be able to acquire does not often transcend the privacy of the committee rooms. Debates on EC/EU affairs have been infrequent in the Bundestag as well as in the Bundesrat. There has also been infrequent use of traditional means of parliamentary interpellation. The most plausible explanation for the infrequency of the use of instruments of parliamentary interpellation is the Bundestag's domestic workload and the lack of party political conflict over EU affairs.[52]

Thus, both Houses of the German Parliament have delegated their powers increasingly to specialised committees and party study groups. The committees have acquired considerable technical expertise. Their right to obtain information has been strengthened. In general, the Federal Government's attitude *vis-à-vis* the committees has been co-operative. Both Houses' ability to cope with the 'flood of papers' from Brussels was improved through the establishment of effective sifting procedures. The Bundesrat's power to commit the Federal Government to a certain course of action in the Council of Ministers has been established at least in some policy areas. Yet the transmission of information to the respective parent chamber, and to the general public, has remained limited.

NOTES

I am grateful to Philip Norton and Mark R. Thompson for their helpful comments on an earlier draft of this article. Any error or opacity remaining is my responsibility alone.

1. Fritz W. Scharpf, 'Versuch über Demokratie im verhandelnden Staat' in Roland Czada and Manfred G. Schmidt (eds.), *Verhandlungsdemokratie, Interessenvermittlung, Regierbarkeit. Festschrift für Gerhard Lehmbruch zum 65. Geburtstag* (Opladen: Westdeutscher Verlag, 1993), pp.25–50.
2. Entscheidung des Bundesverfassungsgerichts, 12 October 1993 (2 BvR 2134/92 and 2159/92). A transcript can be found in *Neue Juristische Wochenschrift* (1993), pp.3047 ff.
3. See, for example, Albert Bleckmann, 'Die Umsetzung von Gemeinschaftsbeschlüssen in nationales Recht im Licht der Beziehungen zwischen den nationalen Parlamenten und dem Europäischen Parlament', *Zeitschrift für Parlamentsfragen* 22, 4 (1991), pp.572–84; Heinrich Oberreuter, 'Das Parlament als Gesetzgeber und Repräsentationsorgan' in Oscar W. Gabriel (ed.), *Die EG-Staaten im Vergleich: Strukturen, Prozesse, Politikinhalte* (Opladen: Westdeutscher Verlag, 1992), p.316; Klaus Pöhle, 'Europäische Union à la Maastricht – Eine ernste Herausforderung für die Parlamente der EG', *Zeitschrift für Parlamentsfragen* 24, 1 (1993), pp.49–63; Suzanne S. Schüttemeyer, 'Funktionsverluste des Bundestages durch die europäische Integration?', *Zeitschrift für Parlamentsfragen* 9, 2 (1978), pp.261–78; Winfried Steffani, 'Parlamentarismus in den EG-Staaten und demokratisches Defizit der europäischen Institutionen', *Zeitschrift für Parlamentsfragen* 9, 2 (1978), pp.233–53.
4. Simon Bulmer, *The Domestic Structure of European Policy-Making in West Germany* (New York and London: Garland, 1986), pp.219 and 235–41.
5. The analysis will be implicitly informed by an information-theoretic model of parliament emphasising the role of committees as extractors and disseminators of information. See, in particular, Keith Krehbiel, *Information and Legislative Organization* (Ann Arbor, Michigan: University of Michigan Press, 1991).
6. See the summary by Jürgen Bellers, 'Parlamentarische Souveränität und europäische Integration' in Raban Graf von Westphalen (ed.), *Parlamentslehre: Das parlamentarische Regierungssystem im technischen Zeitalter* (München and Wien: Oldenbourg, 1993), pp.522–5.

7. Bulmer, *The Domestic Structure*, p.211.
8. Renate Mayntz, 'Executive Leadership in Germany: Dispersion of Power or "Kanzler-demokratie"?' in Richard Rose and Ezra N. Suleiman (eds.), *Presidents and Prime Ministers* (Washington, D.C.: American Enterprise Institute for Public Policy Research. 1980), p.140.
9. Bulmer, *The Domestic Structure*, p.217.
10. For data see Thomas Saalfeld, 'Germany' in George Thomas Kurian and Lawrence D. Longley (eds.), *World Encyclopedia of Parliaments and Legislatures* (Washington D.C.: Congressional Quarterly Press, 1995 [in press]), Table 3.
11. For data see Saalfeld, 'Germany', Table 4.
12. Bulmer, *The Domestic Structure*, pp.222 and 243; Schüttemeyer, 'Funktionsverluste des Bundestages'.
13. Walter Bagehot, *The English Constitution. With an Introduction by R.H.S. Crossman* (Glasgow: Fontana/Collins, 1963), p.152.
14. Bulmer, *The Domestic Structure*, pp.221-2.
15. Bundestags-Drucksache 7/5924, 2 December 1976, p.231.
16. See Wolfgang Fischer, 'Die Europäische Union im Grundgesetz: der neue Artikel 23' *Zeitschrift für Parlamentsfragen* 24, 1 (1993), pp.34-5.
17. Bulmer, *The Domestic Structure*, pp.221-2.
18. Bulmer, *The Domestic Structure*, pp.220-21 (literal quote p.221).
19. Article 2, Act of Ratification of the Rome Treaties. English translation by Bulmer, *The Domestic Structure*, p.225. The first sentence was later amended to read '. . . informed of developments in the Council of Ministers of the European Communities.' This was to take account of the merger of the three Communities. Bulmer, *The Domestic Structure*, p.250, footnote 54. See also Wolfgang Ismayr, *Der Deutsche Bundestag: Funktionen, Willensbildung, Reformansätze* (Opladen: Leske und Budrich, 1992), p.327.
20. Bulmer, *The Domestic Structure*, pp.226-7. Ismayr, *Der Deutsche Bundestag*, p.328.
21. Cf. Krehbiel, *Information and Legislative Organization*, p.262.
22. Ismayr, *Der Deutsche Bundestag*, p.330.
23. Bulmer, *The Domestic Structure*, pp.227-9 (literal quote pp.228-9).
24. Fischer, 'Die Europäische Union', p.35.
25. Georg Ress, 'The Constitution and the Maastricht Treaty: Between Co-operation and Conflict' *German Politics*, 3, 3 (1994), p.49.
26. 'Gesetz über die Zusammenarbeit zwischen Bundesregierung und Deutschem Bundestag in Angelegenheiten der Europäischen Union' (12 March 1993, *Bundesgesetzblatt*, Teil I, p.311) and 'Gesetz über die Zusammenarbeit von Bund und Ländern in Angelegenheiten der Europäischen Union' (12 March 1993, *Bundesgesetzblatt*, Teil I, p.313). The text of the Cooperation Act (Bundestag) is easily accessible in Franz Möller and Martin Limpert, 'Informations- und Mitwirkungsrechte des Bundestages in Angelegenheiten der Europäischen Union', *Zeitschrift für Parlamentsfragen* 24, 1 (1993), p.22 (note 6); see also Ress, 'The Constitution', p.50.
27. Ress, 'The Constitution', p.50.
28. Möller and Limpert, 'Bundestag und Europäische Union', pp.28-9.
29. For a summary see Ress, 'The Constitution', pp.61-4.
30. Ismayr, *Der Deutsche Bundestag*, p.328.
31. Bulmer, *The Domestic Structure*, p.230.
32. 'Kommission des Ältestenrates zur Behandlung von Fragen der Zusammenarbeit zwischen dem Europäischen Parlament und dem Deutschen Bundestag'. Cf. Schindler, *Datenhandbuch 1983 bis 1991*, p.1253.
33. Klaus Pöhle, 'Die Europa-Kommission des Deutschen Bundestages: Ein politisches und geschäftsordnungsmäßiges Novum' *Zeitschrift für Parlamentsfragen* 15, 3 (1984), pp.352-9.
34. See, e.g., Peter Mehl, *Die Europa-Kommission des Deutschen Bundestages: Eine neue Einrichtung interparlamentarischer Zusammenarbeit* (Kehl am Rhein: Engel, 1987), pp.66-7 and p.92.
35. Cf. Schindler, *Datenhandbuch 1983 bis 1991*, pp.1254-5.

36. Ismayr, *Der Deutsche Bundestag*, p.186.
37. Alwin Brück, 'Europäische Integration und Entmachtung des Deutschen Bundestages: Ein Unterausschuß ist nicht genug', *Zeitschrift für Parlamentsfragen*, 2 (1988), pp.221–4; see also Klaus Hänsch, 'Europäische Integration und parlamentarische Demokratie', *Europa-Archiv* No.7 (1986), p.197.
38. Bundestags-Drucksache 11/56, March 1987. See also Schindler, *Datenhandbuch 1983 bis 1991*, p.1254.
39. Ismayr, *Der Deutsche Bundestag*, p.331.
40. Möller and Limpert, 'Bundestag und Europäische Union', pp.31–2.
41. Ismayr, *Der Deutsche Bundestag*, pp.331–2.
42. Ismayr, *Der Deutsche Bundestag*, p.327.
43. Ismayr, *Der Deutsche Bundestag*, pp.328–9.
44. Bulmer, *The Domestic Structure*, p.236.
45. 45.Bulmer, *The Domestic Structure*, pp.236–40 (literal quote p.240).
46. Fischer, 'Die Europäische Union', pp.36–9.
47. Basic Law, Article 23 (new) Sentences 4–7; cf. Fischer, 'Die Europäische Union', pp.42–4.
48. Klaus H. Goetz and Peter J. Cullen, 'The Basic Law after Unification: Continued Centrality or Declining Force?', *German Politics*, 3, 3 (1993), p.22.
49. Ress, 'The Constitution', p.51.
50. Bulmer, *The Domestic Structure*, p.244.
51. Brück, 'Europäische Integration', p.223.
52. Bulmer, *The Domestic Structure*, pp.240–41.

The Italian Parliament and European Integration – Responsibilities, Failures and Successes

PAUL FURLONG

The process of European integration has imposed particular strains and constraints on Parliament in Italy, which were evident even before 1987 but which were exacerbated by the demands of the Single Market project. The pace and extent of institutional change in the late 1980s reinforced existing problems, and in particular greatly increased the difficulties faced by Parliament in adopting the large numbers of directives. These difficulties were part of a wider and more strategic failure, namely the failure of Government and of the political elites to respond to the accelerated economic integration from 1987 onwards. The increased delays and inadequacies of parliamentary procedure were merely one symptom of this, and not new, though certainly more severe than had previously been felt. That they were not new is a commonplace. One commentator has gone so far as to describe the relationship between Parliament and the European Community before 1987 as 'pathological'.[1] For the preceding three decades Parliament did not adopt special procedures for considering European Community business, and adopted a variety of means of ordinary legislation, apparently indiscriminately, for the transposition of EC norms. This included even for a period using decree-laws, an emergency procedure, to transpose EC regulations which should in the event have had a direct effect without the need for transposition in this way.

Despite its lengthy antecedents, Parliament's apparent inability to bring order to its relations with Brussels did not become a major issue until the late 1980s. This was not only because of the limited salience of European integration before then. It was also because of other more general weaknesses for which it was much criticised in the 1970s and 1980s and which occupied public attention much more. As well as being held responsible for governmental instability,[2] Parliament was also periodically blamed for the public sector deficit, for delayed and piecemeal legislation, for protecting its own corrupt members and in general for contributing to

Paul Furlong is Senior Lecturer in the Department of Political Science and International Studies at the University of Birmingham.

the increased gap between the political system and organised society. These two sets of issues, the problems of European integration and the difficulties of the political system, came together at the beginning of the 1990s. The break-up of the established party system between 1989 and 1994 is attributable to this explosive mixture. This is not to deny the importance of judicial activism in exposing political corruption, which was certainly a critical factor, but underlying this was a set of long-term problems centred on the gap between the processes of economic development and the political stagnation of the party system. Of this stagnation Parliament was a highly visible symbol. European integration represented modernisation and economic success. Failure to adapt adequately to the processes of integration undermined not only the parties but also their most visible institution. Fairly or unfairly, it therefore was to Parliament's discredit that, for example, in 1991 the European Court of Justice had before it 288 cases of inadequacy or of failure to transpose EC legislation relating to Italy, by far the largest number brought by the Commission against a Member State. In 1991, a Commission report on the application of Community Law revealed that Italy had the lowest rate of transposition of all Member States, at 76.5 per cent. This report was followed by a public rebuke from Jacques Delors in February 1992, which certainly did not help the governing parties in the parliamentary elections which followed the next month. The withdrawal of Italy from the ERM in September 1992 added to the general impression of failure of the governing classes to adapt to the challenges and opportunities of the new dynamics of European integration. Whether it was directly responsible or not, the European failures of the Italian Parliament were inextricably enmeshed in the more general crisis of the political system.

Thus the crisis of the political system as a whole invested Parliament both directly, because of its alleged policy deficiencies, and indirectly, because of the spectacular disrepute into which the old political parties had fallen. The irony of this is that, as we shall see, by 1991 Parliament had already in place a reformed procedure which enabled it to deal very quickly with the multitude of new directives associated with the Single Market programme, so that by the end of 1992 the backlog of work had been removed and Italy could fairly claim to have implemented almost all the relevant directives relating to the Single Market. By March 1995 it had transposed 190 out of 219 directives, similar to the rates achieved by other Member States. Partly as a consequence, the number of extant Commission cases against Italy for failure of implementation brought before the Court of Justice had dropped to 15. This was too late to help the political parties whose electoral control had already been undermined, but the political system for which they had been responsible for nearly 50 years survived in the established constitutional arrangements, including in Parliament.

THE CONSTITUTIONAL ROLE OF PARLIAMENT

Parliament has important and specific functions in constitutional and political terms. In the debates in the constitutional assembly in the period 1946 to 1948, Parliament was an almost unique point of convergence between the forces of the left and of the right, who for different reasons sought to make it central to the new democracy. Both sides saw in Parliament a means of ensuring that Fascism could not return, but sought different remedies which depended on their different diagnoses of the origins of Fascism. For the Christian Democrats, the largest single party, and for their allies in government, it was important that Parliament should be the main source of law, while for the parties of the left, particularly the Communists, Parliament was identified as the expression of popular will through which societal forces should be able to achieve radical and dynamic progress towards a more egalitarian and just society. Hence the Constitution states unequivocally that 'sovereignty belongs to the people, who exercise it in the ways and within the limits laid down by the constitution' (Article 1), and that 'the legislative function is carried out by the two Houses [of Parliament]' (Article 70). This tension between Parliament and people lies at the heart of the constitutional settlement. The compromise achieved was to retain the 'centrality' and uniqueness of Parliament, particularly in its law-making functions, while at the same time erecting a series of other institutions and procedures which either monitor Parliament's activities or which share in a subordinate way its legislative functions. In the former group are the Head of State (the President of the Republic) and the Constitutional Court, and in the latter are the regional governments and the process of popular referendum. The Constitution also enshrines the separation of powers, so that the main institutions can claim rigorous independence from one another, a claim which Parliament has always been ready to make in its relations with Government. Though the parties of the left sought a sovereign national assembly expressing uniquely the will of organised society, the legislature which developed was in practice highly pluralistic, both in the sense that it contended with other institutions for effective legislative control and in the sense that its internal procedures recognised the right of many different political parties to influence all legislation, through a complex and open legislative process.

PARLIAMENT AND EUROPEAN INTEGRATION BEFORE 1989

Prior to 1987, Parliament had no special procedures to deal with European legislation. In principle, there should not have been major difficulties in establishing the predominance of EC legislation, since Article 11 of the Constitution specifically allows 'such limitations on sovereignty as may be necessary for an international order aimed at ensuring peace and justice among nations'. The implicit application of this article to norms originating from the EC was established by decisions of the Constitutional Court, particularly sentence 183 of 1973. To deal with the increasing volume of material emanating from Brussels, Parliament for many years relied on periodic omnibus laws which gave wide delegated powers to Government to enable it to deal with the detail of international obligations: law 1203 of 1957 relating to the ratification of the Treaty of Rome, laws 871 of 1965 and 740 of 1969 dealing with the transitional arrangements to the Common Market, similar *leggi-delega* in 1970 and 1975, and then in the 1980s laws which authorised the Government to ensure the appropriate transposition of the large numbers of new directives (law 42 of 1982 and law 183 of 1987). This strategy was designed to by-pass the cumbersome parliamentary procedures, with their emphasis on plural points of access. In practice Parliament retained the right to process European legislation in the normal way also, so that the block delegation of powers to the Government became merely an expedient to remove the periodic log-jams to which European legislation was subject as was most other normative activity. It was widely recognised that parliamentary procedures suffered from an excess of legislation, in the sense that for formal reasons it was often necessary to legislate on relatively minor matters whose principles had already been agreed to. So Parliament would sometimes find itself bringing the full force of legislation to bear on directives emanating from the European Commission which merely introduced minor amendments to norms previously agreed. One of the results of this method was that it did not discriminate between measures. Relatively easy issues were in effect slowed down, and it was difficult to concentrate effort on the more contentious issues.

Other difficulties with this *ad hoc* approach were that it left unresolved the increasing tension with the regional governments, who sought the right to involve themselves more closely in all aspects of EC policy formation, and that it left intact the conventional reflex reaction that European legislative business was a matter of international relations and therefore should wait for the often non-existent leadership of the Ministry of Foreign Affairs. Finally, there were no effective means of monitoring and controlling how government enacted the delegated legislation or regulation which resulted, other than the normal parliamentary procedures with all their well-aired deficiencies.[3]

However, through these conflicting pressures and objectives Parliament consistently sought to emphasise its right to have an independent voice, even when it clearly lacked the power of initiative. It was aided in this by the willingness of the backbenchers who belonged to the governing parties to resist party discipline (such as it was), to absent themselves and to use the secret vote against their own ministers. But the Government itself accepted the need for wide parliamentary support on most measures other than votes of confidence and the annual finance bills, and in this sense colluded with Parliament in the creation of two separate majorities – the governing majority, visible only on issues of high salience, and the wider constitutional majority including the Communists whose agreement was used to ensure the passage of ordinary government business. The European business of Parliament thus was part of a pluralistic and complicated web of agreements, and was mainly distinguished by its relatively low returns for politicians and by its relatively low salience.

The first major change in this came in 1987, with the Fabbri law (183/ 1987). As well as ratifying 41 directives immediately and delegating authority to the Government for a further 59, the Fabbri law for the first time obliged the Government to consult Parliament and the regional assemblies over EC proposals and legislation. This was to take place through the Prime Minister's Office, and was the responsibility of the Minister without portfolio (Community Affairs). The Fabbri law also allowed and indeed encouraged the process of 'delegislating', by giving ministries the power to implement directives whose main purpose was to make technical changes to existing directives. In 1988, a wide-ranging and much-debated law (400/1988) reformed the organisation of the Prime Minister's Office, so as to give the Head of Government more resources and wider powers to co-ordinate ministerial activity. One of the measures included in this law was the formal establishment of a Department of Community Affairs, in effect regularising the practice which had developed over the previous few years. The functions of the Minister for Community Affairs were to co-ordinate consultation on EC proposals with ministries, Parliament, regions and major communal governments, to put forward legislation as appropriate, and to report to Parliament on Italy's European policies. The Minister remained subordinate to the Prime Minister and had no independent personnel. Also the Minister had no obvious interlocutor in either of the two Chambers of Parliament, and the problem remained that European legislation had to take its place in the legislative queue behind other bills which might have much greater and more immediate political pay-offs. As already indicated, it was not only

European legislation that suffered in this way. Governments of the period had had great difficulty in securing the passage of their annual Finance Bills and Budgets, and it had been necessary to introduce a 'fast-track' in the parliamentary calendar, in effect a reserved route by which Parliament was obliged to consider and complete the Budget within a fixed time-scale.

The solution adopted for the European legislation was rather different. What provided the final impulse to parliamentary reform in this area was a popular referendum held in June 1989 by which the Single European Act of 1986 and its treaty changes were ratified by an overwhelming popular majority. The referendum was called by the Government as a purely consultative exercise, but its constitutional basis was the subject of vigorous criticism not only from jurists but also from Parliament, which saw the referendum as a highly unfortunate precedent whose objective was to enable future governments to by-pass Parliament. Partly in response to this, the La Pergola law (law 86/1989) established a relatively complete and articulated set of procedures which aimed not only to ensure the rapid processing of European legislation (Single Market and other), but also to place Parliament at the centre of European policy through its monitoring and controlling procedures. The law also was motivated by the need to take action on the backlog of legislation prior to the beginning of the Italian Presidency of the European Council in July 1990.

THE 'LA PERGOLA' LAW 1989 AND AFTER

The 'La Pergola' law of 1989 is named after the Minister for Community Affairs at the time, who was largely responsible for its drafting and who guided it through Parliament. The main provision of the law is the introduction of an annual 'Community Law'. Each year by the beginning of March the Minister for Community Affairs is obliged to present to Parliament a bill which comprises all the legal acts necessary to transpose extant community jurisprudence up to July of the previous year. The law envisages several different kinds of legal instruments: the bill may transpose directives immediately into law, it may delegate power to the Government to legislate (always subject to report to Parliament), it may provide for the directive to be implemented through Government regulation, and it may allow other forms of administrative implementation such as ministerial decree. Also available, though unused, is provision for the regional assemblies to implement directives. As part of the 'Community Law', La Pergola requires the Government, in accordance with the Fabbri law of 1987, to report to Parliament on the extent to which Italian law conforms to European law. This becomes the main criterion, though not the only one, for formal parliamentary scrutiny. The parliamentary process therefore is not intended to be a restricted or minimalist exercise, but one which genuinely investigates the effects of the European directives and makes the appropriate changes to existing domestic norms (or authorises others to do so). La Pergola also requires the Government to report at the same time on sentences of the European Court of Justice which may entail changes to Italian legislation. Separately from the annual Community Law, the Government has to provide a six-monthly report on Italy's participation in the formation of European policy and on Italy's general strategy. As well as these measures, La Pergola incorporates the provisions of an earlier law (871/1965) which require the Government to report annually on all Commission activity relating to the Single Market and to the principles of social and economic cohesion.

With the introduction of the La Pergola law, both Houses of Parliament for the first time gave overall responsibility for all European business to special committees (though the Senate Giunta on Community Affairs had originally been established in 1968). These committees received the reports from Government in accordance with the new law, and acted as the co-ordinating committee for the legislative processes of the annual Community. This special committee had several functions. It presents the annual Community Law to the full Assembly, and therefore has to receive comments from the permanent committees which review all bills in their own subject areas. The most important of these Permanent Committees in the Chamber of Deputies are Committee I, on Constitutional Affairs, and Committee V, on Budget and Treasury matters. On bills, the decisions of these two committees have a binding effect and can override the decisions of the other permanent committees. This appears to apply also in relation to the Special Committee on Community Affairs. There is therefore the possibility of serious conflict between the Special Committee and either or both of these committees I and V, since its role is to apply the principle of compatibility with an external institution whose legislation may override domestic law. Competition between the 'European' Special Committee and the other permanent committees is also possible and has led to significant delays in the new procedures.

Tables 1 and 2 give a detailed breakdown of the legislative activity of the annual Community Law since 1989. This legislation refers to all Community norms, not only those relating to the Single Market, though this was clearly one of the main concerns of the innovation. According to parliamentary regulations (Article 126 in the regulations of the Chamber of Deputies), each permanent committee has to consider the relevant provisions of the bill presented by the Government and report to the special committee within 15 days. The special committee then has 30 days

TABLE 1

ANNUAL COMMUNITY LAW – TYPES OF LEGISLATION

		Type of legislation				
Community Law for year	Completion of procedure	Direct	delegated	by regulation	by admin. act	Total number of measures
1990	Dec-90	6	164	46	98	314
1991	Jan-92	13	52	12	27	104
1992	Dec-92	1	23	7	3	34
1993	Feb-94	3	30	31	82	146
1994	Mar-95	3	23	5	39	70

TABLE 2

ANNUAL COMMUNITY LAW – TYPES OF LEGISLATION, PERCENTAGES

		Type of legislation				
Community Law for year	Completion of procedure	Direct	delegated	by regulation	by admin. act	Total measures
1990	Dec-90	1.9	52.2	14.6	31.2	100.0
1991	Jan-92	12.5	50.0	11.5	26.0	100.0
1992	Dec-92	2.9	67.6	20.6	8.8	100.0
1993	Feb-94	2.1	20.5	21.2	56.2	100.0
1994	Mar-95	4.3	32.9	7.1	55.7	100.0

to present the bill to the full assembly. The functions of the Senate Giunta on community affairs are slightly different from those in the Chamber of Deputies, but the procedure is in essence repeated in both Houses. The entire timetable should therefore be completed in both Houses within three months, by the end of May. In practice, mainly because of disagreements between the special committees and the permanent committees, but also because of pressure of other business, the formal timetable has never been fully adhered to. Indeed, in 1992, the early dissolution of Parliament resulted in the loss of the entire bill. Instead of presenting the bill again, after the elections the new Government presented what became known as the 'mini-comunitaria', which contained only provisions relating to the Single Market and whose purpose was to ensure that Italy had entirely fulfilled its obligations in that respect by the symbolic European deadline of 31 December 1992.

In purely numerical terms, the legislative innovations of the La Pergola law must be accounted a success, in the sense that the parliamentary log-jam has been removed and that procedures are now available to prevent its recurrence. Over 600 directives have been dealt with in the first five years under the La Pergola procedures, nearly as many as in the previous 30 years. There are however some problems with the way European legislation is now handled.[4] One criticism which was made in the first years was that the reluctance of Parliament to proceed by direct legislation (that is, to use the Community Law to pass laws having direct effect) has merely postponed the resolution of the issues. The most unfriendly reading of the innovation was that it was mainly cosmetic, motivated by the twin deadlines of the Italian Presidency of the Council and the symbolic completion of the Single Market programme by 31 December 1992. Some support for this could be found in the continuing propensity to give wide delegated powers to Government – over half of all directives in the first three years were dealt with in this way. Though there is scope for parliamentary scrutiny of the *leggi-delega*, such scrutiny is usually less than rigorous, and on this basis Parliament could scarcely claim to be central to the real processes of policy-making. There was also some suspicion that the log-jam had not been broken, merely shifted into the ministries, where it would remain. On the first point, the excessive recourse to delegated powers, it has to be observed that one of the objectives of parliamentary reform in recent years has been 'de-legislating', already referred to in the context of the Fabbri law of 1987. This was certainly one of the underlying aims of the La Pergola reform. While it is difficult to reach definite conclusions on the basis of only five years' experience, it does seem that after an initial reluctance on the part of the special committee, more directives are now being channelled through the administrative route (over 50 per cent in years 1993 and 1994). It is true, however, that there have been delays in the action undertaken by ministries to follow up the Community laws. By March 1995, directives not processed by the appropriate ministries numbered one from 1990, three from 1991, none from 1992, and a total of 91 from 1993.[5]

It is also arguable that Parliament has created a small band of 'European specialists' in the active members of the special committees. These have in practice very wide powers, subject formally to the scrutiny of the full assembly, which faced with long and complex Community laws has not shown any great propensity to overturn the decisions of the specialists. The full membership of the Special Committee in the Chamber of Deputies is 48, covering all party groups, but research on attendance suggests that the active membership numbers about ten.[6] The difficulty here might be not so much the expertise developed in the subject area, but rather the extent of their power and the lack of publicity within which they work, which might leave the specialists open to undue influence from lobby interests, either directly or working through the permanent committees.

CONCLUSION

Much attention has been focused on the legislative aspects of Parliament's involvement in European integration. This is scarcely surprising, since legislation is Parliament's privileged point of access to the political system, one to which it has always given priority, over other functions such as scrutiny and redress. Though there is not space here to discuss in detail the wider responsibilities of other actors in the political system, the difficulties and successes of Italy's parliamentary procedures for dealing with the EU's normative output have to be seen in the context not only of the turbulence of its politics since 1989, but also of Italy's European strategy. Italy has traditionally been seen as one of the most vocal supporters of European integration, and in recent debates over the future course of European integration, including Maastricht, has tended to favour acceleration in both political and economic integration. This is not only for reasons of genuine belief in the original ideals of the European Economic Community, though this is certainly a factor. It is also because Italy, like France, has been extremely wary of the 'German issue'. Like France, it has identified further integration both as an antidote to potential German domination of a Europe managed on inter-governmental methods, and as a means of binding the newly unified Germany into its traditional relationships with western Europe. This concern over German domination is expressed also through Italy's support for enhanced funds for structural funds and its support for social policy, which are seen as means of achieving the social and economic balance which is one of the original objectives of the Treaty of Rome. That is not to say that Italy has been able to pursue its aims with consistent force or success. Italy is the third largest economy in the European Union, but its political and economic elites feel very strongly its traditional incapacity to make its presence felt. The lack of effectiveness has been even more noticeable in recent years, and results from the uncertainties and loss of status associated with the collapse of the established governing parties, the revelations of widespread corruption in public life, and the difficulties in finding stable replacements for the old parties. In an even more direct way, the devaluation of the lira in September 1992 and its withdrawal from the ERM were not only a blow to Italy's international credibility, they also undermined one of the pillars of Italy's European policy, namely that it must be in the forefront of monetary union. Since the currency instability has continued, the likelihood of Italy's participation in monetary union, its capacity to meet the convergence criteria, have continued to be called into question. In this context, the role of Parliament can only be limited. Italy's failure to meet its legislative obligations under the Single European Act was a source of grave concern and contributed to the decay of the established party system. Nevertheless, the apparent resolution of this problem by technical ingenuity has revealed that there are structural problems underlying Italy's participation in European integration, for which Parliament was more the scapegoat than the villain. Difficulties remain with the new procedures. But what is increasingly obvious is that Italy often fails to make an effective input into European policy-making both at the strategic level (IGCs, for example) but also more prosaically in its routine policy formulation. This is the responsibility not of Parliament, but of an unreformed public administration and of a fragmented ministerial organisation. This is not so much a procedural or technical problem. Rather it concerns one of the categorical imperatives of Italy's old regime (pre-1992), namely the overwhelming requirement for equilibrium among the governing parties. This in turn impeded the repeated efforts to reform or circumvent the central public administration, whose working methods and political regulation unlike those of Parliament remained largely untouched over a long period of economic growth and political development since 1945. If the parliamentary reforms of recent years have unmasked the alibis of the executive branch, that will not have been the least of the benefits to result from them.

NOTES

1. V. Guizzi, L'attuazione delle direttive comunitarie in Italia, paper presented to the Second Congress of the European Legislation Association, Rome 23–24 March 1995, p.1.
2. For a brief discussion of this argument, see P. Furlong, 'Parliament in Italian Politics,' pp.52–66 in special edition of *West European Politics* 13, 3 (July 1990).
3. On the problems of legislation in the 1980s, and a government response, see V. Della Sala, 'Government by Decree: The Craxi government and the Use of Decree Legislation in the Italian Parliament', pp.8–24 in R. Nanetti *et al.*, *Italian Politics – A Review*, vol.1 (London, Pinter, 1988).
4. For a reasoned critique of the procedure then in its infancy, see M. Giuliani, 'Il processo decisionale Italiano e le politiche comunitarie', *Polis* agosto 1992 pp.307–42.
5. Relazione della Commissione Speciale per le politiche Comunitarie, Camera dei Deputati, 13 marzo 1995, p.1.
6. Giuliani 1992, p.331.

The French Parliament and the EU: Loosening the Constitutional Straitjacket

FRANCO RIZZUTO

France has been, and remains, one of the motors behind the post-war political and economic integration of western Europe. It was a French Government that proposed the Coal and Steel Community and the aborted European Defence Community in the late forties and early fifties. Interestingly the latter initiative failed to get off the ground because of a negative vote in the French National Assembly. France was also a key player in the negotiations leading to the Treaty of Rome establishing the Common Market and more recently a leading influence in shaping the Single European Act and the Treaty on European Union. Moreover, successive French governments have not only been key proponents and advocates of an ever closer union but they have also played at times a dominant role in shaping the particular style of decision-making in Europe's evolving institutional framework. For example, the so-called Luxembourg Compromise of 1966 more or less imposed the French preference for inter-governmental decision-making in the Community. The Council of Ministers and the European Council remain, in line with French preferences, the key decisional sites in the European Union. France more than any other member of the Union has been able to combine, some would say mask, the almost single-minded defence and furtherance of national interests with Jean Monnet's vision of the inevitable logic of ever closer union.

The elaboration of France's European policy has been dominated by the Presidency and the Government, thanks to the 1958 Constitution and the Gaullist-inspired tradition of parliamentary non-intervention in the conduct of external relations. The Fifth Republic's Constitution transferred power from Parliament to the Executive and established a strong executive relatively free from parliamentary harassment and interference. Not only does the Government enjoy significant procedural advantages in its dealings with Parliament but Article 34 restricts Parliament's field of law-making and Article 37 asserts that everything not included under Article 34 comes under the executive's power of regulation over which

Franco Rizzuto is Head of Modern European Cultural Studies, Edge Hill University College

Parliament has no control or input. The implementation of treaties and relations with European Union institutions have always been regarded as being within the Executive's sphere of regulation. Further, Article 43 limits the number of permanent parliamentary committees to six for each Chamber and therefore makes it impossible without a contitutional amendment for Parliament to establish new ones. The President is empowered under Article 52 to conduct foreign policy.

Not surprisingly, therefore, the French Parliament's involvement in European Community matters has generated little research interest over the years. Its role was essentially peripheral. Writing in the mid-1970s J.R. Frears[1] concluded that of all the Parliaments of the then nine Member States, the French alone viewed with equanimity or indifference the transfer of its legislative powers to European Community institutions. He found that the French Parliament had neither the means nor the inclination to intervene. There was in fact no procedure or machinery at all in place for the exercise of parliamentary control or scrutiny of executive actions in Community decision-making. He detected no concern or fear among French parliamentarians that the Government was negotiating away national interests and national sovereignty. European Community matters were regarded as foreign policy by parliamentarians, part of the President of the Republic's *domaine reserve*, and therefore out of bounds. He found members of Parliament to be ill-informed or uninterested. Foreign and therefore Community affairs was not a major preoccupation for parliamentarians. They were of limited electoral importance. There was little interest among French parliamentarians for either more information or a specialised committee dealing with Community matters. The Government, through the General Secretariat of the Interministerial Committee for Questions of European Economic Co-operation, itself had evolved methods of formulating, co-ordinating and implementing policy in the Community which allowed no parliamentary scrutiny. Government never felt under obligation to reveal its negotiating position or views on Community matters even in response to parliamentary questions. Members of Parliament who wished to influence Community decisions before they were taken directed their efforts towards the Foreign Ministry, the appropriate technical ministry, Brussels, or interest groups.[2]

In recent years three developments have helped draw the French Parliament from out of the shadows and make it a more interesting and indeed potentially very significant participant. First, the fear among a number of French parliamentarians from the late 1970s that something had to be done to impede the gathering pace of European integration with the concomitant decisional drift away from Paris towards Brussels and Strasbourg, which they felt would turn the French Parliament into little more than a poorly informed rubber stamp. Parliamentarians who were on the whole hostile to the pro-integration policies of successive governments of the Right saw greater parliamentary involvement in the conduct of European Community affairs as a way of slowing down or de-railing the process. This fear gave rise to the establishment, after much government amendment of the draft legislation, in July 1979 of permanent Parliamentary *Délégations* for the European Communities in the National Assembly and the Senate. In many respects they were modelled on the European Affairs section set up by the Senate in early 1973. The section was in no sense an instrument of senatorial control over the government. Its primary tasks were to co-ordinate documentation and assist committees on Community problems. Committees were under no obligation to heed the section's advice. Its principal activities involved collecting documentation in one place, supplying members and officials of the Senate with background papers, providing technical and administrative support for the senatorial members of the French delegations to the European Parliament, liaising with Community institutions and ministries with European responsibilities and undertaking detailed research on European issues that senators might be interested in.

Secondly, the striking quantitative increase in European Community legislation mainly as a result of the enactment of the Single European Act, and the need to incorporate much of it into domestic law,[3] as well as the requirement to ensure that existing and future domestic law was consistent with Community law highlighted the basic failings of the provisions and workings of the 1979 law and gave rise in May 1990 to a law strengthening the role of the parliamentary *délégations*. We consider this below.

Thirdly, one of the consequences of the heated debate over the ratification of the Maastricht Treaty in France was the amendment of Article 88 of the Constitution which now obliges the Government to send Parliament, at the same time as sent to the European Community Council of Ministers and thus prior to a decision, all European Community proposed legislation. Furthermore, Parliament, in or out of session, may now vote on resolutions on matters arising under the provisions of the new Article 88.[4] While resolutions cannot legally bind French governments, they may from time to time have important political consequences. The new article clearly constitutes, as *Le Monde* pointed out, something of a break with the tradition so evident in the 1960s and 1970s of the Executive being the sole player in international negotiations by indicating that the two Houses of Parliament will henceforth be able to table and vote on resolutions and not just express opinions.[5] Interestingly, government attitudes on the issue of greater parliamentary involvement appear to have changed in recent years. For example, in the period since the Maastricht ratification debate governments have complied with the letter of their constitutional obligation to provide Parliament with all European Union proposed legislation in a way they had not really done so before.

LIMITED BEGINNINGS

The 1979 law setting up the parliamentary *délégations* gave them a very limited, if specialised, role – to inform their respective Chambers of the activities of the European Community institutions. Each had 18 members drawn in proportion to the parties' strength in each Chamber. They had to submit their conclusions and advice to the relevant permanent committee and produce for their respective Chambers a sessional report. The on-going scrutiny and investigation of the Government's conduct on European Community policy was to remain firmly in the hands of individual parliamentarians or of the six permanent parliamentary committees of each Chamber. The *délégations* were given no powers of investigation. Moreover, the permanent committees were under no obligation to take any notice of the *délégations*' observations or advice. Members of the *délégations* were unevenly distributed among the permanent committees.

In order for the *délégations* to perform their role effectively, the Government had to provide them, as soon as it obtained them, with all relevant documentation produced by European Community institutions, as well as all information concerning ongoing negotiations. The Government was also obliged to inform the *délégations* of all proposed EC directives or regulations dealing with matters for which Parliament had law-making powers under Article 34 of the French Constitution prior to their adoption by the European Community Council of Ministers.

On the whole, all the available evidence suggests that during the first decade of their existence, their impact was very limited. During the first decade of their existence the Senate *dèlègation* held 137 meetings and published 199 views. The National Assembly met more frequently – 187 times, published 281 views and held 50 hearings. Nevertheless, much of their work was ignored by the permanent committees. Indeed, many parliamentarians were unaware of their existence. Governments rarely provided parliamentary *délégations* with the necessary information and documentation prior to consideration or decision by the European Community Council of Ministers. When they did, it was often so late that the *délégations* had little time to examine the proposed legislation prior to its adoption by the EC Council of Ministers. The *délégations* in fact tended to obtain more information directly from the European Community institutions.

The clause in the 1979 law obliging the Government to inform the *délégations* of on-going negotiations or the French Government's negotiating stance was, for the most part, simply ignored. The appearance before the *dèlègations* of the Foreign Minister or the Minister for European Community Affairs from time to time was the only real concession government made. Furthermore, *délégations* could not advise on the compatibility of proposed domestic legislation with European Community law and thus avoid areas of potential conflict. Nor were they allowed to examine legislation in place in other Member States. On the whole, the permanent committees did not really make use of the expertise of European Community matters gained by the *délégations*. The failure of the 1979 law to link the work of the *délégations* to the law-making deliberations of the permanent committees partly explains this. The general unwillingness of many permanent committee chairs to elevate the importance of the *délégations'* work was also important.

RESPONDING TO THE SINGLE EUROPEAN ACT

A combination of the weaknesses of the 1979 law, the pressures resulting from the requirement to pass countless laws to complete the Internal Market, the growing complexity of many of the issues arising, and the growing debate over the so-called democratic deficit in an increasingly supra-national driven European Community saw the introduction in April 1989 by the Socialist Government of a bill, passed in May 1990, which sought to clarify and strengthen the information-provider role of the parliamentary *délégations*.

While the 1990 law did not alter the essentially supportive/subordinate role of the *délégations*, it did, however, institute a number of significant modifications. The law itself reflected the more cautious line preferred by the proponents of reform in the Senate. This in essence involved four basic changes to the 1979 law which aimed to make the *délégations* more effective. The Senate bill proposed increasing their membership, a wider and more balanced representation of permanent committee members, the institutionalisation of the practice of ministerial hearings, and allowing *délégations* to issue reports and conclusions whenever they felt necessary. The National Assembly bill had on the contrary proposed to increase significantly the powers of the *délégations* by directly involving them in the law-making deliberations of the permanent committees and by making their input obligatory in a number of areas. Indeed, the National Assembly bill sought to transform the *délégations* from providers of information to agencies with the significant role of co-ordinating the activities of the European Communities and the work of the French

Parliament. Under the National Assembly proposals the Government or a permanent committee could consult the *délégations* on proposed Community legislation. The *délégations* could on their own initiative or that of the Government issue opinions on any bill – government or private member's, dealing with matters covered by the activities of the European Community.

In the event, the potentially very powerful co-ordinating role sought by the National Assembly was not acceptable to the Senate whose view was favoured by the Government and was not included in the law. The *délégations* were to remain instruments at the service of Parliament and subordinate to the permanent committees. However, a number of significant clarifications and improvements were introduced. First, the 1990 law implicitly recognises the right of the *délégations* to examine and append observations to proposed EC legislation which is then passed on to the relevant permanent parliamentary committee. Secondly, the *délégations* may be consulted by a permanent or by special parliamentary committees on any Community act or proposal or any proposed domestic legislation covered by the Community. Thirdly, the *délégations* submit to the competent parliamentary committee reports, with or without conclusions. They are able, on their own initiative, to write reports on the issues they consider important.

The size of the *délégations* was doubled from 18 to 36. While membership would continue to reflect differing party strengths in each Chamber, membership would now also have to be drawn in a more balanced way from the six permanent committees. In short, the change means that membership of the *délégations* is more representative both of parties and of permanent committees. This was considered a very important change. Overlapping membership was seen as the most effective way of integrating the work of the *délégations* into the deliberations of the permanent committees. Each of the six permanent committees in the National Assembly and Senate now have anything from three to 12 members who are also members of the *délégations*, with many exercising committee responsibilities. In addition, national parliamentarians who were also members of the European Parliament were no longer barred from membership of the *délégations*. All in all, it was felt that these changes would enable the *délégations* to play a more important role in the work of the various parliamentary committees.

The 1990 modifications, if anything, extended the range of issues to be examined by the *délégations*. The 1979 law had identified for examination only those matters examinable by Parliament under Article 34 of the Constitution. All Community proposals are now to be submitted for examination by the *délégations*. The 1990 law also clarified the issue of the timing of the passing of documentation for examination. The 1979 law had been somewhat imprecise and, in most instances, resulted in the *délégations* having insufficient time to consider proposals prior to their adoption by the EC Council of Ministers. Following the 1990 law, *délégations* are to receive all necessary information at the same time as proposals are submitted to the European Community Council of Ministers. It was felt that this would give *délégations* more time to perform their tasks. The obligation of the Government to provide the *délégations* with all documents produced by various institutions of the Community was re-stated in the 1990 law, as was the obligation to inform them of current negotiations. The 1990 law also incorporated the practice which had developed in previous years of inviting government ministers to appear and give evidence. The *délégations* may also invite French members of the European Parliament to participate in their deliberations. Both government ministers and MEPs may turn down the invitation to attend. The practice of inviting representatives of Community institutions which had developed in previous years was not written into the law, though it remains possible. The two *délégations* are also now able to hold common meetings. The 1990 law also gave the *délégations* more autonomy by allowing them to choose Community matters upon which they wish to issue reports, with or without recommendations for parliamentary action. Moreover, their reports are now more widely available and are considered parliamentary documents in their own right.

RESPONDING TO MAASTRICHT

As was noted above, the amendment in June 1992 of Article 88 of the Constitution following the Maastricht ratification process gives Parliament for the first time the constitutional right to to be informed, to scrutinise, and intervene – via the tabling of resolutions – in the conduct of European Community policy. The translation and implementation of the new constitutional provision have resulted in a number of significant changes in Parliament's rules and procedures when dealing with European Union matters.[6] Perhaps most importantly, the *délégations*' role in proceedings has been formally recognised and indeed significantly strengthened (see Figure 1). Henceforth, in theory at least, their views cannot be ignored by permanent committees as they could, and often were, in the past. For example they must respond to any proposed resolution tabled by the *délégations* within a month of its reception whether Parliament is in session or not. Clearly the relationship between the *délégations* and the permanent committees is crucial. The *délégations*' influence will depend on the acceptance or rejection by the permanent committees of their

FIGURE 1

THE SCRUTINY OF EUROPEAN UNION LEGISLATIVE PROPOSALS BY THE FRENCH NATIONAL ASSEMBLY

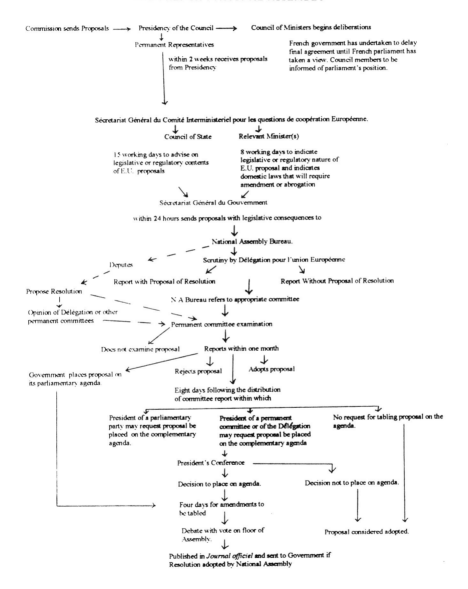

prosposals. The practice has developed whereby the *délégation* will designate as rapporteurs members of the permanent committee to whom may be sent proposed resolutions in the hope that this will make that committee more likely to favour the *délégations'* suggestions. This appears to be a successful development because rejection of a *délégation's* views or proposals has become an extremely rare event. Yet another significant development is the greater willingness of Government to include consideration of such resolutions on the National Assembly timetable.

The new procedures have transformed the *délégations* into gatekeepers. While the Government must make available to all parliamentarians and permanent committees information and proposed European Union legislation, the *délégations* have the primary responsibility of examining proposals and deciding on whether further action is necessary. Even in instances where individual parliamentarians may wish to table a resolution the *délégation* will be asked for its views. Unlike the Senate's *délégation*, the National Assembly's meets monthly and systematically and exhaustively examines and classifies all proposals before it places them into one of four categories. The reports produced following examination of proposed legislation by the National Assembly *délégation* include a number of interesting sections: the legal basis of the proposed legislation; the date of the proposed legislation's transmission to the Council of Ministers; the date it was received by the Presidency of the National Assembly; the relevant procedures to be followed for their adoption; the motives and objectives of the proposed legislation; a judgement by the *délégation* on the applicability of the principle of subsidiarity; an indication of any national legislation which would have to be modified following the European Union's adoption of the proposed legislation; the general responses from interested groups and institutions to the proposed legislation and the stage it has reached in the European Unions decision-making processes; a provisional timetable for its examination; and the conclusions and recommendations of the *délégation*. After completing this process the *délégation* will suggest one of four courses of action.

First, it may propose that no further action is necessary because the proposed legislation is of limited significance or too far down the European Union decision-making process. Secondly, it may find that no further action is possible because the legislation will already have been adopted by the European Union. This tends to apply to around 25 per cent of all legislation before the *délégation*. In instances such as these the *délégation* will produce a summary of the adopted legislation. Thirdly, it may decide that a more detailed analysis of the proposed legislation is necessary and proceed to designate from within its membership rapporteurs to carry it out. The outcome may be the tabling of a resolution. Fourthly, the *délégation* may decide to adopt a definitive position on a legislative proposal which will have as an outcome either the immediate tabling of a proposed resolution or it will directly inform the Government of its views.

During the period between August 1992 and June 1994, the *délégation* in the National Assembly examined 265 European Union legislative proposals. Thirty-eight proposals gave rise to the tabling of 41 resolutions. Of these, 23 were adopted by the National Assembly; 14 after full debate by the whole assembly; nine after examination by permanent committee. Most resolutions were tabled by members of the *délégation*. Of the 23 adopted, 14 were tabled by *délégation* members. They also tabled 25 of the 41, while ten were tabled by the party groups and the remaining six by chairmen of the permanent committees of the National Assembly. The resolutions have tended to divide into three groups. The first group comprises those which call on the Government to oppose the proposed legislation in the Council of Ministers. The second group includes those resolutions suggesting changes of emphasis or quite detailed amendments. The third group of resolutions are more general in content and tend to be comments on a number of legislative proposals in the same policy sector. This evidence also tends to suggest that French parliamentarians other than those who are members of the *délégations* have remained marginal participants in the new opportunities for a greater input afforded by the amendment of Article 88 of the Constitution.

Given the short period of time in which the new procedures have been in operation it is perhaps too early to assess the full impact and effectiveness of the new arrangements. Nonetheless, a number of issues have emerged which are likely to remain significant bones of contention between Parliament and Government. The first major cause of dissatisfaction for members of the *délégations* and other interested parliamentarians concerns the lack of time available to them in order to examine proposed Community legislation. As can be noted from Figure 1, it takes around one month for proposals finally to find their way to Parliament from the Commission. This has meant that in many instances legislation has been adopted by the Council of Ministers before *délégations* have had the opportunity to examine and take a view on the matter. In many other instances legislation has been adopted while the *délégations* or Parliament had it under consideration or were even debating a resolution motion. In these instances Parliament's new constitutional rights were effectively ignored. Moreover, even when Parliament has the opportunity to examine proposed legislation, this takes place at such a late stage in the decision-making process that its ability to influence outcomes is not good. In response to these problems, in June 1994 the Government announced that it would seek to delay Council of Ministers' deliberations on proposed legislation until after the *délégations* of the French Parliament have completed their work. It is unclear at this stage if this has in fact actually ever happened since the announcement.

A second area of conflict between Parliament and Government to have emerged concerns the narrow interpretation given by the Government to Article 88. In effect this has resulted in Parliament not being provided with all European Union proposed legislation. The Government has felt under no obligation to provide Parliament with any information falling under the Commission's powers of delegated legislation, inter-institutional agreements between the institutions of the European Union, or any proposed legislation drawn up as a consequence of the so-called 'second' and 'third' inter-governmental pillars of the Maastricht Treaty dealing with foreign and defence policy and justice and internal affairs matters respectively. It has even failed to provide Parliament with all proposed European Union legislation containing provisions requiring the Parliament's intervention under Article 34. The Conseil d'Etat advises the Government as to the legislative or regulatory nature of proposed European Union legislation. However, the Government does not have to explain the basis for its decision not to refer proposed legislation to Parliament. The chairman of the *délégation* in the National Assembly has suggested that the Government has provided Parliament with a large number of European Union legislative proposals of minor importance or little political significance and withheld a significant number of important proposals.

The influence of Parliament's resolutions on the Government consti-tutes a third area worthy of note. It is clear that the Government is not legally bound in its negotiations on proposed legislation by resolutions adopted by either Chamber of the French Parliament. However, a number of interesting developments have occurred. First, the Govern-ment now includes in the documents of ministers involved in Council of Minister negotiations the resolutions adopted by Parliament. Secondly, once a resolution is adopted by Parliament, the SGCI working with the Minister for European Affairs has to ensure that the contents of the resolution are taken into account by the relevant ministers when formu-lating negotiating positions. Thirdly, the debates on proposed resolutions have provided Parliament with an opportunity to influence the Govern-ment's stance and obtain its views on the matter under consideration. Fourthly, the Government has used resolutions voted by Parliament as a new type of diplomatic weapon in its negotiating tactics. The European Union Council of Ministers is informed of the views of Parliament as expressed in resolutions. As one might expect, the Government has been particularly keen on using those resolutions that strengthen its negotiating position and has tended to ignore those resolutions which did not accord with its views on an issue. At the same time, however, the Government has not been forthcoming in providing Parliament with information on the extent to which it has incorporated its wishes. It is therefore extremely difficult to come to a view on the extent to which the Government pays any attention to Parliament.

Parliament's ability to scrutinise the activities of the Government in European affairs have not been greatly enhanced by the changes since 1992. With the exception of the arangements put in place to give effect to Article 88 of the Constitution, the National Assembly, for example, has no specific procedures in place to deal with European affairs. Members of the National Assembly have to use established procedural means to elicit information from the Government. The only innovation, a sessional debate on the Government's European policy was introduced in 1989. Even resolution debates are timetabled on Monday mornings and Thursday afternoons when members have either not returned from their constituencies or have gone for the weekend. The *délégations* are now provided with minutes of the meetings of the European Council of Ministers but not with any detailed information of the meeting of the Committee of Permanent Representatives (COREPER) or the even more important working parties of the European Council of Ministers. The Government has in fact paid only partial attention to its obligation to provide the *délégations* of both Chambers with information of ongoing negotiations. It has not really been willing to provide Parliament with the means to make an informed input into the formulation of what it considers 'its' policy domain. However, it is unlikely that Parliament, through its *délégations*, will allow the Government the kind of unfettered freedom of action that was a feature of the past. The National Assembly *délégation* following the 1993 legislative elections has to some extent become a potentially very influential home for many parliamentarians who were in the 'no' camp during the Maastricht referendum campaign. They, perhaps more than any other group of parliamentarians, are determined to integrate national parliaments in the European Union's decision-making processes. There is little doubt that the National Assembly's *délégation* has become a far more active parliamentary body since 1993. For example, it produced 54 reports in the 14 months following its reconstitution after the legislative elections and held more than 60 meetings. It had met only 123 times during the previous five years and produced 79 reports. Moreover, there is some evidence emerging that from time to time their reports influence the Government. There has also been an intensification of its links with the European Parliament. This has involved holding meetings with various committees of the European Parliament on specific issues, inviting French members of the European Parliament to give evidence to the *délégation*. French members of the European Parliament are regularly kept informed of the views and positions adopted by the National Assembly on issues of common interest through the liaison office of the French Parliament. Before each session of the European Parliament French MEPs are provided with a sessional dossier containing all French parliamentary documents relevant to the issues on the European Parliament's agenda. In return the *délégation* benefits from a regular flow of information on the activities of the European Parliament which at times is more useful than that provided by the Government. The National Assembly delegation has also sought to maximise the influence and impact of its reports by distributing them very widely. This includes all chairs of permanent committees, the chairs of committees of the European Parliament, the European Commission, to French ministers, to the SGCI, to COREPER, to the ambassadors of other European Union Member States, to the European affairs committees in the parliaments of other Member States, and to journalists and other interested academics.[7]

This short paper has sought briefly to outline how the French Parliament has adapted its internal structures and to a lesser extent its procedures in order to be able to play a more important role in European Community matters. Naturally, a number of issues require further and sustained examination, not least of these, for example, would be an evaluation of the performance of the parliamentary *délégations* and their relationship to permanent committees or the impact on the Government of Parliament's resolutions. What is clear is that since 1979 an increasing number of French parliamentarians and successive governments have recognised the need to respond, via institutional, procedural and constitutional adjustments, to the challenges raised by greater European integration and the completion of the internal market. This has already had, and will undoubtedly continue to have, important and significant consequences for Parliament. Not least of these is likely to be a loosening of the constitutional straitjacket placed on Parliament in 1958.

NOTES

1. J.R. Frears, 'The French Parliament and the European Community', *Journal of Common Market Studies* 12 (1975) pp.140–58.
2. On the role of the Secretariat Général du Comité interministeriel pour les questions de cooperation économique européenne (SGCI) see C. Lequesne, *Paris-Bruxelles: Comment se fait la Politique Européenne de la France* (Paris, Presse de la Fondation Nationale des Science Politiques, 1993).
3. For a useful examination of the broad impact on French politics and institutions of the Single European Act and Maastricht Treaty see R. Ladrech, 'Europeanization of

Domestic Politics and Institutions: The Case of France', *Journal of Common Market Studies*, 32 (1994), pp.69–88.

4. The following is the relevant clause of the amended Article 88 adopted at a special Congress of Parliament at Versailles on 23 June 1992.

Title XIV On the European Communities and the European Union.

Art. 88-4 The government submits to the National Assembly and the Senate, by way of their transmission to the Council of the Communities, proposals of Community acts incorporating provisions of a legislative nature. During sessions, or outside them, resolutions can be voted in the framework of the present article, according to the terms determined by the rules of each assembly.

5. *Le Monde*, 19 May 1993, p.12.
6. For details of the procedural changes as well as a review of the performance and prospects of the new arrangements in the National Assembly see R. Pandraud, 'L'Assemblee nationale et l'Europe; Bilan et perspectives', Rapport d'information No.1436 (Paris, Les Document d'Information – Assemblee Nationale, 1994).
7. Pandrand, 'L'Assemblee nationale et l'Europe', pp.235–47.

The Netherlands: From Founding Father to Mounding Baby

M.P.C.M. VAN SCHENDELEN

The Netherlands was one of the six founding members of the European Community and its forerunners. Until the first enlargement in 1973, it represented more than seven per cent of both EC population and gross domestic product. In political terms it acted as the main broker between the quarrelling Member States of France and Germany; Italy and Belgium were distracted by domestic problems and Luxembourg was less capable of mediating. For that brokerage, the country was rewarded with important positions, particularly (from 1958 to 1977) the Commissioner of DG VI (Agriculture), where 80 per cent of the European budget was spent. Four decades later, the Netherlands represents roughly 4.5 per cent of EU population and GDP and is no longer invited to play a major political role; France and Germany created their special forms of accommodation and new larger Member States (UK, Spain) entered the scene. At best, the country is now the largest of the ten small Member States. The changing political geography of the Union did reduce the importance of the country. But, conversely, for the country the Union has become more important than ever: in 1951 it gained 38 per cent of its national income from exports, but in 1990 the figure was 53 per cent and three-quarters of those exports went to EU countries.

From the beginning, national political culture was much in favour of European integration, not only at mass level (according to Eurobarometer data) but also at elite levels in government and business,[1] though there was a delicate balance between Atlantic and European loyalties. Support for European integration was most clearly expressed in the Government's official preference for supranationalism: the more transfer of powers to the common institutions, the better for both Europe and the Netherlands; the same belief was lately laid down in the Dutch proposals for European Political Union (1991). An element of this belief has always been that democratic (that is, parliamentary) control of European governance should be strengthened by empowering the European Parliament and

M.P.C.M. Van Schendelen is Professor of Political Science, Erasmus University, Rotterdam. The research reported here was made possible by a grant from the Research Centre for Financial Economic Policy (OCFEB) of the Economic Faculty of Erasmus University, Rotterdam, for which the author is most grateful.

not, in the Dutch logic of supranationalism, the national Parliament. The so-called democratic deficit must be solved in 'Brussels'.[2]

In the Dutch bi-cameral parliament, the Second Chamber (Tweede Kamer) – with 150 full-time members – is the most powerful: it is directly elected, forms the Cabinet and has, compared with other parliaments in Europe, a wide range of powers. The First Chamber (Eerste Kamer), with its 75 part-time members, is of secondary importance. This article focuses on the Second Chamber.

The Parliament or – *pars pro toto* – the Second Chamber has both a party system and a committee system. So-called specialists of each party meet in committee and cover a special policy field. To their party they provide cues for voting and other common activities. Every member is a specialist and, in consequence, some sort of a front-bencher in certain policy fields. The real parliamentary decision-making takes place in small and informal meetings of the specialists and the leaders of the government parties and their related Cabinet members; party discipline does the rest.[3]

Since 1979, the year of the first directly elected EP, there has been no dual mandate. A 1993 proposal to re-introduce it for a few members was rejected by the political parties, which have the final say over candidatures. Communication between the national parliament and EP has become scarce and exceptional. Dutch MEPs wanted to have more communication in the 1980s, but got formal refusals, except for guest-status in party meetings. Since 1992 the MPs have shown more interest in communicating with MEPs.[4] They have, however, limited funds to travel to parliaments in Europe, including the EP.[5] The main linkage between the two parliaments is based on a modest circulating recruitment: at election times the parties direct a few MEPs to the national scene and MPs to the EP.

EUROPEAN ACTIVITIES OF THE SECOND CHAMBER 1978–1993

Table 1 provides data on various parliamentary activities regarding European affairs. From the official thesaurus of the Dutch Parliament all items with a reference to the 'European Community' or related terms such as the EP and MEP have been counted for the sessions (from September to September) between 1978 and 1993. Three main categories are distinguished: debates, dossiers, and documents.

The category of debates refers to the number of times a European item was debated in either a plenary or a committee meeting (except closed committee meetings, but including all public ones ['OCV'] and all extended ones ['UCV'], which act on behalf of the plenary). The category of dossiers refers to the number of times a new European theme was put on the Parliament's agenda. The decision to open a new dossier is at the

TABLE 1
SECOND CHAMBER ACTIVITIES REGARDING 'EUROPE'

parliamentary year / category	1978 -79 **	1979 -80	1980 -81	1981 -82 *	1982 -83 *	1983 -84 **	1984 -85	1985 -86 *	1986 -87	1987 -88	1988 -89 **	1989 -90 *	1990 -91	1991 -92	1992 -93	Total
1. DEBATES	20	.13	14	8	14	12	20	12	51	14	68	72	73	73	22	486
2. DOSSIERS	8	11	16	9	11	7	19	13	10	17	21	33	17	23	20	235
3. DOCUMENTS of which	93	115	76	96	97	83	137	154	150	203	350	346	377	385	349	3,431
a) parl. questions	78	71	47	25	28	19	34	17	48	42	39	27	32	38	34	579
b) parl. motions	14	39	19	23	17	21	36	22	20	18	14	22	41	24	29	359
c) parl. reports	0	1	0	20	19	11	14	12	21	32	32	36	40	46	38	322
d) parl. various	0	0	0	2	3	6	5	6	1	4	5	3	3	5	12	55
e) g'ment letters	1	4	10	19	18	13	21	43	34	51	195	213	224	234	206	1,286
f) g'ment reports	0	0	0	2	1	3	3	26	17	34	29	21	17	27	22	202
g) g'ment various	0	0	0	1	3	2	2	3	1	1	2	1	0	2	7	25
h) miscellaneous	0	0	0	-;	8	8	22	25	8	21	34	23	20	9	21	203

*   national election year
** EP election year

discretion of the Presidium and the Clerk and indicates the birth of a new policy theme. The category of documents refers to the number of times a specific document has been produced by either (a member of) the Parliament or (one of) the Cabinet. On the Parliament's side have been distinguished questions to the Government, motions (proposals to make an urgent, but non-binding, request to the Government), reports on consultations with the government, and 'various' (mainly reports from committees on government proposals). On the Cabinet's side are distinguished letters to the Parliament, reports on European affairs and 'various' (mainly memoranda on government proposals). There is also a miscellaneous group of documents with a diffuse or ambivalent character (mainly documents from outside Parliament or Cabinet).

All data are only for the Second Chamber. The reasons for this are that it is the major political chamber, most government documents are the same for both chambers, and the First Chamber has a marginal output of its own (ten per cent of the number of debates and less than one per cent of the number of documents in the Second Chamber).

The table shows an increasing involvement of the national Parliament with European affairs during the 15-year time period. With many ups and downs, there is now much more often debate, new dossier formation, and production of documents than 15 years before. The turning point is the session of 1984–85. The explanation can only be found at the European level: in 1984 the EP drafted the European Union Treaty and got new elections, while in 1985 – as detailed in Philip Norton's introduction – the Commission published its White Paper on Completion of the Internal Market and the Council finally adopted the Single European Act. The national Parliament at that time became more conscious of Europe. For the many ups and downs there is no single explanation, except that in election years MPs tend to be less productive in debate and documents.

The debates have become much more numerous, not only in the plenary but also at committee level. This is partly due to the the accumulative increase of issues, as indicated by the newly formed dossiers, and partly to the change of parliamentary rules in 1986 concerning the functioning of committees (more often extended or public). The sharp decrease in the number of debates in the sessions 1987–88 and 1992–93 is caused mainly by domestic factors, to some of which we shall return.

Government documents, particularly letters and reports, show an impressive growth after the mid-eighties. As we shall see, a large part of the growth has been caused by parliamentary pressure: MPs wanted to have more information on especially the '1992' White Paper. From their side, the MPs produced slightly more reports and motions, but fewer questions than in the past.

THE YEARS BEFORE 1986: NATIONAL COHESION

Except for the direct elections to the EP in 1979, the time period up to 1986 can, from the parliamentary perspective, be seen as relatively monotonous.

Dutch policy-making on 'Europe' was in the hands of a few players. Only four ministries were, to some degree, involved in European affairs: Foreign Affairs, especially its DG European Affairs; Agriculture; Economic Affairs, particularly its DGs on Energy (regarding the ECSC since 1951 and on gas and oil, of which the country is a main supplier, since 1973) and on Foreign Trade; and Finance, especially its DG Treasury (for European monetary policy). Occasionally, the Prime Minister's small Ministry of General Affairs played some role. Other ministries, not to say public agencies and sub-national governments, were hardly or not at all involved.

In the small circles of Europe-oriented ministries, communication and co-ordination was fairly easy to organise. These tasks were the responsibility of Foreign Affairs. In regular meetings of its inter-departmental co-ordination committee ('CoCo') it formulated the so-called national interest and sent it as an instruction to its Permanent Representative in Brussels; in the Permanent Representative's office only the four of the aforementioned ministries had a delegate. This co-ordination procedure was highly effective at home and could be made effective in Brussels where, as already emphasised in this volume, decision-making in the Council of Ministers was based on unanimity.

During this period, the members of the Second Chamber's Committee on Foreign Affairs were the key MPs on European affairs. Many came from the Ministry of Foreign Affairs, some even with a return ticket. The main parliamentary debate on 'Europe' took place once a year in pursuance of the ministry's yearly report. Until 1979 all (at that time 14) Dutch MEPs were members of the Second Chamber and many were members of its Foreign Affairs Committee as well. A survey among them showed that in practice they functioned as a two-way channel between the two Parliaments: as cue-givers on 'Europe' in the national parliament and as Dutch articulators in the EP.[6]

The direct elections to the EP in 1979 did not initially change this relationship between the two parliaments very much. A survey of Dutch MPs in 1979, held after the EP elections, showed strong support for supranationalism: 45 per cent saw the existing transfer of powers as sufficient, 34 per cent as too little, and only 12 per cent as too much.[7] But the MPs did have some self-criticism: 40 per cent felt they had done too little to push the Government to promote Dutch interests at European level, while 50 per cent considered it as sufficient and only one per cent as too much.[8] This peculiar Dutch view, that national interests are best promoted through supranational channels and platforms, was earlier observed by Spinelli.[9]

Another survey among all (then 25) Dutch MEPs in 1981 showed that there was still some communication between the two parliaments, although mainly at the MEPs' initiative and with growing tensions.[10] They saw the MPs as poorly informed about, and weakly interested in, 'Europe' and considered the relationships with the national Parliament as poor and insufficient. The change from a two-way channel to a widening gap between the two parliaments had been predicted and suggestions for bridging the gap had been made,[11] but all that was ignored by the Second Chamber, which held the view that the two parliaments have each their own job to do: the national one controls the national Government and the EP the European Government.

THE YEARS 1986–1991: NATIONAL TENSIONS

For three reasons the year 1986 is a turning point: the Single European Act became a political fact, the '1992' White Paper was set in motion, and the Second Chamber established its Standing Committee on European Affairs.

The SEA, as outlined in the introduction to this volume, brought into practice qualified majority voting in the Council of Ministers for a wide range of socio-economic dossiers. It implied the formal end of the national veto for cases under the co-operation procedure. The '1992' White Paper brought on to the EU agenda an impressive extension of policy domains and items, with many specific proposals to create a single market for capital, labour, products and services. The programme attracted crowds of stakeholders from both the public sector (central and decentralised government, public agencies and bodies) and the private one (both profit and non-profit making bodies). Discovering that the national Government could not provide protection by veto, they wanted to take care of their own interests.[12] The national co-ordination procedure changed from a small circle of participants into a large arena of competitive ministries. Even the question of whether Foreign Affairs should retain the final say was raised;[13] General Affairs (Prime Minister), Economic Affairs and Home Affairs claimed that say too.

Like most other parliaments of the 'old Six',[14] the Second Chamber established a standing European Affairs Committee by the time (1986) that, on the government side, national co-ordination had become less relevant and more difficult to arrange. The Committee's main task was to co-ordinate parliamentary activity in relation to EC affairs.[15] Its major policy focus became the handling of the '1992' White Paper, for both policy formulation[16] and implementation.[17] It pressured the Government to report on the policy plans of the various ministries. But the reports[18] soon attracted all other sorts of party specialists, who refused to accept co-ordination of their activities by others. The Committee, designed to co-ordinate the Second Chamber on EU affairs, in fact hardly achieved any substantial parliamentary co-ordination.

The practice of involvement by other party specialists in EU affairs even became institutionalised in the new information procedure of 1989[19] by which every minister informs the Parliament (that is, the various committees) before and after a council meeting on respectively the agenda and the results. Although in the beginning the procedure was full of shortcomings (for example, agenda presented after the meeting instead of before) and was hardly responded to by parliamentary action, it did bring EU dossiers on to the desks of non-EU party specialists. They discovered, as it were, 'Europe' and sometimes reacted accordingly, for example, by asking the Government about the powers of the EP and European Court of Justice.[20]

The main test for the EA Committee came on the eve of the Dutch Presidency of the Council in the second half of 1991. The Cabinet reiterated its strong belief in the need for more supranationalism (now called 'federalism'), including more powers to the EP,[21] but remained unable to define clear priorities for its presidency: it listed more than 25 'priorities'[22] and thus none at all, but so satisfying all the various ministries and party specialists. The EA Committee did not set clear priorities from its side.

A 1990 survey of Dutch MPs revealed a still high and constant level of support for the transfer of national powers to 'Brussels' (34 per cent favoured more transfer, while 52 per cent saw it as sufficient and only 13 per cent as already too much) and a very positive appraisal of Dutch influence in the Council (74 per cent 'sufficient') and of EU outcomes (98 per cent 'advantageous'), but also a negative opinion on the importance of the EP (71 per cent 'unimportant') and on its own EA Committee as well (49 per cent negative, 28 per cent positive, 13 per cent ambivalent and nine per cent unfamiliar with it).[23] In the rank ordering of prestigious committees, the EA Committee was assigned a low position.[24] According to 81 per cent of MPs, the national Parliament exerted too little influence on the behaviour of the Government in the Council.[25] Asked about their own behaviour, 88 per cent of MPs confessed that 'most MPs insufficiently inform themselves about EU decision making', while 31 per cent claimed to have at least monthly contacts with MEPs (57 per cent sometimes each year, 13 per cent never), but 70 per cent were now in favour of regular meetings with MEPs.[26]

DUTCH BLACK MONDAY

In the past, the Netherlands have had only small disappointments with 'Brussels'. The country got what it wanted and, given its size, even more than that; and it could veto what it disliked. At the end of the 1980s, it experienced some defeats on minor, considered technical, dossiers. A major defeat came with the decision on the location and the chairmanship of the European Bank for Reconstruction and Development (EBRD) in 1990. The country did offer both what it considered the best place (Amsterdam) and the best man (former Minister of Finance Ruding), but both offers were ignored. Prime Minister Lubbers publicly blamed the three large Member States for constituting 'a directorate'.[27] Simultaneously, the Government felt that its once designed and beloved Common Agricultural Policy (CAP) was coming to its end.

Chairing the Council in the second part of 1991, the country presented – on 24 September – the draft Treaty for European Political Union (EPU): strong supranationalism for all existing and new policy fields, with more powers for the EP and the Commission and less for the Member States. Under strong criticism from all Member States (except Belgium), the Netherlands had to withdraw formally the whole proposal one week later, on Monday 30 September. Many were blamed for this political disaster: the Member States which had misled 'The Hague', Foreign Affairs which had miscalculated the Member States, the Under-Secretary of Foreign Affairs (Dankert, the former EP President) who was the principal author of the text, the Permanent Representative for being correct in his predictions, and the Second Chamber for its supranational pressures on the Cabinet. Even more frustrating, the Netherlands now had to draft a much less supranational and more acceptable 'Maastricht' Treaty text.

Officially the Government kept smiling. In its report to the Second Chamber on its presidency, it said it could 'look back not without satisfaction'.[28] But political behaviour came to reflect feelings of frustration. The Second Chamber spent half a year on the ratification of 'Maastricht'. Its EA Committee held a critical public hearing and produced voluminous critical reports.[29] In plenary session in November 1992, the Second Chamber spent more than 25 hours on the Treaty. It also forwarded seven amendments on the ratification bill and 19 motions, most of which were adopted and demanded from the government a stronger parliamentary say in national policy-making on European affairs.

Since 1991, the Second Chamber has increasingly voiced frustration about its role, considered as marginal, in EU affairs. Together with the Cabinet it wants to co-direct national EU policies and more and more it sees both the EP and the national bureaucracy as subordinate, while it refused to give citizens a say by referendum on the ratification of the Maastricht Treaty. It wants to take up, next to the Cabinet, the reins of national EU policy-making. In a short time, it intensified existing procedures and introduced new ones, as follows:

On Implementation of EU Directives

The Chamber intensified the existing procedure of requiring information by the Cabinet on the implementation of EU directives.[30] Many ministries appeared to have a poor performance. By critical questions and debate, members of the EA Committee and other committees pressured the responsible ministers to perform better.

On Council Information

The Cabinet's *rapportage* on Council agenda and outcomes[31] was made more on time, detailed and covering all the various Councils, including those concerning the dossiers on the second and third pillars.[32]

On Any Treaty Building

The Chamber got a new procedure introduced of quarterly *rapportage* of all treaties that were in development, whether related to the EU or not.[33] The Committees on Foreign Affairs and Justice question the relevant ministers.

On Commission Proposals

A procedure started in mid-1991 of Cabinet *rapportage* on the implications of EU Commission proposals for Dutch national law[34] was intensified into the provision of monthly information to the Chamber by the Under-Secretary of Foreign Affairs in his co-ordinating role on EU affairs. The Justice Committee in particular had pressed for this.

On Special Dossiers

On a number of EU dossiers the Chamber showed more than usual interest by demanding information, for example on the Delors II package,[35] the budgetary control on the Commission,[36] and the effects of fiscal harmonisation.[37]

On Representations Abroad

In mid-1993 the Chamber demanded from the Minister of Foreign Affairs a policy plan regarding Dutch embassies in the EU and elsewhere.[38] Cabinet and Chamber shared the view that more direct communications with other EU Member States were needed, not only through the embassies but also directly from the various ministries. The Chamber's EA Committee itself became by 1992 an active participant in the Inter-parliamentary Conference of EA Committees and the EP's Institutional Committee[39] but was soon disappointed by the results.[40]

The new or intensified procedures provided institutional facilities to the MPs to participate more in national EU policy-making. But so far the Second Chamber has behaved in a restrained manner.[41] It has questioned and debated the Cabinet and passed a few (non-binding) motions as well, but does not issue binding instructions to the Cabinet as the Danish Folketing does.

During 1992/93, the position of the EA Committee inside the Chamber was more and more challenged. First of all, all other committees started or intensified their role-playing in EU affairs. Secondly, a special committee of the Second Chamber, led by its chairman Deetman and in charge of making proposals for broad institutional reform, came up with the proposal to limit the number of parliamentary committees to one per ministry,[42] thus proposing the end of the EA Committee (because European Affairs is part of Foreign Affairs). But finally the EA Committee was saved. However, because of the national elections of 1994, the EA Committee lost its chairman (Stemerdink) and some leading figures (such as Jurgens and Van Iersel).

At the same time, concern about the nation's effectiveness inside the EU became more manifest inside the Government. In early 1993 the joint secretaries-general of all Dutch ministries published a critical report on the national co-ordination of EU affairs.[43] Critical issues were seen, among others, as the lack of EU knowledge inside both the Chamber and the Administration, the fragmented ('chaotic') character of Dutch behaviour in Brussels, the neglect of the Commission's so-called draft phase, and the weak organisation of the national co-ordination. Major recommendations included enhancing the administrative level of the co-ordination committee, strengthening the position of the Prime Minister's Office, and a greater reluctance to agree to supranational developments.

The political wound of Black Monday was temporarily healed by the Commission's proposal to give a major Regional Fund subsidy to the flourishing province of Flevoland. But the wound opened again as soon as it became clear that the sum would be halved. And it was deepened by the loss of new dossiers in Brussels, as on HDTV (standardisation and research and development subsidy for Philips), the import of Caribbean bananas, the CAP reform, the disclosure of Council decision-making, the allocation of EU offices in 1993 (Europol as a not particularly attractive prize for the country), and – last but not least – the allocation of the European Central Bank (ECB) to Germany.

In its last report to the Second Chamber before the Spring 1994 national elections, the once supranationally oriented Foreign Affairs Ministry made clear that it did not want to promote qualified majority voting for its own second pillar policy domain; that, at the 1996 IGC, it would fully defend the present Dutch position in the Council; and that it wanted to approach the future of the EU not necessarily by way of supranationalism, but certainly that of pragmatism.[44] At the same time, Foreign Affairs Under-Secretary Dankert voiced in private meetings (for example, Civil Servants' Day in February 1994) his continuing belief in further EU integration; he soon left the Cabinet for an EP position again. The new Cabinet installed a new Foreign Affairs Minister (Van Mierlo) and Under-Secretary (Patijn) who, not having any previous European experience, decided first to take time (until the Summer of 1995) for a reconsideration of Dutch policy positions concerning the EU.

OVERVIEW

Much has changed, particularly in the past few years, in the four-decades-old relationship between the Dutch Parliament and the EU. The main changes so far are of a cultural character. As part of the Dutch system, the Second Chamber increasingly discovers it is of decreasing importance inside the EU. Once a founding father, the country feels that it has become a baby state and wants to protect, or mound, its interests. Once a regular winner inside the EU, it now believes itself to be a loser. The Second Chamber's attitude towards the EU has changed from almost unconditional support for supranationalism to mixed feelings of Europeanism and self-interested nationalism; from supportive trust in EU integration to creeping distrust; and from satisfaction with its own passive position at a distance to an impatient desire to become actively involved. In regard to the EP and the Dutch delegation in particular, the Second Chamber has changed from patronage-like intimacy to critical estrangement. It still believes that the EU has a democratic deficit, but no longer that this is part of only the EP's balance-sheet: part of it lies in its own Chamber.[45]

The cultural changes have yielded some institutional reform. One is the establishment of an EA Committee. The other is the widening and deepening of various procedures to obtain information from the Government and to have a say over its activities in both the Council and the national Administration; by one procedure the Chamber shifted its policy horizon to even the Commission, thus acknowledging the importance of this so-called draft phase. In addition to these formal changes, the Chamber's parties now welcome, more than before, visits by and to MEPs.

The changes can be seen as produced by increasing frustration over the lack of control on influences from the EU. Major factors of frustration on the EU side are the enlargements which reduce the country's share of power; the QMV, by which political losses are suffered; and the policy expansions, which are beyond any span of control. Major factors on the national side are the decline of national co-ordination, by which the Chamber cannot effectively settle priorities; some political drama, such as 'Black Monday'; and some driving political characters, such as Dankert and Jurgens. The various factors have resulted in a more aggressive parliamentary approach to EU affairs.

EVALUATION

Whether the current changes of Second Chamber involvement in EU affairs can be assessed as positive or negative depends on the criteria one chooses. Various are available.

Self-Evaluation

One criterion can be the judgement of the MPs themselves. Explicit sources are the surveys mentioned above. Implicit sources are the structural changes, particularly the establishment of various procedures and the EA Committee. These sources reveal, since the mid-1980s, a growing criticism of MPs concerning the EU decision-making (both in content and procedures), the role behaviour of national ministers (both in Brussels and, on implementation and co-ordination, at home), and the functioning of MEPs.

Words and Deeds

Policy intentions can also be taken as a criterion. The Chamber wanted to have an EA Committee for the co-ordination of its EU affairs, but the MPs hardly want to become co-ordinated. The Chamber demanded more procedures, but most MPs make hardly any use of the facilities and see, apparently, their mere existence as sufficient. They are more restrained in dealing with EU affairs than with home affairs and more than is required by the constitutional code that the Cabinet governs and the Parliament controls the Cabinet.

Adaptive Behaviour

Of the many academic criteria,[46] the need to adapt one's organisation to one's changing environment is a widely accepted one. At the time that QMV came into Council practice and national co-ordination became fragmented, the Chamber established its EA Committee to co-ordinate its actions towards the Cabinet: a stillborn child. While most Dutch public and private organisations only pay lip service to the Government's self-declared leadership in EU affairs and put their main trust in their own capacities of EU lobbying, the Chamber institutionalised procedures to push the Cabinet: a short ride off on a side issue. A recent collection of about 25 case studies of Dutch EU lobbying showed that in only one case was the Second Chamber approached as well.[47] By poor adaptation to its rapidly changing political environment, the Chamber loses relevancy.

Issue Group on Democracy

A parliament might particularly be seen as a sort of pressure group on the issue of democracy. Criteria then are representativeness and effectiveness regarding, in this case, EU affairs. Operational criteria can be derived from management theories of EU lobbying.[48] They range from such questions as the internal organisation and monitoring agenda and arenas to building up coalitions and developing items for exchange and compromise. Viewed in this perspective, the Chamber is performing poorly. Its EA Committee is at best a staff facility, practically unconnected to the line organisation (the other committees). How modest it is – the most advanced step the Chamber made – is shown by its demand to the Cabinet to monitor Commission proposals. But as an issue group on democracy it is, in short, an amateur organisation: without backing from society, poorly organised, with different priorities, unfamiliar with the EU environment, formalistic in its approach, reluctant to build up coalitions with, for example, the MEPs, and arrogant in its belief to be right on 'Europe', to mention only a few basic shortcomings.[49]

Learning Capacity

Weaknesses can become an asset, if they are taken as a source of learning. There exist indeed indications of learning since the mid-1980s. Though the lessons drawn may be too late, insufficient and easy, they indicate some attitude of learning, which is a prerequisite for any improvement. Consequently, there remains room for optimism in the future. But for the time being, the Dutch Second Chamber is far from being an influential player in the field of EU affairs.

NOTES

1. P. Baehr *et al.*, *Elite en Buitenlandse politiek in Nederland* (Den Haag BZ: Staatsuit-geverij, 1978); J.J.A. Thomassen *et al.*, *De geachte afgevaardigde* (Muiderberg: Coutinho, 1992).
2. Document of the Second Chamber of the Dutch Chamber: TK 22583.
3. M.P.C.M. Van Schendelen, *Parlementaire informatie, besluitvorming en vertegen-woordiging* (Rotterdam: UPR, 1975), and, by the same author, 'Information and Decisionmaking in the Dutch Parliament', *Legislative Studies Quarterly*, 2 (1976), pp.231–50; Thomassen, pp.75–87.
4. TK 21427.
5. In 1994 the budget was 355,000 ecu. TK 23628.
6. V. Herman and M.P.C.M. Van Schendelen (eds.), *The European Parliament and the National Parliaments* (Westmead: Saxon House, 1979), pp.141–62.
7. M.P.C.M. Van Schendelen *et al.*, '*Leden van de Staten-General*' (Den Haag: VUGA, 1981), p.173.
8. Van Schendelen *et al.*, 1981, p.174.
9. A. Spinelli, *The Eurocrats* (Baltimore MD: Johns Hopkins University Press, 1966), p.82.
10. M.P.C.M. Van Schendelen, *Het Europese Parlement* (Utrecht: Aula, 1984), pp.84–8.
11. EBN, *Het Europees Parlement na de eerste rechtstreekse verkiezingen* (report committee-Samkalden) (Den Haag: Europese Beweging Nederland, 1979).
12. M.P.C.M. Van Schendelen (ed.), *National Public and Private EC Lobbying* (Aldershot: Dartmouth, 1993).
13. TK 21865.
14. ECPRD, *Bodies within National Parliaments specialising in EC Affairs* (Luxembourg: European Centre for Parliamentary Research and Documentation, 1990).
15. TK 19336-26.
16. TK 20596.
17. TK 21109.
18. TK 20596, also 21240, 21618 and 21623.
19. At first TK 20800, subsequently TK 21501.
20. TK 20596-8.
21. TK 20596-32.
22. TK 22052-1.
23. Thomassen, pp.230–35.
24. Thomassen, pp.89–95.
25. Thomassen, p.234.
26. Thomassen, pp.234–5.
27. M.P.C.M. Van Schendelen (ed.), *Nederlandse Lobby's in Europa* (Den Haag: SDU, 1993), pp.325–8.
28. TK 22052-13.
29. TK 22647-8/11/17.
30. TK 21109.
31. TK 21501.
32. TK 23400-V-38, 23490 and 23641.
33. TK 23530.
34. TK 22112.
35. TK 22677 and 23639.
36. TK 22946.
37. TK 23030.
38. TK 23238.

39. TK 22660.
40. TK 22996.
41. L.M.F. Besselink, 'Het parlement en de Europese besluitvorming', in J.G. Brouwer *et al.*, *Parlement en Buitenlands Beleid* (Zwolle: Tjeenk Willink, 1993), pp.47–83.
42. TK 21427-39/101.
43. BZ, *De organisatie en werkwijze van de Rijksdienst: Buitenlandse Zaken* (Den Haag: Ministry of Foreign Affairs, 1993).
44. TK 23620.
45. E.C.M. Jurgens, *Een onparlementair stelsel* (Deventer: Kluwer, 1993).
46. Van Schendelen, *National Public and Private EC Lobbying*, pp.144–7.
47. Van Schendelen, *Nederlandse Lobby's in Europa*.
48. R. Pedler and M.P.C.M. Van Schendelen, *Lobbying the European Union: Companies, Trade Associations and Issue Groups* (Aldershot: Dartmouth, 1994), pp.6–8.
49. EBN, *De gevolgen van een Europese 'vierde' bestuurslaag* (report committee–Donner) (Den Haag: Europese Beweging Nederland, 1991).

The Belgian Parliament and European Integration

LIEVEN DE WINTER and THIERRY LAURENT

In order to understand the adaptation of the Belgian Parliament to the process of European integration one must first specify the main features of the legislative branch as it evolved within a specific political environment.

First, up until 1995, the Belgian parliamentary system could be characterised in Lijphart's terms as a 'weak' form of bicameralism.[1] The two national chambers are congruent in terms of political composition and structural attributes (committees, leadership offices). Also, they are symmetrical in terms of competences, procedures and activities (initiation of legislation, executive control). Each bill has to be approved by the House of Representatives and the Senate in order to become law. Due to this structural and functional equivalence, the adaptation process of the House as well as of the Senate will be addressed.

Second, over a period of 25 years, successive waves of constitutional reforms have gradually generated regional and community entities that enjoy a power of legislative initiative equal to the one of the national Parliament. Therefore, given the fact that the federalization process has an impact on the relationship of the national Government with EU authorities, it would also be logical to address as well the role played by the legislative assemblies of the communities and regions. However, this adaptation of the sub-national assemblies to European integration will not be developed here as it is yet too early to appraise this process fully.

Third, like any other decision-making process in Belgium, the decision-making on European questions is characterised by very specific features of a political system considered 'the most perfect, most convincing, and most impressive example of a consociation'.[2] In a society characterised by multiple and cross-cutting cleavages, the main political parties, through a permanent process of negotiation, arrive at compromises and pacts that intend to prevent open conflicts between the main well-established societal pillars. Hence, in most policy fields, decisions are based on a large consensus between the main political parties, rather than on a

Lieven De Winter is Professeur Adjoint at the Department of Political and Social Sciences of the Université Catholique de Louvain; Thierry Laurent is research assistant of the Fonds du Développement Scientifique of the Université Catholique de Louvain.

simple majority/opposition pattern. This is especially so for questions of parliamentary reform and for matters related to foreign policy. Furthermore, with regard to the merits of European integration, consensus is exceptionally large among the Belgian political elite as well as among the public at large.[3]

With the end of the Second World War and the emergence of a new 'concert of nations' within a fully bipolarised world, the European idea was relaunched; Belgium became rapidly conscious that the only realistic option permitting it to preserve a place on the international politico-economic scene was to seek alliances with other European countries within new structures. Forced *de facto* to choose between co-operation or oblivion, the small European countries took the initiative. In their eyes, a progressive transfer of sovereignty constituted a better guarantee for freedom and prosperity than the potential obligation to ally with one or another emerging dominant state in the European arena. Following the model of the Economic Union concluded between Belgium and Luxembourg in 1921 (BLEU), the Belgian Government signed a customs agreement with representatives of the Netherlands and Luxembourg, the other 'political dwarfs' preoccupied by their politico-economic future. Hence, for the small European countries, the process of co-operation and European integration began rather early. Also when this process of the European construction became more intense, Belgium made decisive contributions during its most crucial moments. Assured of the importance of Community integration, it has assumed since then a role of mediator trying to bring larger European states to compromise. While avoiding openly opposing the will of the latter, it left an indelible imprint on the process of *rapprochement* between European nations.[4]

Despite the feeble interest of Belgian MPs in foreign affairs,[5] the ambition of Belgian leaders to be first-line actors in the European construction process facilitated the swift adaptation of national political structures to this process. Indeed, when on 9 May 1957, Foreign Affairs Minister Spaak tabled in the House the proposals of ratification for the European treaties, these documents also called for the creation of a temporary EEC committee (a body that eventually could become permanent). A week later the composition of this temporary committee was announced. During the following months, many deputies proposed to transform the temporary into a permanent committee, competent for scrutinising the evolution of the application of the Common Market Treaty. Others opposed this creation, as the Standing Orders of the House only grant the power of control over the Government to the plenary assembly. Moreover, the Government, aiming at a fast ratification of the treaties, did not help or initiate the creation of such a body asked for by deputies. Instead, a compromise was reached. Majority and opposition jointly presented an amendment to the ratification law. It called for annual reports of the Executive to the House concerning the application of the European treaties. Yet, the Government never made such reports. So, four years later, a permanent Committee of European Affairs[6] within the Chamber of Representatives was finally created on the initiative of the House. This self-defence reflex, intended to maintain the link with MEPs, gave the House indispensable control and information possibilities to counterbalance the progressive loss of Parliament's prerogatives.[7] This European Affairs Committee, the first one created in a national Parliament of the Common Market, met for the first time on 16 June 1962.

The new Article 83 of the standing orders of the House stipulated that a European Affairs Committee was to be constituted after each renewal of the House. This committee consisted of 23 members and used the same rules of operation (quorum, meetings behind closed doors) as other permanent committees.[8] Any Belgian MP, member of one of the various European assemblies,[9] could not be a full or even substitute member of this Committee, in spite of the fact that in those days the combination of these functions was very common, if not compulsory.[10] Such MPs could only participate in the proceedings of the Committee with a purely consultative status. Hence, MPs who, due to their accumulation of these legislative offices were probably most experienced and knowledgeable in European matters, were excluded from the committee that was explicitly created for these matters! The motivation for this surprising incompatibility was that the House wanted to avoid MEP-MPs being asked to judge, as members of the national Parliament, their actions as members of the European Parliament. However, MEPs acquired an important informal role as they were in practice responsible for informing the Committee of the positions adopted by European assemblies.

Hence, the role of this Committee was to obtain all information on the consequences of the application of the EC treaties, to supervise their application and to follow the developments within the organisations that the latter created. For this purpose, the Committee acquired knowledge of the reports of the Belgian Government on the execution of the treaties, could summon ministers to attend committee meetings and ask them for explanations.[11] Nevertheless, the Committee did not really exert control on the executive. Ministers appeared before the committee only to inform and assure contact with MPs, but could not be held responsible by the committee.[12] The Committee drafted a report for the House each time that a specific problem discussed within the European Parliament or another European assembly had led to a decision or a resolution that could have implications for Belgian legislation.

The European Affairs Committee was also responsible for examining the annual report made to the House by the delegations of the Belgian Parliament to the European assemblies.[13] Each year, before the Easter holidays, the Committee reported to the House about its activities and findings. In addition, the Committee could report on all questions it judged useful to submit to the House, on all questions the House had submitted to the Committee, as well as on all those demanding the inter-vention of the House by virtue of its constitutional competences. Other permanent committees did not enjoy this right of initiative. At any given time the House could, however, by a resolution taken by absolute majority, debate questions submitted to the Committee when it thought that it would better to discuss the matter in the full House.

In practice, the Committee looked mainly into Common Market problems: customs, transport and agricultural problems, the application of European treaties, negotiations with potential new Member States, and so on. However, despite its apparently large sphere of competence, the European Affairs Committee had only limited success. Indeed, it confined itself essentially to the role of collecting reports drafted by Belgian members of the European assemblies, and itself drafted only a few reports on European questions. This self-restriction explains why the share of the Committee in the overall legislative production of the Belgian Parliament was almost nil.[14] In addition, in the entire course of its existence, this Committee held less than 100 meetings (1962–79). If one excludes the period (1962–63) just after its creation, and the 1977–78 session (the session that preceded the first direct European election), the total number of meetings for remaining sessions drops to 50, or less than four meetings a year.

Several reasons can explain the Committee's low degree of activity. First, the Government did not want any close parliamentary scrutiny of its activities at the European level. Second, the House was reluctant to attribute the necessary formal powers that such a committee would require to accomplish its oversight mission effectively.[15] A similar paradox lay in the fact that from the beginning the House never intended to deprive the regular committees of their subject competence on foreign affairs, economic policies, agriculture, and so on. Also, as Belgian MEPs were also members of their national Parliament, they did not feel the need for rediscussing matters they could discuss in their regular committee in the European Affairs Committee. As a result, most important European matters were discussed within the traditional committees. The impossibility for Belgian representatives to be members of this Committee if they occupied a mandate in an assembly within a European organisation reinforced this tendency. Furthermore, until the 1980s Belgian MPs did not seem to show a very vivid interest in international problems.[16]

The European Affairs Committee finally disappeared in 1979 when the House decided to rationalise its committee system.[17] In the meanwhile, the Belgian Parliament participated in the creation of other instruments of interparliamentary communication such as the Conference of Chairmen of Parliaments of European Member States and of the European Parliament (established in 1975).

THE PERIOD OF TRANSITION (1979–85)

While the various competences of the former European Affairs Committee were transferred to the Foreign Affairs Committee,[18] other measures were taken facilitating the interaction between the Belgian and European parliaments. With the first direct election of MEPs in June 1979, the combination of Belgian and European parliamentary offices became less automatic. Hence a problem arose as MEPs who were not MPs were not allowed to participate in the meetings of national parliamentary committees. However, they could be invited as experts by a parliamentary committee to participate in meetings (having a consultative voice), and make statements on topics previously debated within the European assemblies that were of particular interest to Belgium. Nevertheless, the experience was inconclusive because Belgian MEPs had in practice only access to meetings of the External Relations Committee while they also wanted to participate in committees dealing with agriculture, infrastructure, and so on.

Furthermore, a liaison office was created, intended to facilitate contacts and co-operation between MEPs and MPs. Also, the House's information bulletin to its MPs started to include brief activity reports of the European Parliament in order to facilitate Belgian MPs' access to useful information. Finally, Belgian MEPs were granted the same rights of access to all Belgian parliamentary buildings as enjoyed by national MPs.[19]

Nevertheless, for two years the double-mandate remained the rule rather than the exception,[20] a combination that was enhanced by the physical proximity of the Belgian Parliament and the seat of committees of the European Parliament and the European Community Commission. However, the electoral law of 27 February 1984 instituted an incompatibility between European and Belgian parliamentary mandates. The complete disappearance of the double mandate incited in 1985 the Standing Orders Committee of the House to respond to the request of several Belgian MEPs for access to the Belgian Parliament. A new Article 25 in the Standing Orders stipulated that Belgian MEPs have direct access to the External Relations Committee and access to all other permanent committees on the condition of a preliminary request to the chairman of the committee concerned.[21] The MEPs have only a consultative voice and must restrict their intervention to the matter mentioned in their request. In addition, each member of the European Parliament can, as before, be called or invited to participate as an expert in committee meetings. It is important to note that, at that time, this system of participation had no equal in the other countries of the Community.

THE CREATION OF THE ADVICE COMMITTEE IN CHARGE OF EUROPEAN MATTERS OF THE HOUSE OF REPRESENTATIVES IN 1985

Two factors pushed the Belgian Parliament once more to install a body[22] specifically in charge of European affairs and of securing more structured contacts between Belgian and European parliaments. First, the acceleration of the deepening of the European Community in the beginning of the 1980s increased the pre-eminence of Community law over national law. Second, Parliament became suddenly aware of the fact that, like its equivalents, it was increasingly stripped of its own prerogatives to the benefit of the European and national executives (the latter as the agent for executing European proposals). So, in order to avoid being overtaken by events, the House decided to become a valid interlocutor in the conduct of European affairs.

At the end of November 1984, the President of the House called a meeting of all MEPs and presidents of the parliamentary parties. In February 1985 the Special Committee on Standing Orders and Reform of Parliamentary Activities envisaged two important modifications of the Standing Orders. The first one stipulated that Belgian MEPs could attend all meetings of permanent committees. The second called for the creation of an Advice Committee in charge of European Affairs, inspired by the model of the Europa Kommission of the German Bundestag. This committee was installed in May 1985, in spite of some opposition from deputies who did not want to give to members of other assemblies the opportunity to sit in the House committees.[23]

The new Article 100 of the Standing Orders of the House of Representatives established the formal framework of this permanent committee. Given the disappearance of the double mandate, it was decided to compose the committee of ten members of the House and ten Belgian MEPs. The former are appointed by the House while the latter are appointed by their peers (MEPs elected in Belgium), respecting the principle of proportional representation of party groups. This Committee is chaired *de jure* by the President of the House (who can delegate his prerogatives to one of the vice-presidents). Of the committee's two vice-chairpersons, one is an MP, the other an MEP. Each parliamentary group too small to be represented in this committee can have one of its deputies and one of its MEPs attend committee meetings, but without being entitled to speak or vote. While in principle this committee meets only once a month, the current of events forced it to meet more frequently. For instance, when it had to draft its report on the Maastricht Treaty, it met three to four times a month.

The mission of the Advice Committee in charge of European Matters is to give, either on its own initiative or on the demand of an MP or a Belgian MEP, advice on various questions concerning Europe in general and the European Community in particular. There are three types of

TABLE 1

MEETINGS OF THE HOUSE OF REPRESENTATIVES ADVICE COMMITTEE IN CHARGE OF EUROPEAN MATTERS (BY PARLIAMENTARY SESSION)

Session	N of meetings
O.S. 1961–1962:	5
O.S. 1962–1963:	12
O.S. 1963–1964:	5
O.S. 1964–1965:	4
E.S. 1965:	0
O.S. 1965–1966:	5
O.S. 1966–1967:	4
O.S. 1967–1968:	2
E.S. 1968:	0
O.S. 1968–1969:	2
O.S. 1969–1970:	4
O.S. 1970–1971:	2
O.S. 1971–1972:	1
O.S. 1972–1973:	6
O.S. 1973–1974:	2
E.S. 1974:	4
O.S. 1974–1975:	7
O.S. 1975–1976:	2
O.S. 1976–1977:	0
E.S. 1977:	0
O.S. 1977–1978:	20
O.S. 1978–1979:	3
E.S. 1979:	2

O.S.: ordinary session
E.S.: extraordinary session

questions: (1) questions on institutional and other important political matters; (2) questions of co-operation between the House of Representatives and the European Parliament; (3) questions concerning the status of Belgian MEPs and the reciprocal information of the two assemblies. Nevertheless, one should notice that if the House decides to devote a debate in plenary session to one of these issues, the members of the Committee can in no way participate in debates.

The committee operates in the following way: it receives from the House all approved EC documents. Its working agenda is formally fixed in common agreement with the House, but in practice it usually decides freely which topics merit discussion and elaboration. The House, to which the committee reports are dispatched, then decides whether or not to debate the findings of these reports. Similarly, the Advice Committee also drafts resolutions to be debated by the House in plenary assembly. Hence, it is clear that the fundamental task of the committee is to inform,

TABLE 2

MEETINGS OF THE HOUSE OF REPRESENTATIVES ADVICE COMMITTEE
IN CHARGE OF EUROPEAN MATTERS (MOST RECENT SESSIONS)

A. Public Meetings

Session	Number	Duration	Together with other committee
E.S. 91–92:	12	(22h50)	No
O.S. 92–93:	1	(1h45)	Finance and External Relations Committees
	2	(5h25)	External Relations Committee
O.S. 93–94:	4	(7h30)	No
	1	(4h05)	Defence and External Relations Committees
	3	(3h55)	External Relations Committee
	1	(1h30)	Social Affairs Committee

B. Meetings behind closed doors

Session	Number	Duration	Together with other committee
E.S. 91–92:	12	(22h50)	No
	2	(3h50)	Finance and External Relations Committees
O.S. 92–93:	20	(34h40)	No
	1	(0h45)	External Relations Committee
O.S. 93–94:	8	(14h05)	No
	1	(1h50)	Defence and External Relations Committee
	1	(2h45)	Finance Committee
	1	(2h30)	Social Affairs Committee

O.S.: ordinary session
E.S.: extraordinary session

to incite Belgian deputies to develop an interest in the European construction process and especially draw their attention to the implications
this process has for Belgium.

Although formally any legislative text must be approved by one of
the traditional permanent committees, the Committee increasingly takes
legislative initiatives. Also common meetings with others permanent
Committees (External Relationships, Finances, Defence and Social
Affairs) have become more frequent (see Table 2). Furthermore, when
an interpellation is held in one of the other permanent committees,
members of the Committee are sometimes invited and consulted as
experts.

The balanced composition of the Advice Committee offers a considerable advantage over the other bodies specialising in European affairs. In
theory, the MEPs can raise questions and inform their colleague-MPs of
the importance of certain topics, and this before they are voted on at the
European level. Unfortunately, in practice, the Committee discusses in
most cases texts that are already ratified by Community authorities, given
the fact that the Belgian Government usually transmits European documents very late to Parliament.[24] Hence, as political choices made by the
executive can *de facto* only be challenged *ex-post*, Parliament exerts little
influence. This lack of real *ex-ante* political control downgrades the role
of Parliament to that of a mere rubber-stamping body, transposing more
or less automatically Community rules into internal law.

Different proposals were formulated to correct this situation. In 1990,
the Parliament recommended the strengthening of parliamentary control
over European integration. A law, adopted by the House in May 1991,
reaffirmed this will to institute a system of information between Government and Parliament. It obliged the Government to report to the
Parliament on the state of advancement of normative act proposals of the
European Communities that are pending at the level of the Council of
Ministers and fall under national jurisdiction. Therefore, the law formally
granted Parliament the right of *ex-ante* supervision.

Unfortunately, several events postponed the final approval of this
proposal by both Chambers. Indeed, the anticipated dissolution of the
Chambers in 1991, then the latest constitutional reforms and the signature of the Maastricht Treaty have rendered this proposal partially
obsolete. These events have incited the Senate to amend the bill approved
by the House in order to update and complement it. The amended bill,
returned under the 'navette' system to the House, had not been voted
upon by the House before the chambers were dissolved again on 12 April,
following the announcement of an anticipated general election on 21 May
1995.

In spite of Parliament's slow processing of this bill, the matter is not trivial. Regular contact – before Community decisions are taken – between the Belgian member of the European Council and the Belgian legislature, is in several ways essential to both Chambers. First, it re-introduces a form of political control over the Executive. Second, it gives Parliament the opportunity to voice its opinion on matters on which it had lost authority due to the transfer of competences to the European level. Third, to involve the Belgian Parliament, from the initial phase, in the Community decision-making process can only favour its under-standing of European matters. Therefore, it would also facilitate and accelerate the process of transposition of European directives into internal law, as the Chambers would have already then voiced their view on the question.

The Advice Committee has also enlarged its contacts with the external world, because its role of provider of information implies that it should be well informed. At this level, the Advice Committee can decide to summon members of the national Government. For example, during the parlia-mentary session 1990–91, the Advice Committee heard several ministers and secretaries of state with regard to the problem of the too slow trans-formation of European directives into the Belgian legal order, as well as on other problems related to Europe. Similarly, multiple links were developed with the European Parliament and legislative assemblies of the other states of the European Community. For instance, on the proposal of the Advice Committee, the House organised in May 1987 a parlia-mentary conference on the European Union, in which participated delegates of most European national parliaments and of the Institutional Committee of the European Parliament. A Belgian parliamentary dele-gation went to the Rome parliamentary *Assises*[25] at the end of November 1990. And numerous meetings between the Advice Committee and chair-persons or high-ranking officials of other parliamentary assemblies have taken place in the margin of the discussions on the establishment of economic and monetary union. Similarly, frequent meetings have taken place with members of the Commission of the European Community. Mr Van Miert, European Commissioner, as well as some high officials of the Commission, have made various statements on political union and on economic and monetary union. Finally, the Advice Committee maintains links with similar bodies of other Member States of the European Union, by participating in all conferences of bodies concerned with European affairs in the parliaments of the Member States (COSAC). It regularly invites delegations of specialised bodies of others European countries and honours invitations for visits made reciprocally by these bodies in the other states.

THE CREATION OF THE SENATE ADVICE COMMITTEE IN CHARGE OF
EUROPEAN MATTERS

Even if a lot of senators were for a long time in favour of the creation of a
European Affairs Committee similar to the one in the House, up until
March 1990 the different proposals made in the previous decades had no
concrete result. It was in response to the appeal of the Conference of
Presidents of Parliaments of Member States and of the European Parliament held at Madrid in May 1989, that the Belgian Senate finally created
an Advice Committee in charge of European Matters. This conference
had in fact underlined the necessity of a body specialized in Community
affairs within each Chamber of each Member State.

There were long discussions concerning the organisational features of
this committee within the committee responsible for this creation. It did
not want to copy entirely the characteristics of the Advice Committee of
the House of Representatives, especially not with regard to its mixed
composition. The Senate did not want to allow 'thirds' (in this case MEPs
elected in Belgium) to become effective members of a body of the Senate.
Hence, the new Article 62bis of the Standing Orders of the Senate stipulates the committee is composed of 22 senators. However, when the
Committee is holding joint sessions with the Advice Committee of the
House, the number of senators is limited to ten in order to insure parity
with the House delegation (10 MEPs + 10 Representatives + 10 Senators).
In order to maintain a direct connection with Belgian members of the
European assemblies, it was decided to invite such members to participate
in proceedings of the Committee, but without being entitled to vote.

Like its corollary in the House, the purpose of the Senate Advice
Committee is to give advice on European questions, either at its own
initiative or at the request of the President of the Senate or of a permanent
committee. The Advice Committee transmits its advice to the plenary
session of the Senate or to the concerned permanent committee. Moreover, at least once per year it has to draft a report to the plenary assembly
on the state of progress of the transposition of European rules into the
internal legal order. The Committee meets approximately twice a month.
About a third of its meetings are held jointly with its corollary of the
House. The fact that activities and job definition of the two committees
are very similar justifies these joint meetings. In addition, by avoiding
redundant separate meetings, the rather scarce resources of both advice
committees are not wasted.[26]

Like the Advice Committee of the House, the one in the Senate maintains various contacts with the different authorities affected by or involved
in the European construction process. It has heard several representatives

of the Belgian Government, of the Belgian members of European Communities authorities (more specifically of the Commission) with regard to the evolution of political and economic union. Furthermore, the committee participates also in activities of the COSAC and invites delegations of similar specialised bodies of the Member States.

The third institutional reform phase of the Belgian State (that was voted in 1993) complicates the functional identity of this committee. The modification of the Senate in terms of the status, composition, objectives and role in the legislative process, will necessitate a reorientation of the mission of the Senate Advice Committee. The growing prominence of the regions in Belgium (and in Europe in general) will most likely transform the Advice Committee into a liaison agency connecting authorities at the subnational level (regions) to those at the supranational level (European Union).

A NEW FRAMEWORK OF PARLIAMENTARY PARTICIPATION IN ORDER TO FIGHT THE DEMOCRATIC DEFICIT

The various intergovernmental conferences on economic, monetary and political union have shown that the Belgian Parliament (as its homologues) is willing to participate, parallel with the Government, in the European decision-making process at all levels. Thus, during the elaboration of the European Union treaty, the Chambers have – before the start of these conferences – heard ministers, expressed their chambers' position in a memorandum and asked the Government to underwrite this position. Then, during the negotiations, they have examined the main issues at stake and reconfirmed their previously defined priorities. After the Maastricht summit, the Government informed the Chambers of the final content of the agreement. Finally, the Chambers evaluated the treaty after its ratification. Hence, the House was not only kept informed, but also allowed to formulate an opinion *after* expression of the Community decision. Contrary to the restricted role it played during the conclusion of the Single European Act five years earlier, this time the House determined its position in a resolution *before* the Act was considered by the European Council of Luxembourg in June 1991. Therefore, during the negotiations phase, the position of the Belgian government is now more strictly scrutinised by Parliament.

This growing participation of parliamentary authorities is formally expressed in the most recent constitutional reforms. Indeed, the new Article 168 of the Belgian Constitution specifies that the Chambers are to be kept informed, from the opening round of the negotiations intended to revise the treaties, about the progress of the negotiations and of the content of the treaty before its signature. Similarly, a law of 5 May 1993 grants the same right to the legislative councils of the communities and regions. Contrary to the classical international treaties, the EC treaties are obliged to obtain the preliminary approval of Parliament.[27]

Finally, a bill dealing with the transposition of European texts prompted a new clause to the law enacted on 8 August 1980. This clause concerns the information provided to the chambers and councils with regard to normative act proposals of the European Commission. Its Article 92quater states that from their transmission to the European Council of Ministers, proposals on regulations and directives and possibly also on the other normative acts of the Commission are to be transmitted to the concerned Chambers and regional/community councils. This tool allowing Chambers to participate in the elaboration of the European law is increasingly used by the Parliament, examining more and more frequently proposals for regulations and directives. These various dispositions present a double advantage. First, their obligatory character strengthens the existing yet underdeveloped parliamentary participation. More generally, by *de facto* reinstating political control of the Government, they will necessarily strengthen the dialogue between the Belgian Parliament and the European and national executives. This will be helpful in reducing the democratic deficit.

However, despite this apparent dynamism, Parliament has urgently to legislate more clearly on the subject. So far, in case of violation of the Government's obligation to inform Parliament, the only applicable sanctions are purely political. This only increases the democratic deficit. In the present situation, the desire to be kept informed before any adoption of a definite position by the Council of Ministers may remain wishful thinking.

Moreover, even if the latest constitutional reforms constitute significant progress in terms of keeping Parliament informed, they also complicate the situation, by expanding once more the legislative powers of the federated entities. Indeed, the majority of violations currently committed by 'Belgium' fall under the competence of regional authorities. Hence, the federal Government is responsible to European authorities for matters that are no longer legislated by the federal Parliament. Moreover, the community and regional councils feel less concerned by European integration than federal Chambers, and are not likely to cope with this problem in a homogeneous way. In addition, no text states specifically what procedures will be used to associate the community and regional legislative bodies. Hence, one risks a situation of a total absence of rules, or at least of strong judicial heterogeneity and improvisation at this level. The example of the last revision of EC treaties is significant.

The participation of federated entities at intergovernmental conferences was based purely on *ad hoc* agreements. This absence of formalised dialogue or co-operation with communities and regions councils is somewhat worrying. Indeed, in an important number of sectors daily affected by European decisions (agriculture, environment, energy, and so on), the competences of federated entities are often larger than those of the federal State. Furthermore, policies developed by the Maastricht Treaty in the margin of European institutions enlarge the scope, and therefore the problem, of mandatory participation of the sub-national level. The process of co-operation, little routinised as it is based on *ad hoc* meetings, often turns out to be conflictual. It is therefore imperative that federate and federal entities co-ordinate their action, rather than base the elaboration of the position of Belgium solely on the laborious process of interministerial co-operation. In the latter case, one can fear that the Chambers (federal and federate) would turn again into passive actors within the process of European construction, and aggravate the problem of the democratic deficit.

CONCLUSION

Despite the creation within the Belgian Parliament of various special bodies intended to deal with European affairs, until recently these matters have *de facto* always been handled by the regular Foreign Affairs Committee. Nevertheless, as previously stated, different indicators like the multiplication of joint meetings, show clearly that the current advice committees in charge of European matters have become more and more prominent in processing European affairs. They demand that the dialogue and decisions on the European level should be detached from the sphere of the regular foreign policy.

By attempting to facilitate the interpenetration of Belgian and Community rules, the advice committees in charge of European matters fulfil a very important function with regard to European integration. This is done, first, by adapting national law to European realities; second, by controlling the implementation and transposition of European law into the Belgian legal order; and, finally, by becoming an increasingly privileged partner in the elaboration of the position defended by Belgium as a member of the European Union authorities. This way, democratic control on Community decisions is somewhat restored.

Functioning for ten years, the Advice Committee of the House can look back on a substantial experience, much richer than its equivalent in the Senate whose mission in the future is full of uncertainties. The recommendations – that in the beginning were often limited to technical remarks

– have become increasingly political. The Advice Committee of the House also asserts its solidarity with other parliamentary authorities: on the one hand, by supporting the European Parliament in its aspirations to be gradually more and more involved in the decision-making processes of the European Union and, on the other hand, by pursuing the strengthening of interparliamentary co-operation.

Although they constitute today an indispensable tool, the advice committees remain very dependent on governmental goodwill. Indeed, their 'information' problem is essentially caused by the national executive's monopoly over information coming from the European level, and the lack of transparency of the European decision-making process, with a Council of the European Union that sometimes intentionally withholds information. The fact that advice committees frequently do not handle a dossier in time is usually due to the fact that too often the Government does not transmit in due course relevant proposals of directives, regulations or other texts produced by the European Commission. Hence the House Advice Committee regularly insists that the House *as a whole* puts pressure on the Executive to transmit the requested documents. The Advice Committee of the House has also repeatedly insisted on organising a general debate in the plenary session of the House, before each European Council of Heads of States and Governments, in order to determine the position of the national legislature on the various matters that will be dealt with at the European level. It has also requested that the Government no longer decide without taking into account the advice formulated by the Parliament during the aforementioned debates. Even if usually these appeals remain inconsequential and have no judicial value, they nevertheless force the Executive to reflect on the usefulness of collaboration with the Parliament for all matters concerning Belgium's participation in the European integration process. This way, the Advice Committee undeniably helps to reduce the democratic deficit which yet too often characterises decision-making in European matters not only at the level of the European Union, but also at the national level.

Finally, it is difficult to forecast the future of this type of body, given the fact that the structure of Europe is in evolution, and that the Belgian State most likely will undergo further institutional changes. The policy process in Belgium is characterised more by disjointed incrementalism than by a linear process. Problems are dealt with as they arrive on the political scene, but are usually solved by a compromise, valid for only a limited duration. Despite the fact that there is a large consensus that the federalisation of the Belgian State has reached its conclusion or at least requires a breathing space, a further evolution towards confederalism cannot be excluded. If this occurs, the already large competences of the communities and regions assemblies will most likely be enlarged again, and those of the two federal chambers restricted. In case of such a power shift to the sub-national legislative authorities, one can question the significance of the role that the present advices committees, and the federal Parliament as a whole, will be allowed to play in the process of European integration.

NOTES

1. After the May 1995 general elections, the stipulations of the new constitution (voted in 1993) will install a House of Representatives predominant in terms of legislative production and governmental control, while the Senate will be transformed into a Federal Chamber, basically competent for problems concerning the relations between federal and regional/community authorities.
2. A. Lijphart, *Conflict and coexistence in Belgium* (University of California, Berkeley: Institute of Universal Studies, 1981).
3. For further details, see P.-H. Claeys, N. Loeb-Mayer and G. Van Den Berghe, *European or National* (Leuven-Bruxelles: Katholieke Universiteit Leuven – Université Libre de Bruxelles, 1980); P.-H. Claeys, N. Loeb-Mayer and G.Van Den Berghe, 'Belgium', in J. Lodge (ed.), *Direct Elections to the European Parliament* (London: Macmillan, 1986), pp.51–73; J. Ackaert, L. De Winter and M. Swyngedouw, *Belgium: An electorate on the Eve of Disintegration*, pp.53–72 in C. Van Der Eijk, M. Franklin (eds.), University of Michigan Press, Ann Arbor (forthcoming), 1996.
4. The activities of Belgian elites towards European integration were inspired by the principle of 'unity in diversity', which, given the high degree of ethnic and regional heterogeneity of the country, also characterises the institutional development of national political structures, i.e the process of multiplication of institutional structures at different levels.
5. See R. Coolsaet, *Histoire de la politique étrangère belge* (Bruxelles: Vie Ouvrière, 1988), pp.155, 164, 165, 253, 254.
6. 'Commission des Affaires européennes' or 'Commissie voor Europese Zaken'.
7. The introduction of a new chapter V in the House Standing Orders was voted on 8 February 1962.
8. But, contrary to the latter, this committee designated itself its Bureau and President and vice-Presidents. Article 12 of the Standing Orders stipulates that the House Chairman and vice-Chairmen preside *de jure* over the committees of which they are members.
9. This did not only apply to the 'pure European' assemblies, but also to the Inter-parliamentary Council of the BENELUX, the Council of Europe Assembly and the West-European Union Assembly.
10. For the cumulation of the office of MEP and national political positions, see W. Dewachter, L. De Winter, 'Het verlies van het machtspotentieel van een zwak parlement. Onderzoek aan de hand van de Belgische afgevaardigden in het Europees Parlement (1952–1979)', *Res Publica*, XXI (1979), pp. 115–25, and M. Verminck (1985) 'Le Parlement européen de 1979 à 1984' *Res Publica* XXVII: 2–3 and 287–96.
11. In 1965, the Harmel Government created a position of State Minister to European Affairs in order to assist the Foreign Minister as far as European matters were concerned.
12. However it did raise a constitutional problem. Since 1945, the minister of the department concerned by the topic of a bill discussed in a parliamentary committee usually attends the relevant meetings. However, Article 88 of the Belgian Constitution grants the right to claim the presence of a minister exclusively to the legislative assemblies. So,

the competence given to the European Affairs Committee (and not to other permanent committees) in order to fulfil its role seems to be unconstitutional. See H. De Croo, 'Une initiative belge: la Commission des Affaires Européennes de la Chambre des Représentants', *Revue du Marché Commun*, nr. 64, December 1963, pp.476–9.

13. The calendar of reports of the delegations was established by the committee. However, the delegations were equally composed by the two Chambers, half of the MEPs coming from the Senate.

14. In the activity reports of parliamentary committees published by the House at the end of each session (in Parliamentary Documents), one finds – apart from the reports – less than ten resolutions and bills for the period concerned (1962–79).

15. The Committee specified that it wanted to draw the Government's attention to recommendations coming from European Parliamentary Assemblies in order to avoid decisions taken at the level of Governments running counter to the aforementioned recommendations. So it aimed at imposing on the Government, a member of the European Executive, what the European Parliament was not yet able to impose directly upon the European Executive.

16. According to Coolsaet (1988: 253–254) during the sixties and the seventies the contribution of the Parliament was insignificant with regard to European Integration and other important aspects of Belgian foreign politics (e.g. Atlantic relations and détente). Foreign Affairs were exclusively determined by the competent minister and his immediate collaborators.

17. Also the modification of the relationship between the European and national Parliaments, following the first direct elections of MEPs, necessitated modifications of the role of the committee. Hence, amendments were introduced in October 1979. A supplementary report was made public in December. Finally, Article 83 was abolished yet without creating a substitute committee. See E. Toebosch, *Parlementen en reglementen*, (Bruxelles: E. Story-Scientia, 1991, p.116.

18. In December 1981, this committee became the External Relations Committee.

19. Hence, MEPs could also have access to the parliamentary library and research services and easily maintain direct contacts with their national colleagues.

20. Before the 1981 general elections, 66 per cent of the Belgian MEPs combined their European office with a national parliamentary office. However, after those elections, only 12.5 per cent still combined both offices.

21. The President of the House is informed of that request. Even if the Chairman of the concerned committee accepts the request, the committee (even the External Relationships one) can always decide the contrary during a debate behind closed doors.

22. 'Comité d'avis de la Chambre chargé de questions européennes' or 'Adviescomité van de Kamer voor Europese Aangelegenheden'.

23. However, a new article 25 in the Standing Orders was created in order to state precisely the limits of the participation of MEPs in Belgian House committees. See Toebosch, pp.116–17.

24. Also in other permanent commissions of the House, MEPs only rarely participate.

25. Conference of national parliaments held on 27–30 November 1990 on the role of European and national legislative powers in the construction of the Union. See the chapter in this volume by Martin Westlake.

26. Each Advice Committee has only one secretary (and not always full time) at its disposal. It has no research staff at all, while regular committees have at least have one 'documentalist'.

27. For more developed information, see D. Nagant De Deuxchaines, *Le renforcement du caractère démocratique de la Communauté Européenne*, in F. Delperee (ed.), *La Belgique fédérale* (Bruxelles: Bruylant, 1994), p.455.

The United Kingdom: Political Conflict, Parliamentary Scrutiny

PHILIP NORTON

The United Kingdom became a member of the European Community on 1 January 1973. The events leading up to its membership were far from trouble free. The same can be said of the period of its membership. The UK was a late and reluctant member. It has remained in many respects a reluctant member.

The United Kingdom has differed from most of its European neighbours in that it has enjoyed a notable longevity in its constitutional arrangements. The last time England was invaded successfully was in 1066. The last time it had a major constitutional upheaval was in 1688, and even then the continuity of institutions was stressed. The differences extend beyond constitutional history to the nation's role in world affairs. At the beginning of the twentieth century, the country was at the heart of an empire – an empire that was still in existence in the wake of the Second World War. Britain also has a tradition of acting as a balancer in power relationships in Europe, distancing itself from efforts to build supreme European powers and taking sides only to restore order. This history has shaped British attitudes towards the post-1945 movement for European integration.

In the late 1940s and early 1950s, Britain was preoccupied with economic and social reconstruction. European integration had an appeal to some politicians as a broadly desirable aspiration but it was not seen as a political imperative and not something to be accorded priority over reconstruction. Nor was it seen as a goal to be pursued if it threatened the interests of the empire, now redeveloped as the Commonwealth, nor if it threatened Britain's capacity to determine its own future. The Labour Government of Clement Attlee declined to take part in negotiations leading to the Treaty of Paris. It was suspicious of the supranational element of control. A later Conservative Government under Sir Anthony Eden declined to take part in the negotiations leading to the Treaty of Rome. Relative economic prosperity and an unwillingness to share power with continental neighbours helped keep Britain clear of entanglement with the three European Communities.[2]

Philip Norton is Professor of Government, University of Hull. For reading and commenting on a draft of this article he is indebted to Andrew Griffin, Michael Pownall, Robert Rogers, Mark Shephard and Martin Westlake.

Changed political and economic conditions in the late 1950s and early 1960s encouraged a number of politicians and civil servants to see the European Communities in a new light.[3] Britain's place on the world stage was in question. The Commonwealth was not proving a body easily amenable to British leadership nor one that offered a great growth in trade. The 'special relationship' with the United States was proving less than special in the wake of conflict over the Suez crisis of 1956 and the cancellation by the USA of the Blue Streak rocket in 1960. The economy was not showing the same growth rate as those countries in the EEC and was experiencing problems by the early 1960s. Membership of the EC began to look more attractive. It offered a market of 180 million people and potentially a new platform on which the United Kingdom could again establish a position as a world leader.

During the latter half of 1960 'a considerable evolution in thinking had taken place within the British Government',[4] an evolution spurred by pressure from the US government, keen to see a more united western Europe.[5] On 31 July 1961, Prime Minister Harold Macmillan told the House of Commons that Britain was applying for membership. The application was vetoed by President de Gaulle of France, who viewed the United Kingdom as still being too closely tied to the United States. A second application was lodged in 1967 by Labour Prime Minister Harold Wilson. In 1969, formal agreement to open negotiations was reached and those negotiations were conducted and completed under a Conservative Government elected in 1970. Most of the terms of membership had been agreed by October 1971 and the Treaty of Accession was signed early in 1972. The legal basis for membership was provided by the European Communities Act 1972, which was introduced in the House of Commons in February and completed all its stages by the summer recess. The United Kingdom became a member of the EC on the first day of the following year, almost 15 years after it first had an opportunity to do so.

THE PARTY RESPONSE

Both the Labour and Conservative parties were initially reluctant to become involved with the EC. The Conservative Party changed tack in 1961 and thereafter remained an advocate of membership. The Labour Party was initially opposed to membership, with Labour leader Hugh Gaitskell being a vocal opponent. His successor, Harold Wilson, swung the Labour Party behind the application for membership in 1967, but then led his party in opposition to membership – on the terms negotiated – in 1972. The Labour Government elected in 1974 renegotiated the terms of membership and then advocated support for continued membership in a referendum it called in 1975 (although cabinet collegiality was waived during the referendum campaign and some prominent cabinet ministers played an active part in the 'no' campaign). After its return to opposition in 1979 the party swung against membership and in its general election manifesto of 1983 called for British withdrawal from the EC. Since then, it has moved back towards support for membership and for greater British involvement. The Conservative Party under Margaret Thatcher and her successor has adopted a more sceptical stance, supporting continued membership but wary of further moves toward political and economic union.

From the beginning of the 1950s, both parties have also been internally divided on the issue. Those divisions have been marked in the House of Commons. Half-a-dozen Conservative Members of Parliament (MPs) refused to back a motion in 1950 calling for Britain to take part in the negotiations leading to the Treaty of Paris. More than 20 failed to support the first application for membership in 1961. When a motion approving in principle British membership was put to the House of Commons in October 1971, 69 Labour MPs voted for it and 20 abstained from voting – the rest of the party voted against – while 39 Conservatives voted against it, the rest voting for it.[6] The second reading of the European Communities Bill in 1972 was only achieved by the Government making the vote one of confidence – and even then 15 Conservative MPs voted against and a further five abstained from voting.[7] Those internal divisions have not abated as a consequence of membership. The issue of 'Europe' continues to split both main parties, most visibly so in the case of the Conservative Party.

The response to the Maastricht Treaty in 1992 and 1993 revealed the depth of the divisions in the Conservative Party. Critics on the Conservative benches opposed the bill throughout its passage.[8] They maintained their opposition in 1994 during the passage of the bill to ratify an increase in the EC budget. On both issues, Prime Minister John Major was forced to resort to votes of confidence to ensure that the Government got its way. The critics were not confined to the Conservative Party. Forty Labour MPs defied their party to vote against the 1994 bill.

The critical lobby in the Conservative Party was notable not only for being vocal in the 1990s but also for its growth in size. One analysis has identified four basic groupings in the party on the issue of European integration: anti-Europeans, who are opposed on principle (usually but not always on constitutional grounds, opposing any diminution of the UK's capacity to take independent decisions) to membership of the EU; Euro-sceptics, who support membership in order to achieve a single market but not for going beyond that; Euro-agnostics, who have no fixed view on integration but who believe in taking a stance that is in the best interests of Britain at the time; and Euro-enthusiasts, who have a principled belief in European integration.[9] There are similar variations on the Labour side, with some on the socialist wing of the party seeing the Community as a capitalists' club and a potential brake on a socialist government in Britain and others on the political right who oppose encroachments on British sovereignty. Others adopt a more pragmatic (Euro-agnostic) view while some – essentially the social democratic element of the party – support the concept of European integration.[10]

The debate over Maastricht brought together anti-Europeans and Euro-sceptics. As the debate progressed, more and more Euro-agnostics also began to adopt a critical stance towards greater integration. The issue of a single currency maximised opposition on the Conservative benches. Euro-agnostic John Major sought to tread a fine line between opponents and supporters of greater integration, but with his opinions veering more toward the former rather than the latter. On the Labour side, John Smith (who was one of the 69 Labour MPs to vote for EC membership in 1971) pushed his party towards a more supportive stance, a line maintained (following Smith's death in May 1994) by his successor, Tony Blair – leading a party that a decade earlier had supported British withdrawal from membership.

The details of Britain's constitutional, international and political history are important not only for explaining Britain's lateness in joining the European Community but also for explaining the continued debate between and within the parties on the issue of European integration. That history and the continuing contentious debate on European integration are important also in explaining the parliamentary response to membership and to the pressures for further integration. They help to explain what may appear a paradox. That is, that in dealing with European secondary legislation both Houses of Parliament have introduced important mechanisms of scrutiny – at least as and generally more extensive than those introduced by other national parliaments – yet appear reluctant to integrate UK MEPs in that process and, furthermore, in responding to primary legislation (treaty amendments) Parliament, primarily the House of Commons, has conveyed the impression of being a reluctant partner. This apparently negative stance in dealing with primary legislation has obscured a largely constructive approach to the consideration of secondary legislation.

THE PARLIAMENTARY RESPONSE

When the European Communities Bill was completing its passage through the House of Commons, it was known that the measure would have significant constitutional implications, but it was not clear how they should or could be tackled. No provision was made at that stage for parliamentary involvement in EC matters. Instead, it was left to both Houses to decide how to proceed.

Both Houses established committees to advise them on how to respond to the new situation.[11] Each committee recommended the creation of some form of permanent committee to scrutinise proposals from the Commission. Each House subsequently established a committee. There, though, the similarity ends. The committees in the two Houses differ significantly from one another. In one, the emphasis is on breadth. In the other, the emphasis is on depth.

The House of Commons

In its scrutiny of EC matters, the House of Commons concentrates on documents drawn up by the Commission for submission to the Council of Ministers or the European Council, although its orders of reference include any document submitted by one EC institution to another (thus including, for example, EP amendments and Court of Auditors reports) and any document relating to EC matters deposited in Parliament by the Government. Once a document is received by the UK Government, the Government deposits it in both Houses of Parliament and within ten working days must also deposit an explanatory memorandum, signed by a minister, on the document's implications for the United Kingdom and the Government's policy towards it. The documents and memoranda are available not only to Members of Parliament but also to the public.

All the documents are sent to the Select Committee on European Legislation. The Committee was established in 1974 and has 16 members. It is chaired by a member of the main opposition party. It meets once a week and is required under a standing order of the House 'to report its opinion on the legal and political importance of each such document and, where it considers appropriate, to report also on the reasons for its opinion and on any matters of principle, policy or law which may be affected' and to make recommendations for the further consideration of each such document – in other words, to say whether or not the document should be debated and, if so, in what forum.

It is up to the select committee to determine what constitutes legal or political importance – there are no definitive guidelines – though the principal criteria are the effect on existing UK law, contentiousness and financial implications. About 1,000 documents a year are now deposited and considered by the committee. Most – about two-thirds – are deemed not to raise issues of legal and political importance. These include factual reports, minor amendments, proposals for consolidating existing legislation, and proposals which have little or no impact on UK law and which do not raise wider issues. About a third are considered to raise legal or political issues of importance, but not all of these are recommended for further debate. About 90 documents per year are recommended for further consideration.[12]

The committee is empowered to take evidence, though most of the evidence is received in written rather than oral form. It examines witnesses – usually ministers – seven or eight times a year. It is also empowered to appoint sub-committees and occasionally – but only occasionally – does so. (In 1994, it appointed one to consider the relative competences of Member States and the EC in road safety.) It is also permitted to hold meetings jointly with the equivalent committee in the Lords but it has not used the power for many years, though there is co-operation between the two committees in monitoring the process of scrutiny. It can appoint specialist advisers, but relies principally on its own staff.

Until 1991, documents recommended for debate were either referred to standing committees, appointed on an *ad hoc* basis, or debated on the floor of the House. About 20 documents, usually of a technical nature, were considered in standing committees and the rest – the majority – were taken on the floor of the House. The standing committees attracted little interest, were usually poorly attended, and each was restricted to meeting for a maximum of two-and-a-half hours, though few meetings used up that amount of time. Debates on the floor were usually held late at night (after ten o'clock), suffered – like the committees – from poor attendance, and in most cases were limited to one-and-a-half hours in duration.

In order to improve scrutiny, and to reduce the burden on the floor of the House, two new permanent European standing committees were created in 1991. One (Committee A) deals with documents affecting agriculture, transport, environment and the Forestry Commission, and the other (Committee B) deals with all other documents. Unless the House (on the motion of a minister) decides otherwise, a document recommended for debate is automatically referred to the appropriate committee. Each committee has 13 members (though any MP can attend and seek to speak, though not vote) and is distinctive in that, prior to the usual debate on the documents, the relevant minister can be questioned for up to one hour. Each committee considers a motion on the document (or documents) before it: the motion is a government motion but may be amended. The motion is usually agreed by the committee, but not always. (The Government was defeated on the Court of Auditors Report on the Environment and, in December 1994, on reform of the agrimonetary system.) The chairman reports to the House the resolution agreed by the committee or, in the case of a motion being defeated, that the committee has come to no resolution.

In the 1992–93 session, European Standing Committee A considered 33 documents in 24 meetings and European Standing Committee B dealt with 55 documents in 30 meetings. (Documents dealing with the same subject can be, and are, taken together. Usually there are only two or three, but Committee B at one sitting dealt with ten documents on carbon dioxide emissions and energy.) The Government then tables the equivalent motion – or, if it chooses, a different one – and the House then approves, or rejects, the motion without debate. On at least one occasion – on the issue of the compulsory wearing of seatbelts – the Government has exercised its power to table a motion in terms other than those agreed by the committee.

The purpose of the scrutiny undertaken by the House is principally to influence the stance taken by UK ministers in the Council of Ministers. Ministers are constrained in what they can agree to in the Council prior to completion of scrutiny by the House. The House passed a resolution in 1980 limiting what a minister could agree to, a limitation modified and reinforced by a further resolution in 1990. Under the terms of the 1990 resolution, a minister should not give agreement to any proposal for EC legislation which has not completed its scrutiny process in the House. However, agreement may be given if the minister considers the proposal confidential, routine or trivial (or is substantially the same as a proposal on which scrutiny has been completed), or if the select committee has indicated that agreement need not be withheld, or for 'special reasons' (such as the need to avoid a legal vacuum or to take decisions during the summer recess), in which case the minister should explain the reasons to the committee or House at the first opportunity to do so. Some documents – usually less than ten per cent – are agreed before the scrutiny stage is completed by the House.[13] Where this happens, the requirement for an explanation by a minister is taken seriously by MPs and ministers can be subject to an uncomfortable time in the House. The chairman of the European Legislation Committee may write up to 25 letters a week to ministers about the handling of documents and the discharge of the Government's scrutiny obligations and many more letters are written at official level.

The work of the select committee has been complicated by the co-operation and now the co-decision procedure introduced under the SEA and the Maastricht Treaty. To take account of the co-decision procedure, the committee in a special report in 1993 recommended that the common position should be notified by the Government to the clerk of the committee and that, if the EP proposes amendments to the common position, the amended text (and the Commission's opinions) should be deposited with the committee, along with an explanatory memorandum. If the Council does not approve the EP's amendments, or if the conciliation committee approves (or fails to approve) a joint text, the committee should be informed. If the Council confirms the original common position, the text should be notified to the clerk of the committee.[14]

So much for the specified scrutiny procedure covering each document. Apart from the consideration of these documents by the Select Committee on European Legislation, it is also open to departmental select committees – created by the House in 1979 to examine the expenditure, administration and policy of government departments – to consider EU issues that impinge on departmental responsibilities. Each week, a paper is circulated by the Select Committee on European Legislation to the departmental select committees informing them of relevant European legislation. However, relatively little time is given over by the committees to European issues. A proposal to establish a committee with specific responsibility for EC matters was rejected by the Procedure Committee of the House in 1989 and the existing departmental committees devote most of their time to domestic issues. However, the Foreign Secretary and Home Secretary do now appear before the foreign affairs and home affairs committees respectively before each meeting of the European Council and some committees, such as the trade and industry committee and the environment committee, have considered some specific European issues. None, though, considers EU issues on any systematic or regular basis.

It is also open to MPs to raise EU issues in Question Time and debates. A fixed 20-minute slot for European questions in Foreign Office question time – held once a month – was abandoned in 1985. The House now holds two general debates each year prior to the meeting of the European Council and there are debates on the EC budget, agricultural price fixing, and fisheries. On occasion there are separate debates on Court of Auditors reports. There are also the debates on EC documents at the recommendation of the EC Legislation Committee.

Some links have also been established with EC institutions and the institutions of other Member States, most notably by the EC Legislation Committee. Every six months, the Committee visits the Presidency country for discussions with members of the Government and Parliament and each year travels to Brussels, Strasbourg and Luxembourg, visiting not only the Commission and the EP but also the European Court of Justice and the Court of Auditors. There is also a briefing from the UK Permanent Representative on each visit. The House of Commons, though, affords no formal status to MEPs in its activities, other than access to the Palace of Westminster and the galleries. British MEPs can attend meetings of their party committees in the House but enjoy no privileges within the House itself.

The House of Lords

The scrutiny of EC documents undertaken by the House of Lords differs in form and extent to that undertaken by the House of Commons. Once documents and explanatory memoranda are received, they are referred to the European Communities Committee. The Committee, first appointed in 1974, has 24 members and meets fortnightly. It is chaired by a peer drawn usually from an opposition party (until 1994 it was chaired by a Labour peer and since November 1994 has been chaired by a Liberal Democrat) and has much wider terms of reference than its Commons counterpart. It is appointed to consider documents and to report on those which it considers raise matters of principle and policy, and also on other questions to which the Committee believes the attention of the House should be drawn. As such, it can – and does – comment on the merits of proposals as well as consider trends in EC policy making. The Committee can, and does, appoint specialist advisers to assist it in particular enquiries. The advisers are often senior figures and may be drawn from diverse sources. In one enquiry an adviser of Italian nationality – a former senior economist in the Commission – was appointed.

Most of the work of the Committee is conducted through sub-committees.[15] The number has varied, but there are presently six. Sub-Committee A, for example, deals with finance, trade and external relations. Each sub-committee has nine or ten members, comprising two or more members of the full committee and a number of co-opted members. As a result, over 60 members of the House are actively involved in committee work. Co-opted members are appointed on the basis of their particular interests and expertise; party affiliation is not the overriding criterion. A rotation rule applies, each member serving up to four years and the chairman of a sub-committee for three. Sub-Committee E, dealing with law and institutions, is always chaired by an independent law lord (a judge appointed to the House to serve in its capacity as the highest domestic court of appeal). In February 1995, the Committee was given leave to appoint *ad hoc* sub-committee to consider preparations for the 1996 IGC. Its members include a former head of the civil service, two former diplomats, two former cabinet ministers, two former MEPs and a former EC commissioner.

Each week, the chairman of the Committee does a 'sift' of the documents received from government departments, sorting out the less important documents (Sift A) from the more important documents requiring further consideration (Sift B). In this task, he is helped by a legal adviser as well as by the clerk to the committee. Documents from Sift B are sent to the appropriate sub-committee, which is free to conduct inquiries or to clear the documents without further scrutiny.

When inquiries are undertaken they may be full-scale inquiries, entailing the questioning of witnesses and consideration of extensive written evidence. Evidence in such cases will be sought from interested parties, inlcuding representatives of trade and professional organisations, pressure groups, Commission officials (on occasion commissioners) and MEPs, including committee *rapporteurs* (that is, authors of specific parliamentary reports). Most of the evidence is taken in Westminster, but on occasions sub-committees have taken evidence in Brussels or Strasbourg and have travelled to other Member States. Other inquiries may be undertaken on a much smaller scale, often confined to correspondence with the relevant government department. The use of correspondence has grown, not least as the EC law-making process has become speedier and more complex.

The reports of the Committee – embodying analysis and recommendations as well as the evidence taken – are published, as (since 1987) are copies of correspondence with government departments. The publications are formally prepared for the House but – as with reports from the European Legislation Committee in the Commons – copies are sent to the Government, the Commission, the European Parliament, the UK Permanent Representative, the EU Presidency-in-Office, and European committees in other national parliaments.

The Committee decides whether the reports are made for the information of the House or for debate. It makes about 20 to 30 reports a year, with the majority recommended for debate. Where they are recommended for debate, a debate is arranged before the proposal to which the report relates is agreed in the Council of Ministers. Such debates occupy a relatively small proportion of the time of the House – usually less than five per cent each session – with most debates lasting less than three hours. On occasion, though, some debates are extensive. The report on economic and monetary union and political union was debated in November 1990 for almost eight hours.

The House has no structure of departmental select committees, and the task of looking at developments and the broad direction of policy within the EU rests with the European Communities Committee. Some sub-committees will look at issues beyond those contained in specific documents. On occasion an *ad hoc* inquiry into issues that span the remit of two or more sub-committees has been undertaken, as happened in 1986 on the implications of the Single European Act.[16] Recent years have seen the publication of substantial reports on fraud against the EC budget, enlargement, and the enforcement of competition rules.

Like its Commons counterpart, the Committee has developed links with EC institutions. The chairmen of the main committee and sub-committees visit Brussels every two or three years to meet the EP President and the officers of EP committees to discuss matters of common interest. The committee clerks attend on occasion plenary sessions of the EP and keep in contact with officials of the Commission and Parliament. Sub-committee members also visit Brussels on occasion for informal discussions, in particular meetings with national parliamentarians convened by committees of the EP. Such contacts are generally viewed as productive. 'One has the impression that informal contacts keep committee members abreast of the direction of thinking within Community institutions and the likely, most worthwhile, areas for inquiries.'[17] However, like the Commons, no formal status is accorded in the House to UK MEPs, the only difference between the two chambers being that the Lords accords MEPs access to some dining facilities.

The House prides itself on the quality of the work it does in the field of EC legislation and its reports have been widely acknowledged as authoritative, including by members of the Commission and the EP.[18] However, like its Commons counterpart, it has no role that is formally recognised by the treaties and at a practical level is conscious of the increased difficulties generated by the co-decision procedure and the two new pillars of the Union.[19] It now considers in draft documents emanating from the home affairs and justice pillar and may be alone among parliamentary bodies in the EU in carrying out a detailed study of the draft convention on Europol. However, the more pillar documents there are – they are few in number at the moment – the greater the burden on the committee.

The work of the Committee thus differs from its Commons counterpart. The European Legislation Committee in the Commons goes for breadth – considering every document deposited – and reports quickly. The EC Committee in the Lords goes for depth, concentrating on a few documents and taking time to consider them. Rather than competing with each other, the two complement one another. Between them, they serve to fulfil what is essentially an informing function.[20]

ANALYSIS

What, then, explains the particular features of the parliamentary response to membership of the EC – the features that are at the heart of the paradox identified earlier: that is, committee-based scrutiny of EC documents almost from the time of joining the Community and a reluctance to integrate to UK MEPs into that process, and an apparent reluctance to contemplate further integration within the EU?

The parliamentary response can be explained in terms of constitutional, political and practical factors. Parliament had fought to assert its ascendancy over the executive authority – the king – in 1688. The Glorious Revolution of that year, and the resulting Bill of Rights of 1689, confirmed the doctrine of parliamentary supremacy in terms of English law.[21] The doctrine is a judicially self-imposed one, stipulating that no person or body, other than Parliament itself, is recognised by the courts as having the right to override or set aside the legislation of Parliament. There are no legal limits to the legislative authority of Parliament. One of the precepts derived from the principle is that no Parliament can bind its successor.

Membership of the EC constituted a significant challenge to legislative supremacy both in relation to the executive authority and to the courts. Under the terms of membership, policy-making competence in various sectors was to pass to the institutions of the Community, legislation passed by those bodies would not require the assent of Parliament, and the courts were to have the power to give precedence to EC law over municipal (that is, domestic UK) law.

The full constitutional implications of these changes have yet to be fully worked through and realised. However, at the level of EC legislation, there was – in the immediate wake of membership – an awareness that Parliament should at least seek to retain some role. Given its historic role as a law-effecting body, it was difficult for many parliamentarians to accept a passive part in the process by which measures of public policy were approved.

The pressure for some form of parliamentary involvement was compounded by a political consideration. Membership of the EC had been contested within both main parties. That disagreement did not disappear once the UK had become a member of the EC. Opponents of EC membership took a critical view of the institutions of the Community. The EP was seen at the time as a 'talking shop' of little use and one anyway that opponents of EC entry were not prepared to concede should be given more powers. For them, there was a need for some form of scrutiny by the people's elected representatives and that was best achieved through national parliaments. Hence the emphasis on the Parliament at Westminster, not the EP at Strasbourg.

The initial parliamentary response to membership was thus to establish mechanisms for scrutinising EC documents. The precise mechanisms were the result of practical needs. Neither House was highly specialised. Both were chamber-oriented institutions, making little use of committees, and certainly very little use of permanent committees. The creation of EC committees was thus not a natural consequence of existing practice but rather the consequence of necessity. Given the sheer volume of EC legislation, there was no way that scrutiny could be achieved on the floor of the House. Each House thus resorted to a dedicated committee.

The implementation of the Single European Act consequently had less of an impact than on most other national legislative chambers. EC committees were already in place. In so far as the Single European Act was to have an effect, it was in contributing to the eventual creation of the two European standing committees in the House of Commons. The effect of the SEA was to facilitate more regulations and directives, thus increasing the burden on an already heavily burdened House. The standing committees were designed to help reduce the burden on the chamber.

The constitutional and political imperatives also dictated the attitude towards the status of British MEPs – and towards demands for increases in the power of the EP. Many critics of the EU have viewed legislative power as a zero-sum game. If the power of the EP is increased, then the power of the national Parliament is presumed to decrease. There is thus opposition to an expansion of the powers of the EP. This was apparent in 1977 during the passage of the European Assemblies Election Bill, when the Government agreed to an amendment to the bill requiring any future treaty amendment increasing the powers of the EP to be subject to parliamentary approval. It was also reflected in the opposition of some Conservative MPs to the passage of the European Communities (Amendment) Bill in 1992 to give legal effect to the Treaty on European Union, a bill necessitated in part by the provisions of the 1977 Act. It is also reflected in a survey of Conservative MPs in 1994. 82 per cent of those questioned strongly agreed or agreed that the 'key to closing the "democratic deficit" is strengthening the scrutiny by national parliaments of the EU legislative process'. (Reflecting their scepticism of the EP, 62 per cent disagreed or strongly disagreed with the suggestion that the EP should be given the right to initiate EU legislation.) A majority – 56 per cent – also favoured passage of an Act establishing explicitly the ultimate supremacy of Parliament over EU legislation.[22]

Not surprisingly, given the constitutional context and the prevailing political attitudes on the part of members of the governing party, parliamentarians have displayed some territorial protectiveness in their dealings with MEPs and have been reluctant to accord them any formal position in relation to parliamentary committees or, indeed, any parliamentary activity. A proposal from the Lords EC Committee in 1978 that, following direct elections, a European Grand Committee should be formed comprising British MEPs and members of the EC committees in the two Houses fell on barren ground.

The reluctance to accept a European Grand Committee also derives from the third variable – a recognition of certain practical constraints. There is the recognition on the part of a number of parliamentarians – and of MEPs – that even if it is desirable in principle to have greater links between the national and the European Parliament there are practical limitations to achieving such links. The workload of British parliamentarians is heavy. This is especially so in the case of MPs but is also increasingly true of active members of the House of Lords. MPs in particular are having to be more severe in their allocation of time to parliamentary responsibilities. MEPs also are subject to increasing demands on their time. There are obvious logistical problems to commuting from, say, Edinburgh to Brussels and then trying to work in meetings in London as well. There are similar problems for MPs in the event of any collective or collaborative committee being established and meeting regularly in Brussels. In the words of one former MEP, who also is a member of the House of Lords, 'You can't be in two places at the same time'.

The differences in dealing with European issues between the two Houses may also be explained primarily in constitutional, political and practical terms. The House of Lords is an unelected chamber, and limited by statute in terms of its powers to delay legislation. Given both its composition – with many peers pursuing non-political careers – and its own recognition of political inferiority, the House is less prone to persistent partisanship than the House of Commons. It has concentrated instead on more detached scrutiny of legislation, being variously able – often, but not always – to draw on the expertise of its members.

The House of Commons labours under a greater burden of business than the Lords (the Lords does not discuss financial legislation) and consequently has to spend more time in session. Since 1979, it has also had in existence the departmental select committees, absorbing the time and interests of more than 150 MPs. The result is that the House of Lords has had somewhat greater scope for giving time to EC matters than the House of Commons. Whereas other business – including the work of select committees – has tended to limit the time for consideration of EC matters in the Commons, the reverse situation has pertained in the House of Lords. At the end of 1992, the Lords voted (though only just – the vote was tied) to reduce the number of EC sub-committees from six to five. (When the EC Committee was first appointed the number of sub-committees was seven.) Many peers, including ministers, felt that the sub-committees had been taking up too much time of the members and thus restricting the opportunities for the House to do other things. The number of sub-committees, as we have seen, is now six again, but the House has begun making greater use of committees in other areas.

The political explanation is to be found in the fact that the issue of EC membership has been less contentious in the House of Lords than in the House of Commons. This difference was marked in the 1970s and 1980s. Whereas in the House of Commons the passage of the European Communities in 1972 was a fraught and difficult one, in the Lords it had an untroubled passage. The preceding October the House had approved the principle of EC entry by 451 votes to 58. The difference between the Houses has been less marked in the 1990s, with some critics of the EU making their voices heard on the floor of the House – partly but not wholly a consequence of the elevation to the upper house of leading opponents of further European integration, such as Margaret, now Baroness, Thatcher and Norman, now Lord, Tebbit. Some critics of the EU and further integration also now serve on the EC committee and on the special *ad hoc* sub-committee.

The continued debate in and between parties about the future of the European Union and Britain's place within that Union has ensured that European integration has remained a subject of conflict among parliamentarians. In the Commons, it has meant that debate of European issues is conducted in largely adversarial terms, limiting the capacity of the House to debate constructively. That conflict has also meant that the Government has preferred to avoid floor debate, wanting to keep to as few as possible the occasions when votes on 'Europe' take place. That has been notable especially when the Government has had a small overall majority, as has been the case since April 1992 with the Government of John Major. Some debates, though, cannot be avoided. The conflict has encouraged heated debate on those occasions when primary legislation – treaty amendments – has been brought before the House.

The 1972 European Communities Bill was fought bitterly by opponents of membership. So too was the 1978 European Assembly Elections Bill. The 1992 European Communities (Amendment) Bill – the Maastricht Bill – took up 163 hours in committee in the House of Commons, passing into law a year later than planned by Government. The 1994 bill to give effect to a treaty obligation to increase the size of the European budget was passed only after the Government made its passage a vote of confidence. (Eight Conservative MPs who failed to vote with the party had the party whip withdrawn.)[23] The House of Commons may exert relatively little impact on EC legislation, but the Government has to anticipate parliamentary reaction when agreeing to any change in the treaties. In the House of Lords, the element of conflict is more obvious than it was before, but still not on a scale of that in the House of Commons. The effect of the conflict on primary legislation is to emphasise the splits in British parties about further European integration. The conflict masks the solid and substantial work done within Parliament in scrutinising secondary legislation.

CONCLUSION

For constitutional and political reasons, Parliament has – for most of the period since the UK joined the EC – sought to scrutinise EC documents and to influence deliberations within the Council of Ministers. The attempt has not been altogether unsuccessful. Both Houses have established committees to undertake scrutiny of EC documents and the two committees effectively complement one another. Both benefit from the provision of explanatory memoranda, a provision not common in other systems. Both committees have built links with EC institutions and committees in other national parliaments. The substantial reports produced by the Lords EC committee are informed, usually extensive and regarded by some MEPs as superior to reports produced by EP committees. The European Standing Committees in the Commons have an opportunity to submit ministers to searching questions on EC documents. (Though the opportunity is not much used, it tends to create a testing environment for ministers when it is.) The requirement by the House of Commons that ministers do not agree to documents in the Council of Ministers until the scrutiny process in the House is complete is an important constraint and one envied by some other national parliaments.

   Constitutional factors have nonetheless limited the capacity of both Houses to have a continuous and substantial impact in the making of European legislation. Neither House has any power to negate Commission proposals. That they share with other national legislatures. They are also limited in practical terms in the amount of time and resources they can devote to European issues. The House of Commons has a heavy workload – a world leader in terms of the number of hours it sits each year – and the House of Lords, also increasingly busy, is seeing demands from some peers for more time and committee work to be given over to domestic issues.

   Furthermore, the work done in both Houses in terms of scrutiny is overshadowed by the popular perception of a parliament that is divided over and essentially hostile towards further European integration. Opponents of further integration have been able to exploit a small government majority in the Commons to push the Government to adopt a sceptical stance towards integration, especially in the run-up to the 1996 IGC. The UK is often portrayed in this debate as the odd one out. That portrayal is rather too stark. Ironically perhaps, some of the factors motivating scepticism on the part of parlilamentarians are also responsible for generating a parliamentary means of scrutiny that renders the UK Parliament distinctive, though again not quite the odd one out, among national parliaments. Perhaps regrettably, the solid work of parliamentary scrutiny attracts less attention than the political divide over the future direction of the European Union.

NOTES

1. See H.J. Morgenthau, *Politics Among Nations*, 2nd edn. (New York: Knopf, 1993).
2. See A. King, *Britain Says Yes* (Washington DC: American Enterprise Institute, 1977), pp.2–7.
3. See S. George, *An Awkward Partner* (Oxford: Oxford University Press, 1990), pp.29–35, and D.W. Urwin, *The Community of Europe* (2nd edn., London: Longman, 1995), pp.117–20.
4. M. Camps, *Britain and the European Community 1955–1963* (Oxford: Oxford University Press, 1964), p.325.
5. Camps, p.336.
6. See P. Norton, *The Constitution in Flux* (Oxford: Basil Blackwell, 1982), pp.157–60. Most of these opening paragraphs derive from this work.
7. P. Norton, *Dissension in the House of Commons 1945–74* (London: Macmillan, 1974), pp.404–6.
8. See, for example, A. Jones, 'Parties, Ideologies and Issues: The Case of the European Community', in L. Robins, H. Blackmore and R. Pyper (eds.), *Britain's Changing Party System* (London: Leicester University Press, 1994), pp.75–92, and D. Baker, A. Gamble and S. Ludlam, 'The Parliamentary Siege of Maastricht 1993: Conservative Divisions and British Ratification', *Parliamentary Affairs* 47, 1 (January 1994), pp.37–60.
9. P. Norton, 'The Conservative Party from Thatcher to Major', in A. King (ed.), *Britain at the Polls 1992* (Chatham NJ: Chatham House, 1993), pp.40–42. For a more complex typology, see N. Ashford, 'The Political Parties', in S. George (ed.), *Britain and the European Community: The Politics of Semi-Detachment* (Oxford: Clarendon Press, 1992).
10. See Ashford, 'The Political Parties', and also Norton, *The Consititution in Flux*, pp.263–7.
11. The Foster Committee in the House of Commons and the Maybray-King Committee in the House of Lords. See H.N. Miller, 'The Influence of British Parliamentary Committees on European Communities Legislation', *Legislative Studies Quarterly* 2, 1 (1977), pp.47–9.
12. In the 11-year period 1978 to 1988 inclusively, the number averaged just over 88. The figures ranged from 71 to 107 but for most sessions did not veer that much from the average. See *The Scrutiny of European Legislation: Fourth Report from the Select Committee on Procedure*, Session 1988–89, HC 622-I, p.x, para. 12.
13. See *The Scrutiny of European Legislation*, p.x, para. 15.
14. *First Special Report from the Select Committee on European Legislation*, Session 1993–94, HC 99. See also *Second Special Report*, Session 1993–94, HC 739.
15. See D. Shell, 'The European Communities Committee', in D. Shell and D. Beamish (eds.), *The House of Lords at Work* (Oxford: Oxford University Press, 1993).
16. Until 1991, such inquiries were undertaken at the discretion of the EC committee. Since 1991, priorities for and the balance in committee work in the House have been determined by the liaison committee.
17. D. Shell, *The House of Lords* (2nd edn., Hemel Hempstead: Harvester Wheatsheaf, 1992), p.227.
18. See, e.g., C. Grantham and C.M. Hodgson, 'The House of Lords: Structural Changes',

in P. Norton (ed.), *Parliament in the 1980s* (Oxford: Basil Blackwell, 1985), pp.126–8; T.StJ.N. Bates, 'Select Committees in the House of Lords', in G. Drewry (ed.), *The New Select Committees* (Oxford: Oxford University Press, 1985), pp.50–52; and *Report from the Select Committee on the Committee Work of the House*, House of Lords, Session 1991–92, HL Paper 35-I, pp.24–7.

19. See *House of Lords Scrutiny of the Inter-Governmental Pillars of the European Union*, 28th Report of the Select Committee on the European Communities, House of Lords, Session 1992–93, HL Paper 124.

20. P. Norton, *Does Parliament Matter?* (Hemel Hempstead: Harvester Wheatsheaf, 1993), pp.126–7.

21. P. Norton, 'The Glorious Revolution of 1688 and 1689: Its Continuing Relevance', *Parliamentary Affairs* 42, 2 (April 1989), pp.135–47.

22. D. Baker, I. Fountain, A. Gamble and S. Ludlam, 'What Tory MPs Think About Europe', *Parliamentary Brief* 3, 3 (Dec. 1994), p.98.

23. The scale of this action was without precedent. See P. Norton, 'Whipless MPs: Working Without the Whip', *The House Magazine*, 9 Jan. 1995, pp.10–11.

The Folketing and Denmark's 'European Policy': The Case of an 'Authorising Assembly'?

DAVID ARTER

In a statement displaying an unimpeachable regard for what used to be known in British trade union circles as 'relativities', Erik Damgaard has characterised Denmark as a 'fairly complex system with rather weak minority governments and a fairly strong parliament'. The Danish Folketing, he asserts, 'has certainly not declined in recent decades'. It might be added that in the shape of the Market Relations Committee (*Folketingets markedsudvalg*), renamed the European Affairs Committee on 4 October 1994 – which mandates the negotiating stance of government ministers in the Council of Ministers and, in line with article 7:1 of the Parliamentary Standing Orders, 'co-ordinates the Folketing's handling of EU matters' – Denmark has possessed a widely admired parliamentary organ which attracts as many delegations of foreign experts to the Christiansborg Palace in Copenhagen as visit the Commissariat du Plan in Paris. Most recently, moreover, the 'Danish model' served as the point of departure for the Nordic European Free Trade Association (EFTA) members[2] – the Tiitinen Committee in Finland (which reported in April 1994) and the Swedish Commission of Inquiry the previous year – in their deliberation of ways of adapting existing parliamentary procedures to the contingencies of EU membership.[3] It is against this backdrop of the established reputation of the Market Relations Committee (MRC) and its successor, the European Affairs Committee (EAC) that the present article examines the Folketing's role in the national EU decision-making process and asks whether it could reasonably be depicted as a strong policy influencing assembly in relation to EU matters.

PARLIAMENTARY ADAPTATION AND THE EVOLUTION OF THE MRC–EAC

Four main stages in the adaptation of the Folketing to the challenges of European integration may be identified: the emergence of a purpose-specific committee, the MRC, in 1961; its formalisation and institutionalisation by law in 1972; the extension of the MRC's powers in 1986; and

David Arter is Professor of Nordic Politics, University of Aberdeen.

its redesignation and reorganisation which took effect in October 1994.

The creation of a parliamentary standing committee to oversee Community legislation significantly pre-dated Danish accession to the Common Market and was associated with the country's first (unsuccessful) application (along with Britain) in 1961. Then, the Market Relations Committee operated as essentially a deliberative forum in which to review the various options in Community policy and discuss the possible terms of Denmark's future admission. Acting in an advisory capacity it pre-empted some of the duties of the Foreign Affairs Council (*Det udenrikspolitiske nævn*) – a permanent organ set up by law in 1923 – which the Government is required to consult before every important foreign policy decision is taken. Importantly, the inception of the MRC pre-dated the adoption of a system of permanent, specialist committees in the Folketing in 1972 – the year in which, in the first of the four EC-related referenda between 1972 and 1993, the Danes voted to join the Common Market.

The MRC's position was formalised and institutionalised in connection with Denmark's third and successful application to join the Common Market. Article six of the 1972 Accession Treaty obliges the Government to report to the Folketing on developments in the European Communities and to notify a committee of Parliament of proposals for Council decisions that will become directly applicable in Denmark and whose implementation requires action by the Folketing. The MRC's new status was confirmed following a political crisis in 1973 when the Social Democratic minority Government's Minister of Agriculture concluded a highly unfavourable provisional price agreement for Danish export bacon without gaining the Folketing's backing, a fact which provoked the Liberals (Venstre) and Conservatives to put down a motion of no confidence in the cabinet. A compromise hammered out between the Social Democrats, Radicals (Radikale Venstre) and anti-EC Socialist People's Party served to save the Government's bacon (!), but at the expense of significantly strengthening the *de facto* role of the MRC as a parliamentary control mechanism.[4] Indeed, in its first report, unanimously adopted by its members on 29 March 1974, the MRC stated that the Government shall consult with it on EC policy questions of 'major political importance' and prior to negotiations in the Council of Ministers on 'decisions with a wider significance' it should submit a mandate for negotiation. The interpretation of the terms 'major political importance' and 'decisions with a wider significance' has evolved to such a point that the present convention is for the cabinet to present a mandate for negotiation on practically all legal documents before their adoption in the Council of Ministers.

The *de jure* powers of the MRC were extended as a by-product of the events leading to a second national EC referendum in Denmark on 27 February 1986. When the main opposition party, the Social Democrats, announced they would vote against acceptance of the Single European Act – the Radicals had earlier indicated their intention to do the same – Poul Schlüter, heading a minority non-socialist coalition, surprisingly deployed the referendum as a tactical weapon against the refractory Folketing majority rather than call the expected general election.[5] The ploy worked to good effect; 56.2 per cent of voters ultimately favoured ratifying the Single European Act and the Government thus maintained its tenuous grip on office. However, widespread (at times exaggerated) anxiety at the prospect of exponential political integration – particularly among the Radicals there was opposition to the European Political Community (EPC) Treaty – prompted a desire to ensure there were adequate signalling mechanisms enabling the Folketing to debate major developments in the Community. Accordingly, the MRC's position was consolidated in such a way that a minority of two-fifths of its members was empowered to require a Commission proposal to be given the equivalent of a first reading on the floor of the Folketing (at which principles and generalities could be considered) after which the matter would return to the MRC. In fact, floor debates, held at the MRC's instigation, have been highly technical and attracted little public attention.[6]

The re-christening of the MRC, which became the European Affairs Committee (EAC) in October 1994, stemmed indirectly from the narrow Danish rejection of the Maastricht Treaty at the third 'European' referendum on 2 June 1992 and concern expressed both during and after the campaign about the so-called democratic deficit and the need for greater transparency (openness) in EU decision-making. Accordingly, one of the stipulations of the seven-party 'National Compromise' – foisted on the Schlüter bourgeois minority Government by the opposition-based Social Democrats, Radicals and Socialist People's Party[7] – was that Danish EU decision-making procedures should be reformed so as to involve members of the Folketing and general public to a greater extent.[8] This in turn was a response to the 'No' campaign's insistence that there was an incipient 'crisis of democracy' in Denmark which certainly struck a chord among voters.[9] Following the Edinburgh Summit of December 1992, which spelt out Denmark's exemptions under Maastricht, and in the run-up to the second Danish referendum approving Maastricht on 18 May 1993 (see Table 1), a large majority of Folketing members favoured three measures designed to 'democratise' the domestic management of EU business. First, there was support for the creation of an 'EU-Council' (EF-råd), comprising representatives of organisations, expert opinion and individual members of the public, which would advise on matters of EU importance.

Next, there was solid backing for the setting up of a European Documentation Centre in Parliament whose task it would be to advise citizens on where to obtain more information on EU issues as well as to respond to concrete questions. The present practice is that the Ministry of Foreign Affairs forwards three copies of all Commission proposals as soon as they appear in Danish to the Secretariat of the EAC and they are registered and filed in the EU Documentation Centre and, therefore, are at the disposal of the general public. Finally, a majority of parliamentarians favoured the staging of regular press conferences after the weekly meetings of the MRC.[10] About 95 per cent of the memoranda received by the EAC are currently accessible to the general public and they are also routinely forwarded to members of the press corps.

TABLE 1

'EUROPEAN' REFERENDA IN DENMARK, 1972–93

Date	Issue	% Yes	% No
2 October 1972	EC membership	64.0	36.0
27 February 1986	Single European Act	56.2	43.8
2 June 1992	Ratifying Maastricht	49.3	50.7
18 May 1993	Edinburgh exemptions	56.8	43.2

The EAC (like its predecessor, the MRC) comprises 17 full members (and 11 deputies who also have the right to participate), chosen so as to reflect the partisan balance in the assembly as a whole, and it constitutes one of the 24 standing committees of the Folketing. As such the EAC can, and very occasionally does, function as part of the legislative process, for example, when rules governing elections to the European Parliament are being considered. The ratification of the Maastricht Treaty in 1993 and the enlargement of the Union in 1994 were dealt with by the EAC. When it does function in a legislative role, the formal quorum rules applying to other parliamentary standing committees apply, that is, at least half the members should attend; otherwise, the expectation is simply that half the opinion in the assembly should be present. Unlike other Folketing committees, but in common with the Foreign Affairs Council, the EAC does not produce written reports, nor does it make recommendations to the Folketing. As mentioned, however, it can instigate a Folketing debate on a Commission proposal. During the 1980s, the convention developed that the chair of the MRC was not recruited from one of the governing parties, so absolving the cabinet from any charge of not being prepared to subject the main lines of its Community policy to adequate examination.

The EAC meetings, which take place weekly throughout the year (except August) are usually held on Fridays, before meetings of the Council of Ministers on Mondays and Tuesdays and after the Thursday session of the EU cabinet committee. They normally last between two and five hours and have a detailed agenda. It is the right of a minister (or the EAC chair) to require members, where necessary, to maintain secrecy on matters discussed in the Committee. In practice, the confidentiality rule is applied only exceptionally when the position of other countries is being debated and when Danish ministers are receiving their (oral) mandate for a particular stance in Brussels.

THE GOVERNMENT'S OBLIGATION TO INFORM AND CONSULT THE FOLKETING ON EU BUSINESS

In accordance with Article 6, paragraph 2, of Denmark's EC accession law, and the obligation to inform and consult parliament, the Foreign Ministry transmits all Commission proposals to the EAC and, with the exception of technical matters, there is also an accompanying memorandum evaluating the proposal in respect of national law and setting out the way it will be handled in the EU. EAC agendas comprise items relating to the next two meetings of the Council of Ministers in so far as (i) they concern EU regulations that will apply directly to Denmark (ii) deal with regulations that require Folketing consideration and ratification and (iii) are otherwise regarded as important (the EAC can, of course, place items of its own on the agenda). Although the relevant minister is present at EAC meetings, civil servants are precluded. The government's negotiating aims are presented verbally and discussion also embraces a written statement clarifying the legal and economic implications of the measure. In the EAC a negative majority is required, that is, the Government's line is followed if delegates representing a majority of Folketing seats (viz 90) do not oppose it.

In seeking to evaluate the Folketing's role in scrutinising and sanctioning Government responses to Commission proposals – that is, in shaping Denmark's 'European policy' – it is important to emphasise that, in a real sense, cabinet consultation with the EAC is based as much on convention as legal prescription. The EAC's terms of reference are imprecise: the rules dating back to 1972 allude, as mentioned, to the MRC dealing with market issues of 'essential political importance' and decisions (to be taken in the Council of Ministers) that possess 'wider significance'. Within these broad and inevitably subjective limits, the Government is able in principle to determine which Commission proposals it puts before the EAC. Significantly, there is no formal provision enabling the EAC to take the initiative and request a statement from the Government or an

administrative body – a restriction which has been intermittently criticised by committee members, especially those opposed to the EU. True,
the MRC/EAC has possessed and exercised the right to veto the Government's negotiating stance in Brussels, but in practice several institutional
factors have conspired to consolidate the position of the Committee as an
inspection body.

First, the longevity of the MRC–EAC – which pre-dates a system of
specialist standing committees in the Folketing – has vested it with a
preponderant, if not quite monopolistic role in the parliamentary deliberation of EU measures. The role of the other Folketing committees in EU
decision-making, in short, has been relatively weak and although the
EAC may request a special statement from another standing committee
this is a relatively rare occurrence. In practice it has been confined to the
Committee on the Environment and Regional Planning, from which
statements are regularly requested. Since Maastricht, to be sure, MRC–
EAC links with the other Folketing committees have increased somewhat,
but its contacts with interest groups outside Government and Parliament
have been far more extensive and provided an important signalling
mechanism in alerting committee members to EU issues of imminent
note.

Second, the MRC–EAC has derived considerable authority from the
'heavyweight' composition of the committee. Parties have assigned their
senior figures – former ministers, party leaders and the like – to membership of the Committee which, accordingly, has become a highly prestigious
body. Equally, these leading politicians have generally had little time to
devote to the 'small print' of EAC matters and in consequence have relied
heavily on the deliberations and expertise of party colleagues. Thus, in
line with standard Nordic practice, there is preliminary discussion of
forthcoming EAC business in the respective parliamentary party groups
and their internal policy committees and EAC delegates have also availed
themselves of specialist advice from the standing committee spokesmen
in their parliamentary groups. Equally, although EAC members normally
consult their parliamentary groups they can, as senior figures, commit
their parties unilaterally where necessary.

Finally, established practice has witnessed a readiness on the Government's part to delegate effective scrutiny powers to the MRC–EAC, a
fact which goes a good deal of the way to explaining why legislative-
executive consultation on Community policy in Denmark has generally
functioned smoothly enough. Thus, in recent years, the flow of information to EAC members and, by extension, its 'scrutiny potential' has
increased significantly; the EAC authorises the negotiating stance of
Danish ministers in meetings of the Council of Ministers and this is rarely

automatic; there are now procedures for cross-checking that the minister has remained within the confines of his mandate; and, finally, both prior to and after European Council meetings, the Prime Minister briefs the EAC in person.

The most important items on the EAC's agenda are Council of Ministers' meetings and the agendas distributed to EAC members by the Ministry of Foreign Affairs largely correspond to those of Council meetings. They are transmitted to EAC members in several 'editions' – the first ten days before its meetings and the second four days beforehand, the latter indicating those items on which the Government expects to seek a mandate for negotiation. The agenda contains references to the number of Commission proposals and to complementary memoranda – the so-called 'notes' provided by the relevant government department and dispatched to the EAC by the Ministry of Foreign Affairs – which provide the basis of the EAC 'reading'. The vast majority of the EAC's documentation in fact originates in the Ministry of Foreign Affairs, although it also receives written requests directly from interest groups.

Since October 1994, the Government has been under an obligation to present the EAC with a set of so-called 'basic notes' on those new Commission proposals which relate to levels of Danish protection in the fields of health, the environment, the labour-market and consumer affairs. These 'basic notes' are supplied as quickly as possible after the Commission has submitted the proposal. Furthermore, when a Commission proposal is entered on the agenda of a Council meeting, the Ministry of Foreign Affairs produces a 'topical factual note' at least one week before the relevant EAC meeting. This is often done in the form of so-called 'collected notes' in which each of the items at the appropriate Council meeting is described.

Prior to all negotiations on important political matters, the relevant minister gives the EAC a verbal presentation on his/her initial policy stance. Fresh developments in the bargaining process, moreover, may require the minister to obtain a renewed mandate from the Committee – consequently meetings can take place at short notice and at inconvenient times – and the outcome of continued talks is again presented to the EAC. More typically, the Danish minister in the Council of Ministers contents himself with making a reservation for subsequent parliamentary approval in the EAC. The minister may in fact find it tactically desirable to aver to the Folketing's Standing Orders and request that a matter be postponed until it has been submitted to the EAC.

In any event, approximately one week after the Council meeting, the Danish minister in question submits a set of minutes to the EAC and since 1993 these have been public documents. The Folketing's EU representative in Brussels, moreover, forwards to the EAC the press release issued by the Secretary-General of the Council of Ministers which contains information on how the individual Member States have voted, something which enables EAC members to check whether the minister has kept within the guidelines of his negotiating mandate. On occasions, committee members wil put in written questions so as to get a fuller explanation of matters in the minutes and if the issue is of sufficient political import the minister may be called for cross-examination. Matters of principle can also lead to an interpellation being tabled and the Government will then be required to negotiate a major debate in the Folketing. Incidentally, since 1984, short-hand minutes of EAC meetings have been taken, so ensuring that members are familiar with the precise content of the negotiating mandate. The minutes are forwarded to the party spokesmen on the EAC and other members can go through them in the Secretariat.

Before European Council meetings, the Prime Minister appears before the EAC to give an account of the topics to be discussed and the Government's position on them. One or more rounds of questioning follow during which senior members present the party line. Very exceptionally, when the European Council is expected to take substantive decisions, the Prime Minister seeks acceptance for a negotiating stance and, in any case, appears again after the summit meeting to report on what transpired. Again, questioning and possibly even a debate on one or two matters are possible.

THE EAC AND THE PARTY POLITICS OF INSPECTION AND CONTROL

Whilst institutional variables contribute to a partial understanding of the inspection and control powers of the EAC, its real influence can only be comprehended in the wider dynamic context of the party politics and legislative culture of the Folketing. Significantly, the period of Danish membership of the EC/EU has coincided with, and conflict over European integration contributed to, both the collapse of the traditional party system and a transformation in the parliamentary culture. The party system has been more fragmented and the legislative culture less consensual and these developments have had important implications for the extent of real control exercised by the MRC–EAC over the Government's 'European policy'.

Opposition to Danish membership of the EC was, it appears, of only secondary importance in explaining the proliferation of parliamentary parties that followed the seismic election of 1973. The first after accession, this saw the number of parties gaining representation in the Folketing more than double (from five to 11) and the percentage share of the vote polled by the 'four old parties' – Social Democrats, Radicals, Liberals and Conservatives – drop to 58.1 compared with 80.8 two years earlier. True, the Communists and Justice Party, which returned to the Folketing after nearly a decade and a half in the wilderness, both opposed the EC during the 1972 referendum and they joined the Socialist People's Party, which at the time Denmark joined the Community had been the only anti-EC party in the Folketing. But electoral support for the four expressly anti-market parties (the three aforementioned plus the Left Socialists – who did not make it to Parliament) at 14.0 per cent was only very slightly up on their performance (13.8 per cent) two years earlier and well down on the 36 per cent of Danes who opposed membership at the 2 October 1972 referendum.

In other words, popular suspicion and hostility towards the Community were reflected primarily in divisions within established parties rather than support for new ones. Glistrup's Progress Party, which achieved a sensational breakthrough in 1973, was anti-tax rather than anti-EC and the Centre Democrats, who under Erhard Jakobsen split from the Social Democrats six weeks before the election, were strongly 'pro-Europe'. Of the four historic parties, the Social Democrats and Radicals, although formally in favour of the EC, were divided on the issue at both parliamentary and grassroots levels, leaving only the Conservatives and Liberals as staunch 'marketeers' and even then a small minority of their voters remained opposed. A clearer barometer of popular sentiment on 'Europe', and the prospect of increased political integration in particular, than that afforded by the Folketing party system was support for the 'People's Movement Against the EC'. This claimed one-quarter of Denmark's 16 seats at the European Parliament elections in 1979, 1984, and 1989 and the People's Movement, together with the anti-Maastricht 'June Movement', still claimed one in four Danish votes at the European Parliament election of June 1994 – even though the Edinburgh exemptions to Maastricht had been approved at a popular referendum a year earlier.[11]

Over and above conflict on the European issue, the increasingly fragmented party system after 1973 further complicated the already difficult task of assembling majority coalitions and, in challenging the pragmatic, compromise-based norms that had become integral to the Danish parliamentary culture, also made the Government's task in building legislative majorities more problematic. The structure of the 'traditional' multi-party system in Denmark dictated that majority government necessarily involved coalitions. Thus, although comfortably the largest single party (with 34.6 per cent of the poll in September 1994 – see Table 1), the Danish Social Democrats, unlike their fraternal parties in

Norway, Sweden and Finland, have never obtained a parliamentary majority; indeed, no party since the Liberal Reform Party (Venstrereform-partiet) in 1901–6 has done so. Traditionally, however, majority coalitions were routine enough and accounted for 40 per cent of cabinets in the period 1945–73.[12] All this changed after the 1973 election. Since then, there has been only one majority government compared with eight minority governments between 1973 and 1995, including a growing number of minority coalitions. The present Social Democrat, Radical and Centre Democrat coalition under Poul Nyrup Rasmussen has the support of 76 of the Folketing's 179 members (see Table 2).

TABLE 2

THE DANISH GENERAL ELECTION, 21 SEPTEMBER 1994

	%		SEATS
PARTY	1994	1990	1994
Social Democrats	34.6	37.8	63
Radicals	4.6	3.5	8
Conservatives	15.0	16.0	28
Centre Democrats	2.8	5.1	5
Socialist People's	7.3	8.3	13
Liberals	23.3	15.8	44
Christian People's	1.8	2.3	0
Progress	6.4	6.4	11
Unity	3.1	1.7	6
Others	1.0	3.5	1
			Total 179

Furthermore, whilst minority cabinets are necessarily engaged in building majority legislative coalitions with one or more parties outside government, the accentuated party conflict of the 'new party system' contributed to a more adversarial parliamentary culture in which minority governments could no longer count on external support in the way they could before 1973.[13] This was particularly true during the period of so-called 'footnote politics' between 1982 and 1988 when Schlüter's 'four-leaf clover' minority coalitions of Conservatives, Liberals, Centre Democrats and Christians were regularly defeated on EU issues by the Socialist People's Party, Social Democrats, Radicals and Left Socialists in opposition. The Schlüter cabinets lost 108 out of 1356 final divisions and in all but three cases – recourse to a popular referendum on the issue of the Single European Act in February 1986 was one – the Government accepted defeat with a view to staying in office. During this period the Folketing was clearly a strong policy influencing (even policy making) assembly on EU matters – Damgaard notes that it was the opposition parties and not the Government that in practice made decisions – and in this situation the MRC proved a particular thorn in the Government's side.[14]

CONCLUSIONS

In the routine situation of minority government, the MRC–EAC has been able to exercise significant *political* control over the Danish executive in relation to important EU questions. During the Ankers Jørgensen Social Democratic minority cabinets of the late 1970s and early 1980s, there were four 'anti-market' parties represented on the MRC and by dint of thorough preparation they contrived substantially to protract meetings and sustain the essentially political character of the organ. They were also able to work through the anti-EC members of the European Parliament in Strasbourg. During the period of 'footnote politics' the MRC was the principal organ of the opposition in modifying the Government's negotiating stance and securing Danish 'footnotes' (exemptions, reservations, qualifications and so on) to European agreements.[15]

The degree of control exercised by the MRC in the *technical* inspection of EU policy has been significantly less for two obvious reasons. First, the committee staff is very small. The EAC's secretariat, headed by a clerk, assisted by a deputy clerk and four clerical staff, is responsible for planning the Committee's work, keeping its records and producing minutes of its meetings. There is an EU Counsellor attached to the EAC and, supported by a lawyer, his task is to provide analyses of EU proposals both for the EAC and its individual members. Plainly though, it is very much a case of one man in a minefield of European measures. Second, EAC delegates receive the second edition of agendas only four days before meetings and in consequence find it difficult to assess the implications for Denmark of marginal adjustments to, say, the CAP. They rely heavily on specialist colleagues in their parliamentary groups and other Folketing committees.

In terms of the Folketing committee system as a whole, in fact, there was relatively little institutional adaptation in over three decades until Maastricht. Thereafter, although the MRC was renamed and revamped, its powers remained essentially unchanged. The EAC still does not have the right of initiative in requesting an explanatory statement. Moreover, it continues to carry almost exclusive responsibility for the deliberation of EU questions. Since Maastricht the Government has been required to inform the Foreign Policy Committtee – in addition to the EAC – on matters relating to a common foreign and security policy (pillar two) and the Legal Affairs Committee on matters pertaining to pillar three. Furthermore, beginning in the 1994–95 Folketing session, the 'factual notes' on Commission proposals prepared by the Ministry of Foreign Affairs have also been distributed to relevant standing committees. However, the onus is on an individual committee to determine whether to take up an EU matter and, if it does, the committee may then put supplementary written questions, it may require the minister to attend for cross-examination and it may make a recommendation to the EAC. Perhaps the primary purpose of this parallel flow of information has been to provide an EAC member with a basis on which to discuss matters with his party colleagues on the appropriate specialist committee. It bears restatement that the EAC's task is to co-ordinate the Folketing's work on EU matters and it is the only standing committee entitled to mandate a minister's negotiating stance in the Council of Ministers. Despite its 'Euro-specific' character, moreover, the MRC/EAC is a permeable body, its behaviour dictated by the partisanship of the senior politicians that make up its membership. It has not generated a corporate identity; rather, it has served as a mouthpiece for the expression of interparty conflict.

Nonetheless, the partisan balance in the assembly has ensured that in EU matters, the Folketing remains a strong policy influencing assembly. Thus, at the end of a decade of bourgeois minority government, the Schlüter cabinet was effectively obliged to accept the National Compromise initiated by the opposition-based Social Democrats, Socialist People's Party and Radicals which provided the Government's negotiating stance at the Edinburgh summit in December 1992. Following confirmation of Denmark's exemptions by the summit leaders, a Social Democratic-led majority coalition under Rasmussen between January 1993 and September 1994 – the only one since 1973 – supervised the second referendum on Maastricht in May 1993. The trend towards the 'normalisation' of the Danish party system was confirmed at the polls in September 1994. The Justice and Communist parties have long since departed the parliamentary stage, whilst the Christians failed to negotiate the two per cent threshold and lost their footing in the Folketing. The 'four old parties' polled a combined 77.5 per cent, only a fraction short of their total share in 1971. Yet the return to minority government continues to hold out the prospect of the Folketing being able to exert telling influence on Denmark's EU policy.

Above all, the record of the EAC in influencing the Government's stance at intergovernmental conferences looks set to ensure that the run-up to the Maastricht review IGC in 1996 does not lack interest. In addition to seeking a negotiating mandate from the committee, which it keeps constantly informed of developments as the IGC progresses, the EAC is furnished beforehand with all written proposals from other EU

TABLE 3

COMPOSITION OF DANISH GOVERNMENTS AFTER THE SECOND WORLD WAR

1945	Buhl (all-party)*
1945–47	Kristensen (Liberals)
1947–50	Hedtoft 1 (Social Democrats)
1950–53	Eriksen (Liberals and Conservatives)
1953–55	Hedtoft 11 (Social Democrats)
1955–57	Hansen 1 (Social Democrats)
1957–60	Hansen 11 (Soc Dems, Radicals & Justice Party)*
1960	Kampmann 1 (Soc Dems, Radicals & Justice Party)*
1960–62	Kampmann 11 (Soc Dems & Radicals)*
1962–64	Krag 1 (Soc Dems & Radicals)*
1964–68	Krag 11 (Social Democrats)
1968–71	Baunsgaard (Radicals, Liberals & Conservatives)*
1971–72	Krag 111 (Social Democrats)
1972–73	Jørgensen 1 (Social Democrats)
1973–75	Hartling (Liberals)
1975–78	Jørgensen 11 (Social Democrats)
1978–79	Jørgensen 111 (Social Democrats & Liberals)
1979–82	Jørgensen 1V (Social Democrats)
1982–88	Schlüter 1 (Cons, Libs, Centre Democrats & Christians)
1988–90	Schlüter 11 (Cons, Libs & Radicals)
1990–93	Schlüter 111 (Cons & Libs)
1993–94	Rasmussen 1 (Soc Dems, Radicals, Centre Dems & Christians)*
1994–	Rasmussen 11 (Soc Dems, Radicals & Centre Democrats)

* notes majority government. The Social Democratic-Radical cabinets of 1960–64 relied for the narrowest of majorities on the MP for Greenland who was made Minister for Greenland.

Member States. As Bjørn Einersen has argued, the 'EAC can have a major impact on the stand which the Danish government takes at inter-governmental conferences'.[16] This is particularly so when, as is usually the case, the cabinet has only minority support in the Folketing, but even a majority coalition cannot count on automatic approval of its negotiating stance.

One final point. The documents of the EEA are forwarded to the Danish members of the European Parliament who also receive agendas of EAC meetings. It used to be the case that material stamped 'confidential' was only distributed to MRC members and, when in doubt, there was a tendency for material to be marked 'confidential' if only to minimise the risk of leagues made up of anti-EU MEPs and their counterparts on the MRC.[17] Agreements between EAC members and MEPs within particular parties can still constitute an effective two-pronged offensive to a government's EU stance. In so much, a Government must pay heed to the partisan balance not only in the Folketing, but also among the Danish delegation to the European Parliament in Strasbourg.

NOTES

1. E. Damgaard, 'Denmark: Experiments in Parliamentary Government', in E. Damgaard (ed.), *Parliamentary Change in the Nordic Countries* (Oslo: Scandinavian University Press; 1992), p.47.
2. At a referendum on 16 October 1994, the Finns voted 57.0–43.0 per cent in favour of full EU membership and the Swedes did likewise by a margin of 52.2–46.9 per cent (0.9 per cent blank ballot papers) on 13 November 1994. Both left EFTA on 1 January 1995. In contrast, on 27–28 November 1994 the Norwegians voted for the second time (initially in September 1972) to reject joining the EU. The negative majority was 52.3–47.7 per cent. Both Iceland (which has not applied for EU membership) and Norway, however, have access to the EU's single market through the European Economic Area (EEA) agreement, which came into operation on 1 January 1994.
3. Komiteanmietintö 1994:4, *Valtiosääntökomitea 1992:n mietintö* Euroopan unionin vaikutukset Suomen valtiosääntöön. Ulkopoliittisen päätöksentekojärjestelmän uudistamistarpeet ja tavat (Valtioneuvoston kanslia: Painatuskeskus, 1994), pp.214–16. 'Riksdagens roll i EG samarbetet' SOU:14, pp.231–47.
4. J. Fitzmaurice, 'The Danish System of Parliamentary Control over European Community Policy', in V. Herman and R. van Schendelen (eds.), *The European Parliament and the National Parliaments* (Farnborough: Saxon House, 1979), p.217.
5. D. Arter, *The Politics of European Integration in the Twentieth Century* (Aldershot: Dartmouth, 1993), pp.163–8.
6. Damgaard, 'Denmark: Experiments in Parliamentary Government', p.41.
7. 'De skrev Danmarkshistorie', *Nordisk Kontakt* 10 (1992), pp.37–9.
8. *Det Radikale Venstre* Newsletter 3, Nov. 1992, pp.3–4.
9. See, for example, 'Et-JA med løftet pegefinger', *Midtjyllands Avis*, 19 May 1993, p.2.
10. 'Mere Åbenhed på vej', *Tema/Fagbladet* 17 (1993), pp.4–5.
11. 'Over halvdelen af den danske vælgere stemte ved EU-valget' *Nordisk Kontakt* 6 (1994), pp.18–21.
12. On the shift to a 179-member Folketing in 1953, see D. Arter, 'One Ting Too Many: The Shift to Unicameralism in Denmark' in L.D. Longley and D.M. Olson, *Two Into One: The Politics and Processes of National Legislative Cameral Change* (Boulder, Colorado: Westview, 1991), pp.77–142.
13. E. Damgaard, 'Danmarks Nye Folketing', in Krister Ståhlberg (ed.), *Parlamenten i Norden* (Åbo: Åbo Akademi,1990), pp.1–20.
14. Damgaard, 'Denmark: Experiments in Parliamentary Government' (1992), pp.34–35.
15. Contrast the anodyne conclusion of Kenneth E. Miller that, 'For the government, the MRC provides a useful forum for discussion of Community affairs and committee decisions reveal to the government before it makes an important decision whether a Folketing majority will support it'. K.E. Miller, *Denmark: A Troubled Welfare State* (Westview: Boulder-San Francisco-Oxford: Westview, 1991), p.178.
16. The Secretary of the European Affairs Committee, Bjørn Einersen, was invaluable in providing information on the recent work of the committee.
17. D. Arter, *The Nordic Parliaments: A Comparative Analysis* (London: Hurst, 1984), pp. 369–78.

Irish Parliamentary Culture and the European Union: Formalities to be Observed

EUNAN O'HALPIN

Relations between the Irish Parliament (Oireachtas) and the European Union have, until very recently, been characterised by a combination of neglect and ignorance. This stands in marked contrast to the consistently high level of public and political support for Irish membership over the last two decades, as evidenced in the clear two-to-one pro-Europe results in constitutional referenda on Irish accession in 1972, on the Single European Act in 1987, and on the Maastrict Treaty in 1992. It also appears anomalous given the enormous impact which membership has had on the Irish economy and society, and the highly public preoccupation of successive governments and of the Irish policy system with obtaining the maximum possible slice of funds from every EU programme. Other countries are equally as diligent at pursuing their national financial interests at EU level, but it is doubtful whether the exercise is quite as public as it is in Ireland, where no politician or significant interest group is in any doubt about the imperative to increase the country's take from Europe.[1]

Why, given this high general level of political awareness, has the Oireachtas as an institution formally been so conspicuously uninterested in EU affairs for most of the period since Irish accession? Explanations can be found in the development of Irish parliamentary culture since independence in 1922, in the nature of the Irish policy-making process, and in the receptivity of European community institutions to interest-group representations – for Irish farmers, to take an obvious example, the real action is now in Brussels, not in Dublin. This discussion, however, will focus specifically on the Oireachtas.[2]

IRISH PARLIAMENTARY CULTURE, 1922–95

The Irish Constitution provides for an Oireachtas consisting of two houses, the Dail and the Seanad, together with a directly elected head of state, the President. The President's legislative role is confined to the signature of bills, or very exceptionally to their referral to the Supreme

Eunan O'Halpin is Associate Professor of Government at Dublin City University.

Court for advice as to their constitutionality. As the directly elected lower house the 166-seat Dail is pre-eminent; the 60-seat Seanad or Senate, composed partly of members elected by a bizarre franchise of local politicians, graduates of the two oldest universities, and sitting members of the Oireachtas, and partly of nominees of the Taoiseach (Prime Minister) of the day, is hamstrung by its lack of a popular base, and by the deliberate neglect of successive governments.[3] Since its establishment in 1922 the Irish State has employed an electoral system based on proportional representation, with the single transferable vote and multi-seat constituencies. This appeared a recipe for a complex multi-party system in which the Parliament would be untameable and strong and the Executive consequently rather weak, dependent for survival on constant appeasement of various parliamentary groupings. In practice the system has developed rather differently. Ireland has enjoyed a pattern of highly stable governments, with an average span between elections of three years. These governments have traditionally exercised unfettered dominance in the Dail and Seanad. For example, non-government bills have virtually no chance of becoming law – less than a dozen have been passed since the present Constitution was enacted in 1937 – and ministers have been very reluctant to accept any amendments to draft legislation. Most TDs (MPs) not members of the Government spend the bulk of their time and energy on party and constituency matters; discussion of policy options, or the detailed examination of Government proposals and activities, get little attention because the structures and the culture of the Oireachtas for long inhibited such activities. The use made of parliamentary questions, in theory one of the few worthwhile instruments with which any TD can trouble the Government, illustrates the practical priorities of Irish parliamentarians. While the volume of such questions has grown spectacularly over the years, from something under 4,000 annually in the 1930s to over 16,000 annually by the 1980s, these are almost always used to air the grievances of individual constituents against some part of the state machine, not to extract information on policy issues or on administrative performance from the Government.[4] Studies of the Oireachtas, including one by this writer, arguably exaggerate the dominance of the executive over the legislature by focusing on the published record of proceedings, so discounting the informal powers which individual TDs and senators may possess and exercise in private outside the chamber, perhaps before a measure is even publicly proposed.[5] Nevertheless, it remains the case that party discipline, the pressures of constituency business, and its own conventions, timetable and procedures combine to make the Oireachtas appear a rather lackadaisical institution. It is probably also significant that Fianna Fail, since 1927 the Dail's largest

and most disciplined parliamentary party and the one which has pre-
dominated in government since 1932, for decades regarded Oireachtas
reform as a zero-sum game inimical to the interests of strong government.
Fianna Fail's poor showings in the general elections of 1989 and of 1992
saw the party for the first time obliged to participate in coalition governments, something which had previously been anathema to it. The party's
hesitant shift towards a consensual style of governance has been reflected
in a sudden public enthusiasm for parliamentary reform.

The Oireachtas's weakness as a parliament has been reflected in the
antiquated and cumbersome way in which it has customarily discharged
its business. Deputies and senators receive only meagre office accommodation and secretarial support, there are no parliamentary research
facilities other than a notoriously underdeveloped library, and there is no
money to pay for research assistance. Until the 1980s, when the Fitzgerald
coalition embarked on a somewhat haphazard experiment in procedural
reform, the Oireachtas had nothing akin to a substantial committee system
either to deal with draft legislation or to scrutinize Government policy
and actions.[6] In the spring of 1993, however, important innovations were
announced in Oireachtas procedures. A number of new committees were
established, including one on Foreign Affairs, covering key policy areas.
For the first time, such committees were empowered to shadow the
activities of the relevant government departments. With one exception,
they were also given an enhanced legislative role: the task of handling
draft legislation at the third (committee) stage, where bills are considered
in detail, was generally to be delegated to them. These developments
represent a considerable and to date largely unremarked change in the
way that bills are dealt with, facilitating detailed discussions between
ministers, backbench TDs and senators and, so far as can be judged,
engendering a much greater willingness by ministers to take on board
suggestions and formal amendments put by committee members than is
customary when the third stage of a bill is taken by a committee of the
whole House. The 1993 initiatives were part of the deal which brought the
Labour Party into a coalition government with Albert Reynolds' Fianna
Fail Party; ironically, that alliance collapsed on precisely those issues of
transparency and integrity which had prompted Labour insistence on
parliamentary and other reforms in the first place. The political crisis
which brought down the Reynolds coalition in November 1994 has,
however, *inter alia* produced unanimous agreement amongst party leaders
that Dail procedures must be further changed and its working hours
extended to strengthen both its legislative role and its powers of scrutiny.[7]
The coalition headed by John Bruton is pledged to make further changes
in the committee system designed to make it more effective. While it

remains to be seen if the changes mooted will have that result, there is little doubt that committee work has finally won recognition as a central feature of Oireachtas work.

The Establishment of the Joint Committee on the Secondary Legislation of the European Communities

Ireland joined the EC in 1973 after a constitutional referendum in which the people subordinated Irish to EC law. That decision was given effect in the European Communities Act 1972. This act gave Government the discretion to decide whether to implement Community legislation by introducing a bill in the normal way, or effectively to by-pass the Oireachtas by having the relevant minister make a statutory instrument. Two important balancing steps were also taken under the act: the Government was required to report twice yearly to the Oireachtas on EC developments, and a joint Dail/Seanad committee on the secondary legislation of the European Communities (CSLEC) was established. Composed of TDs, senators and all the Irish MEPs, whether holders of a dual mandate or not, its function was to supervise the implementation of EC decisions where domestic legislation was required and to review all statutory instruments made by ministers under the 1972 act. Any statutory instrument not confirmed by an act of the Oireachtas within six months would lapse.

These measures suggested that the Oireachtas would be a vigilant assessor of Irish membership; in fact, as any student of the Oireachtas's performance as scrutineer of national government might have predicted, they presaged two decades of endemic neglect of European Community affairs by the national parliament. In 1973 the CSLEC was given the additional power to review Commission proposals for legislation, and the provision requiring Oireachtas confirmation of statutory instruments, widely criticised as unworkable, was removed. Although the opposition argued that the CSLEC should be allowed to propose amendments to such regulations, the committee was instead given the draconian power to recommend the annulment of any regulation to the Dail and Seanad. In fact neither this power, nor the committee's right to examine Commission proposals, was ever exercised.[8]

MEPs and the Oireachtas

One of the CSLEC's first disappointments was the realisation that the automatic inclusion of all MEPs as members did little to facilitate communications between the Oireachtas and European institutions. In the rather acid words of one CSLEC member, the impact of the first MEPs was 'lessened by very irregular appearances, and by the temptation to air their frustrations and grievances to the other members of the Joint Committee in the hope of rallying support for improvement in the conditions under which they labour'.[9] When the CSLEC was reconstituted after the 1977 general election, MEPs were given rights of participation but not of voting. In reality problems of timing and distance made their attendance a rarity. For all the awareness of and interest in European affairs generated in the Irish public mind MEPs, whether 'dual mandate' holders or not, might as well have been delegates to some harmless inter-parliamentary forum. This phenomenon was, of course, not peculiar to Ireland: until the first direct elections to the European Parliament took place in 1979, MEPs throughout the EC were exposed to the unanswerable charge that no one had voted for them, and that as the recipients simply of national party patronage they had no legitimate call on the public's loyalty or interest. Direct elections, while they disposed of the first argument, have done very little in Ireland to counter the second. It is clear from survey and election data that, despite the consistently high level of public support for Irish membership of the EU, the public takes only a half-hearted interest in elections to the European Parliament. However vigorously the 15 Irish MEPs seek to keep in touch with their constituents, they cannot hope successfully to compete for attention with the 166 TDs and the many hundreds of local politicians whose primary political activity in the intensely localist world of Irish politics is to nurse their individual vote by their absorption in constituency affairs.[10] While MEPs remain members of their national parliamentary parties, furthermore, and while many have held a dual mandate, there is precious little evidence to suggest that they either attempt to or succeed in enhancing their party colleagues' awareness of what is happening in Brussels or Strasbourg. Indeed, in 1991 the CSLEC itself reported on the marked 'dissatisfaction with their isolation from the national parliament' felt by Irish MEPs.[11]

The Performance of the CSLEC, 1973–92

The early hopes that the CSLEC would both play a crucial role in the integration process and serve as a 'fore-runner for other similar committees relating to Irish domestic legislation' quickly faded.[12] It was dogged by the esoteric and technical nature of its deliberations, far removed from the normal fare of Irish parliamentarians, for most of whom it was a complete backwater: it is no coincidence that the one member consistently singled out for praise by officials, academics and other observers was a strictly part-time politician who was a leading expert on European law, the then Senator and since 1990 President Mary Robinson.[13] In practice, while one commentator has praised its 'diligent habits', the Committee 'took a number of years to establish working procedures, links with government departments and adequate staffing', its impact was very limited and its work was generally far in arrears.[14]

From 1983 to 1987 the CSLEC also faced competion for resources, for active members and for parliamentary attention, because of the plethora of committees with more glamorous – if ephemeral – remits established under the Fitzgerald coalition. Amongst these was one with a foreign policy focus, the Joint Committee on Co-operation with Developing Countries, which offered rather more scope both for travel and for moralising than did the CSLEC. While most of these rivals disappeared in 1987, the CSLEC did not gain much from their demise. Although chaired from 1987 to 1992 by Peter Barry, a former foreign minister with extensive experience of European affairs, its work remained essentially technical and obscure, the object of little comment or controversy despite the enormous sweep of the European measures which it was expected to scrutinise.

Underlying its superficially impressive though uneven output of reports – 59 from 1973 to 1977, 94 from 1977 to 1981, none between 1981 and 1982, 36 between 1983 and 1987, and 14 between 1987 and 1989 – was the reality that these got virtually no parliamentary attention: between 1973 and 1991 CSLEC reports were discussed by the Dail on only three occasions, although the Seanad did rather better with 41 debates.[15] Furthermore, while periodic efforts were made to eliminate the backlog of material to be considered, the Committee was generally in arrears with its work and so was unable to devote much time to the potentially far more promising activity of considering and influencing proposals before they actually became Community law. The fact that most of its work was retrospective did nothing to enhance its status in the Oireachtas. In addition, its relatively large number of publications was not necessarily an indicator of effectiveness: while the respective contributions of members and officials is masked by the fact that the work of sub-committees was done entirely in private, the published record suggests that many of these reports were almost entirely the work of the committee secretariat, with little input from the actual members. The CSLEC's consideration of draft reports was also often cursory: as an example, its meeting of 11 December 1991 to discuss and adopt a document on the reform of the Common Fisheries Policy, a subject of considerable importance to Ireland, took just 25 minutes.[16]

As integration gathered pace in the late 1980s, the inadequacies of the review processes put in place under the 1972 Act became manifest. The CSLEC's perpetual difficulties in doing its work and in gaining parliamentary attention were only one symptom of a continued lack of Oireachtas interest in European affairs, despite the broadening of the integration agenda and growing awareness that some other national parliaments played a far more active part both in monitoring the EC and in analysing EC policy options and issues. Debates on the Government's obligatory twice yearly reports to the Oireachtas on European affairs were, in the Committee's own words, 'infrequent, tardy and unsatisfactory . . . diffuse and cursory'.[17] This dismal state of affairs eventually prompted the CSLEC in 1991 to a review of its own remit and performance. The outcome was a trenchant analysis of the Oireachtas's response to EC membership, marred only by some special pleading: although the record pointed at the very least to a want of urgency amongst committee members in the face of Oireachtas neglect – after all, they were not debarred from raising its plight – the CSLEC declared that it 'feels that it has performed modestly well . . . having regard to its present Terms of Reference'. It was grievously underresourced, and its remit was hopelessly outmoded and restrictive, confining it to a largely retrospective and cursory look at secondary legislation and precluding it from examining 'macro issues' crucial to EC development such as 'GATT and the effects of German unification'. The Committee called for its relaunching as a 'European Community Affairs Committee', with resources and powers comparable to analogous bodies in most other EC national parliaments, and with mechanisms for ensuring timely and appropriate Oireachtas consideration of its reports and recommendations. This would give it 'a new lease of life' and would safeguard 'democratic accountability'.[18]

Despite its forthright tone, this report might well have gone the way of most of its neglected predecessors. In 1992, however, two unrelated events precipitated important changes in the way that the Oireachtas addressed European affairs. The first was the Maastrict Treaty. Its provisions on enlargement had obvious long-term implications for Ireland in terms of political developments, of the distribution of EC financial resources, and of shifts in policy in areas of particular importance to Ireland such as agriculture. These were matters of intense concern to every elected politician. The second factor influencing developments was the outcome of the November general election, which left a weakened Fianna Fail under Albert Reynolds seeking a new partner to form a coalition government. The Labour Party was able to fix a comparatively high price for entering government. Amongst its less onerous demands was the rapid establishment of a joint Dail and Seanad Foreign Affairs committee. There was already a vague consensus on the need for such a forum, born partly of the realisation that most other parliamentary democracies appeared far better equipped in these areas, and partly of a desire to cast more public light on the traditionally secretive foreign policy process.[19]

THE JOINT COMMITTEE ON FOREIGN AFFAIRS AND OVERSIGHT OF EU MATTERS, 1993–95

The Joint Committee on Foreign Affairs (JCFA) was duly established in May 1993, with a mandate which included EU matters. The CSLEC was then reconstituted as a sub-committee on EU legislation.

The new JCFA was chaired by Brian Lenihan of Fianna Fail, a man vastly experienced in government who had been Minister for Foreign Affairs on two occasions, and had served as Tanaiste (deputy Prime Minister) from 1987 to 1990. He had also been one of the first Irish MEPs. Most members of Fianna Fail had something of a guilty conscience about the almost Stalinist treatment meted out to Mr Lenihan during the 1990 presidential election when, while Tanaiste and the party's candidate for that office, he had been ignominiously dismissed from the Fianna Fail/ Progressive Democrat coalition Government in order to ensure its survival.[20] His nomination to chair the new Committee was, consequently, seen partly as a gesture of reparation to a party stalwart, and it probably did something to legitimise the Committee's activities in Fianna Fail eyes. Mr Lenihan was, furthermore, personally popular with members of all parties in the Oireachtas, and consequently well placed to ensure goodwill towards the Committee and to promote consensus in its proceedings.

The JCFA's appeal and its potential importance was also demonstrated in its composition. Nora Owen TD, deputy leader of Fine Gael, the second largest party in the Oireachtas, became its vice-chairman, while amongst its members was Proinsias De Rossa TD, the highly regarded leader of the radical Democratic Left party who had served as a dual mandate MEP from 1989 to 1992. Taken together these factors suggested that, in stark contrast to previous experiments in procedural reform, all the parliamentary parties were genuinely committed to securing the success of the new Committee. Its prospects were further enhanced by the fact that the new Minister for Foreign Affairs and Tanaiste, the Labour leader Dick Spring, had an active personal and party interest in facilitating its work.

The JCFA also benefited from some innovations in procedures and practices. Its chairman was paid a considerable allowance, underlining the expectation that it would quickly become a diligent agent of parliamentary oversight. It was given the important power, one frequently denied to Oireachtas committees, to appoint sub-committees, and it was provided with administrative support on about the same scale as that previously afforded to the CSLEC. The work of reviewing secondary legislation previously done in decent and tardy obscurity by the CSLEC was taken up by the new EU legislation sub-committee under the chairmanship of Gerry Collins, a former foreign minister who is one of the few remaining holders of a dual mandate. While the sub-committee was confronted with the familiar problem of an immense backlog of documents to consider – 217 awaited its attention at its first meeting – it resolved to adopt a proactive approach rather than simply to sift chronologically through the pile of material before it, in order to 'examine pending legislation where we would have a meaningful input'.[21]

The Committee's unusual status in the Oireachtas was also marked by an extraordinary innovation: all MEPs elected on the island of Ireland, including those representing United Kingdom constituencies in Northern Ireland, were given the right to attend and to participate, though not to vote on legislation unless they were simultaneously members of the Oireachtas. This right of attendance has, predictably, not been exercised by Ulster Unionist MEPs: whatever the arguments for tactical co-operation on EU issues of common concern such as the CAP, any participation by them in the Committee's proceedings would be seen by their electorates as an acknowledgement of the legitimacy of the Republic of Ireland's constitutional claim to Northern Ireland. While MEPs from the Republic have no such inhibitions, problems of time and travel have continued to act as a drag on frequent attendance. There are indications, however, that some cross-fertilisation has begun: an example is a recent presentation to the JCFA's Sub-committee on Co-operation with Developing Countries by Niall Andrews MEP, who urged his Oireachtas colleagues to develop 'contacts and communication' with the European Parliament's Development Committee.[22]

The new Committee, unlike the earlier CSLEC and the Joint Committee on Co-operation with Developing Countries of 1983/7, was fortunate both in the broad terms of its remit and in the timing of its creation. Since the mid-1980s the domestic controversy over the Single European Act and more recently the Maastricht Treaty, in combination with the spectacular politicisation of the issue of European Union development in Ireland's nearest and most closely observed neighbour, Britain, have rendered EU affairs a more mainstream consideration in Irish political life. Many members of the Oireachtas have become participants in the activities of the influential Institute of European Affairs, established in 1991 precisely to increase Irish awareness and understanding of developments in and prospects for the EU. Print and broadcast media coverage of Oireachtas proceedings has also increased markedly in scope and depth since the mid-1980s, and this has provided an additional incentive to members of the Oireachtas to put more time and effort into committee proceedings.

The JCFA has been assiduous as well as fortunate since its establishment. In particular, it served as the key parliamentary forum for the analysis of the Maastricht Treaty and for the discussion of the implications of enlargement, and the report which it prepared with the help of advisers and of an academic consultant formed the basis for the full Dail's debate on enlargement in 1994 during the passage of legislation amending the European Communities acts. It has also fulfilled an important representative role in relations with other national parliaments, with the governments of other countries inside and outside the EU, and with EU institutions. The somewhat eclectic list of foreign representatives who appeared before the committee in the course of 1994 includes the Cuban Ambassador to Britain, the Portuguese, Polish, British and Hungarian Ambassadors to Ireland, one European Commissioner, and Prime Minister Benazir Bhutto of Pakistan. As well as enhancing Oireachtas awareness of developments throughout the EU, these contacts lent additional prestige to the activities of the JCFA and its sub-committees.

As an offshoot of the JCFA the EU legislation sub-committee benefited in some respects from the parent committee's success. Like the JCFA, it was sometimes able to adopt a proactive approach: for example, as the GATT negotiations reached their culmination it heard the views of the former European Commissioner Ray MacSharry, who had struck the Blair House deal on agriculture with the United States which cleared the way for the wider treaty. This, however, illustrates another point, the potential for overlap between its activities and that of its parent: the JCFA has itself frequently spent time on EU business. The Government has now addressed this by deciding to establish a separate European Affairs Committee concerned both with policy and with legislation precisely to ensure that EU affairs are examined as a whole. When appropriate this Committee will hold joint sessions with the JCFA, in which case the chairman of the JCFA will preside.[23] While these developments reflect the growing interest of Irish parliamentarians in foreign policy issues in recent years, the new arrangements do nothing to obviate the danger that the European Union committee will be left with the drudgery of scrutinising mounds of proposed or enacted European legislation while the JCFA flits from one interesting policy question or distinguished visitor to another.

CONCLUSION

The response of the Oireachtas to Ireland's accession to the EC for many years was half-hearted and inadequate. The work of the CSLEC, and the requirement that the government report twice yearly to the Oireachtas, were for long treated simply as formalities to be observed. The Oireachtas itself was permeated with a culture which took the absolute dominance of the executive for granted and which discouraged backbench activism, the pursuit of cross-party consensus on any issue, and the rigorous investigation of the activities of Government. A combination of logistics and domestic apathy saw MEPs, other than those who held a dual mandate, conspicuously isolated from Oireachtas affairs, envied by their domestic colleagues for their incomes but completely ignored on policy issues. However, recent years have seen a marked growth in Oireachtas awareness of the significance of EC affairs for national political and economic development. This has coincided with changes in the pattern of domestic politics, with the emergence of coalitions as the dominant model of government and with a modest strengthening of the legislature's powers of oversight and enquiry through specialist committees such as the JCFA. Cumulatively, these factors have produced a marked shift in the Oireachtas's treatment both of EU affairs and of broader foreign policy issues. That trend now appears irreversible.

NOTES

1. Brigid Laffan, "'While you're over there in Brussels, get us a grant'": The Management of the Structural Funds in Ireland', *Irish Political Studies* 4 (1989), pp.43–58.
2. At the time of writing, the Oireachtas committee system is in a state of flux. The new Fine Gael/Labour/Democratic Left coalition Government elected in December 1994 following the extraordinary political crisis which brought down the Reynolds coalition is committed to further reforms in the committee system, but the precise shape which those reforms will take is unclear.
3. John Coakley and Michael Gallagher (eds.), *Politics in the Republic of Ireland* (2nd ed., Dublin: PSAI Press/Folens), 1993, pp.143–5.
4. Coakley and Gallagher, *Politics in the Republic of Ireland*, pp.137–8.
5. Eunan O'Halpin, 'The Dail committee of public accounts, 1961–80', *Administration* 34, 2 (1985), pp.483–511, and 'Oireachtas committees: performance and prospects', *Seirbhis Phoibli* 7, 2 (1986), pp.3–9.
6. For contrasting assessments of the 1983/7 experiments see O'Halpin, 'Oireachtas committees', and Audrey Arkins, 'The committees of the 24th Oireachtas', *Irish Political Studies* 3 (1988), pp.91–8.
7. *The Irish Times*, 5 and 6 Dec. 1994.
8. Mary Robinson, 'The Role of the Irish Parliament', *Administration* 22, 1 (1974), p.16.
9. Robinson, 'The Role of the Irish Parliament', p.21.
10. Coakley and Gallagher, *Politics in the Republic of Ireland*, pp.151–6.
11. Committee on the Secondary Legislation of the European Communities, *Review of the Functions of the Joint Committee on the Secondary Legislation of the European Communities* (Dublin, Stationery Office, 1991), p.15.
12. Robinson, 'The Role of the Irish parliament', pp.16 and 21.
13. In the course of preparing this paper I spoke on an off the record basis with a number of public servants with knowledge of the work of the CSLEC and of the Joint Committee on Foreign Affairs.

14. Arkins, 'The committees of the 24th Oireachtas', p.93; Brigid Laffan, 'Putting European Law into Practice: The Irish Experience', *Administration* 37, 3 (1989), p.214.; Patrick Kelly, Brigid Laffan, and Maurice Manning, 'Ireland', in Heinrich Siedentopf and Jacques Ziller (eds.), *Making European Policies Work: The Implementation of Community Legislation in the Member States* (London, Sage, 1988), p.398.

15. CSLEC, *Review of the Functions of the Joint Committee*, p.10.

16. Joint Committee on the Legislation of the European Communities, *Proposals for the Reform of the Common Fisheries Policy* (Dublin: Stationery Office, 1991).

17. CSLEC, 'Review of the Functions of the Joint Committee', p.7.

18. Ibid., pp.16–24.

19. Ibid., p.14; interviews.

20. On this see Eoin O'Sullivan, 'The 1990 presidential election in the Republic of Ireland', *Irish Political Studies* 6 (1991), pp.85–98, and Brian Lenihan, *For the Record* (Dublin, Blackwater Press, 1991).

21. *Parliamentary Debates: Joint Committee on Foreign Affairs, Wednesday, 14 July 1993* (Dublin: Stationery Office, 1993), cols.151–64.

22. *Parliamentary Debates: Joint Committee on Foreign Affairs, Wednesday, 2 November 1994* (Dublin, Stationery Office, 1994), cols.207–10.

23. The first reference to such an approach which I have come across was made by Prionsias De Rossa TD, now Minister for Social Welfare. *Parliamentary Debates: Joint Committee on Foreign Affairs, 13 September 1994* (Dublin: Stationery Office, 1994), col.3.

Spain: The Cortes and the EU – A Growing Together

CARLOS CLOSA

Accession to the EC was an old Spanish aspiration. An application for membership was first made in 1962, although it was rejected because of the lack of democratic credentials of the Franco regime. Instead, a preferential agreement was negotiated and the country had to wait until 1977 when the return of democracy permitted a successful application. Accession negotiations were long and difficult, and full membership was only achieved in 1986. The prospect of EC membership was one of the stabilising elements in the transition towards democracy, by acting as a selective incentive for it. Membership meant, for political elites and public opinion alike, the return to the Western world from which the country felt excluded. The EC had a legitimising effect on the new Spanish democracy because of Community members' permanent criticism and rejection and occasional condemnation of Franco's regime. This, and more specifically the exclusion from membership, was exhibited by Spanish Democratic opposition as proof of the lack of legitimacy of Franco's regime. Logically, US support of Franco's regime provoked the opposite perception of NATO. This readiness to integrate was reflected by the inclusion, in the 1978 Constitution, of Article 93, which allows constitutional powers to be vested in international institutions.

PARLIAMENTARY ADAPTATION: FROM ACCESSION TO THE TEU

The Spanish Cortes is a bicameral parliament where the lower chamber, the Congress, represents the people and the upper chamber, the Senate, is a chamber of territorial representation. The 350 deputies in the Congress are elected through a system of proportional representation, with the provinces serving as the constituencies. Four senators are selected directly in each province through a plurality system, producing 200 senators. The remaining senators are designated by the assemblies of the

Carlos Closa is Lecturer in Politics at the Universidad Complutense de Madrid and is currently Research Fellow at the European University Institute (Florence).
Part of this research is based on data drawn from the Archive of the Congress. Interviews were held in May 1993; October 1993 with Don Pablo González Mexía, official from the Comisión Mixta; and in November 1994 with Don Mariano Daranas, Chief Official of the Comisión Mixta.

Communidades Autónomas according to population. Therefore, two different territorial entities are represented by the Senate. This, together with the Senate serving as an ineffective second reading chamber (despite formal equality with the Congress), has provoked demands for constitutional reform.

Democratic parliamentary tradition, interrupted for 40 years, has been restored and redeveloped in parallel with EC membership during three legislatures: the 3rd (1986–89), 4th (1989–93) and 5th (1993–). Between 1982 and 1993, the Socialist Party governed with the backing of an absolute parliamentary majority. From 1993, the socialists do not have an absolute majority of seats and they are supported by the Catalan nationalists. Given the accession date (1986), parliamentary adaptation is related not only to the changes required to cope with the Constitutional Treaties but also to the Single European Act that was incorporated from the outset as part of the Community *acquis* negotiated by Spain. Initially, Parliament was more concerned with the elaboration of a new constitution and the normalisation of public life, which was under involutionist threats until 1983. Therefore, there was only a marginal interest in integration, which has been reflected in the way Parliament collectively adapted, both in procedural and substantive terms. This may explain why parliamentary changes dealing with general instruments for information and control have been limited. EC matters are dealt with in plenary sessions through normal parliamentary procedures. Topical matters related to the EC/EU are included in other debates such as the annual State of the Nation debate and non-scheduled debates follow the information rounds that the Government, on its own initiative, uses to inform the Congress of European Council meetings. During the 5th legislature, prime ministerial conferences *a posteriori* have been institutionalised. This applies to ordinary meetings of the European Council; the Prime Minister has reported on only one extraordinary meeting (Birmingham 1992). However, to date EC policy has not been the object of specific debate. Other general control and information procedures, such as interpellations, questions and motions, have been seldom used, although there is a growing tendency towards using them. Given the ease of procedure in tabling written questions, this is by far the most frequently used instrument.

The specific instrument of the Cortes for control and information is the standing committee for EC matters, the *Comisión Mixta del Congreso de los Diputados y del Senado para las Comunidades Europeas* (Joint Committee of the Congress and Senate for the European Communities; hereafter *Comisión Mixta*), constituted by a 1985 bill.[1] The creation of the *Comisión Mixta* was not foreseen in the initial draft proposal and it was

TABLE 1:

CORTES OUTPUT ON EU AFFAIRS (1986–1994)

Legislature

	Type activity			III	Group or Committee	IV		V	
P L E N A R Y	Non-legislative proposal in plenary session	Total	3	PP 2 Mixto 1	1	IU	1	PSOE
		T A W L	1 2		1		1	
	Interpelations	Total	5	PP 3 CiU 1 Mixto 1	1	IU	-	
		T Tra W N.a.	3 1 1		1			
	Motions	Total	-		2	IU 1	-	
		N.a.			2	PP 1		
	Oral questions in plenary session	Total	16	PP 7 PSOE 1 PNV 2 CiU 2 CDS 1 Mixto 3	8	PP 3 CiU 3 PSOE 1 PNV 1	4	PSOE 2 IU 2
		T W L N.a.	11 3 2		5 2 1		2 2	
	Written questions with written response	Total	97	PP 74 CDS 6 CiU 4 Mixto 12 PSOE 1	29	PP 18 CDS 1 IU 2 Mixto 6 CiU 2	6	PP 6
		T L N.a.	94 2 1		29		6	

Source: Own elaboration. Data have been drawn from the Congress Archive Data Base.
Data of the Fifth Legislature do not cover the whole period, just between June 1993
and November 1994. The *Comisión Mixta* data have been searched using *Comisión
Mixta* as keywords. Therefore, all acts are taken into account. All the Cortes
remaining activities regarding EC/EU affairs have been extracted using EC or EU
as search keywords. Therefore, there may be omissions in the total results owing to
the use of different keywords to classify EC/EU related acts.

TABLE I: continued

			Total/sub						
OTHER COMMITTEES	Oral questions	Total	11	Agri. 9 / Soc. 1 / FA 1	12	Agri 9 / Indu 7 / Soc 1 / FA 1		
	Hearings	Total	16	Bud. 15 / Economy 1	17	Bud 14 / Soc 1 / FA 1 / Res 1		
COMISION MIXTA	Non-legislative proposals	Total 1 / A / W 1 / N.a. / L	CiU	3 / 1 / 1 / 1	PP 2 / IU 1	2	Joint 1 / PP 1	
	Oral question in Committee	Total 10 / T 8 / Tra 1 / W 1 / I	PP 7 / CiU 2 / CDS 1	26 / 9 / 13 / 4	PP 23 / IU 2 / CDS 1	17 / 11 / 2 / 4	PP 16 / IU 1	
	Hearings (government)	Total 15 / T 11 / W 2 / NH 2 / L / I	PP 9 / Mixto 1 / Gover. 5	60 / 42 / 8 / 7 / 1	PSOE 1 / PP 27 / CiU 7 / Gov. 12 / CDS 3 / IU 2 / Com 6 / Joint 1	33 / 25 / 2 / 6	PP 11 / PSOE 4 / IU 4 / CiU 1 / Gov. 10 / Com. 6	
	Hearings (officials and authorities)	Total 12 / T 10 / W 1 / L 1 / I	PP 9 / PSOE 1 / Mixto 1 / Gover. 1	72 / 30 / 24 / 7 / 1	PSOE 29 / PP 17 / CiU 10 / Gov. 7 / CDS 4 / IU 2 / Com 3			
	Hearings (specialists)	Total / T / W / L / I		73 / 29 / 25 / 16 / 1	PSOE 14 / PP 6 / CiU 26 / CDS 11 / IU 13 / Com 1			

Legend:
T = Transmitted
W = Withdrawn
L = Lapsed
I = Included in other initiative
N.a. = Not accepted
NH = Not held

Political groups:
PSOE: Socialist
PP: People's Party
IU: United Left
CiU: Catalan Nationalist
CDS: Centrist Group
Mixto: Joint Group
Joint: Joint initiative by all groups
PNV: Basque Nationalist
Gov.: Executive initiatives
Com.: Initiatives from the Comisión Bureau

Committees:
Agri. = Committee on Agriculture, Cattle and Fisheries
Soc. = Social Affairs Committee
FA = Foreign Affairs Committee
Bud = Budget Committee
Res = Research and Technology Committee

incorporated after an amendment presented by the Popular Group.[2] Initially, this committee was composed of a fixed number of members, with the Congress – reflecting its larger size – having a larger representation than the Senate. This produced a very rigid structure and later revision established that the membership would be agreed in a joint session of the bureau of both chambers. The result has been a considerable enlargement of membership, from 15 members in the 3rd legislature to 37 in the 4th and 39 in the 5th. Membership is drawn from all political groups proportional to their size. This raised some problems when sub-committees were created after 1989: each sub-committee had ten members and this created difficulties for those groups with a small number of members. Arrangements were made so that they could be represented by members not on the Committee.

The initial wording of the bill allowed representation only for formal parliamentary groups. Given the fragmentation in the Congress after the 1986 election and some splits in electoral coalitions, there was one huge group that brought together the various parliamentary groupings that individually did not qualify for designation as formal groups.[3] Consequently, the 1985 bill was amended to allow the presence of the minor aggregations within this grouping.

The distribution of posts within the *Comisión Mixta* is as follows:

Chairman: Government
1st Vice-Chairman: Senator from government group
2nd Vice-Chairman: Deputy from the largest opposition group
1st Secretary: Deputy from the government group
2nd Secretary: Opposition deputy

The President of the Congress, or someone delegated permanently by the President, is chairman of the Committee. Traditionally, the position has been delegated to the First Vice-President of the Congress, who usually belongs to the major parliamentary party. However, in the 5th legislature, an opposition deputy – Sr Marcelino Orejo, from the People's Party – was delegated to hold the position. This can be explained by the necessity of the governing party to share parliamentary power, given its minority status, as well as by the standing of the candidate – a former General Secretary of the Council of Europe and a current Commissioner.

There is no quorum for holding sessions, although 50 per cent + 1 of the members must be present for a vote to be held. Decisions are reached by a simple majority, for which each group has a number of votes proportional to its total number of deputies and senators. Other standing committees use a vote per person system.

The powers of the *Comisión Mixta* were laid down in the 1985 Act but the measure was amended in 1988, providing for a greater involvement in European affairs. This change was largely an accidental consequence of an attempt to change representation on the committee. The functions of the Committee can be described as follows:

Legislative Functions

The *Comisión Mixta* is not a legislative committee. However, it was empowered to examine the 15 legislative decrees issued by the Government to adapt Spanish legislation immediately after accession. This legislative function was extraordinary and, in practice, it became a form of *a posteriori* control on Government: the *Comisión Mixta* produced an opinion on each of the legislative decrees after their publication. These opinions did not have any political relevance nor were they discussed in a plenary session.

Control on Government and Information Powers in General

The *Comisión Mixta* was empowered to receive information from the Government on its main lines of policy in the EC. The two main instruments for the exercise of this function are the questions and hearings involving members of the Government and officials. There is a growing use of both questions and hearings: questions doubled in number in the period between 1989 and 1993 and the same happened with hearings. Most of the hearings held have been the result of Government initiatives, the Ministry of Foreign Affairs or the Secretary of State for the European Communities informing the Committee before a European Council meeting. Hearings involving people other than officials and members of the Government have also grown significantly in number, pointing towards a higher profile of the function of providing information. These hearings, though, tend to be of a general character and have taken the form of general debates rather than serving to ensure some form of control.[4]

Informative Powers in the Preparation of EC Legislation.

The initial powers given to the *Comisión Mixta* were very limited. It could receive information from the Government on EC legislative projects that might affect areas on which the Cortes had reserved the right to legislate (that is, fundamental issues of development of the Constitution). This provision excluded the greatest part of EC legislation and limited the autonomy of the Committee.

The Committee gained some element of formal autonomy when the 1988 reform empowered it to produce reports on draft Regulations, Directives and Decisions submitted by the Commission to the Council.

The records of Congress show that the Government sends all Commission proposals every 15 days. The Government's obligation is limited to sending Commission documents: sending accompanying Government reports and studies on proposed measures is not expected. There are no formal channels of communication between the *Comisión Mixta* and the Spanish Permanent Representation. This may help explain why the Committee makes limited use of the power to produce reports, despite the recommendations of some legal specialists that it should be more active in examining the normative proposals.[5]

Informative Powers in the Implementation of EC Law

These powers were initially framed in vague terms. The 1985 bill empowered the *Comisión Mixta* to receive information from the Government on the activities of EC institutions concerning the application and implementation of Spanish accession. The 1988 reform specified and sharpened the object of control: the Committee might receive information from the Government on the decisions and agreements reached within the Council of Ministers. Apart from this, the Government provides the information explicitly requested by MPs as well as documents it may consider pertinent. (These documents are supplied by the Secretary of State for EC affairs.) Most of the documents volunteered by the Government concern major initiatives, such as the Convergence Plan. The Government showed its readiness to keep the Committee informed when it called for an extraordinary cycle of ministers' hearings (held in June 1992) to provide information on the repercussions of the Maastricht Treaty.

Relations with the EP and other National Parliaments.

The first Spanish MEPs were national MPs designated by the Cortes, but the electoral law was changed in order to prevent a dual mandate in the 1989 elections. The reform of the law setting up the *Comisión Mixta* authorised it to establish relations with EP bodies, but these relations have had a very low profile. A delegation from the Committee visited the EP twice (in April 1988 and January 1989) and, on the second occasion, a working meeting was held with the EP's Committee on Institutional Affairs. There was an attempt to create a procedure for maintaining contact with Spanish MEPs through working and informative meetings decided on by common agreement between the Bureau of the *Comisión* and the leaders of the Spanish delegations in the EP. Joint sub-committees could have been created on specific issues. However, the initiative came to nothing and no such meetings are held. Documents are received from the General Secretary of the EP by the General Secretary of the Congress.

The *Comisión Mixta* was empowered in 1988 to maintain relations, for the purposes of co-operation and sharing information, with the equivalent committees in other national parliaments. This activity has been kept to a minimum: the *Comisión* merely notified its constitution to the relevant committees in other EC parliaments and it met a delegation from the Dutch committee.[6] Currently, meetings are held only through the COSAC once a year.

Reporting to Either Chamber

For this function, the Committee may appoint *ponencias* (sub-committees) which are collective organs (that is, there is no single rapporteur). The sub-committee is entrusted with the task of producing a report that is submitted to the Committee and, after its approval, it becomes a document to be submitted (eventually) to the plenary session. The *ponencias* are not permanent: they last for one legislature. Characteristically, they do not have a very technical character, serving instead as arena in which most of the political bargaining is conducted.

During the 3rd legislature, the *Comisión Mixta* created a reporting sub-committee on the implementation of the secondary legislation required by the Accession Act. Three sub-committees were established during the 4th legislature: two *ad hoc* reporting sub-committees and a non-reporting one. The non-reporting one was the *ponencia* on the Accession Treaty and the SEA, heir of the sub-committee appointed in the previous legislature. The range of issues dealt with by this sub-committee (familiarly known as the *Ponencia* of the Internal Market) was very broad and, in fact, it assumed most of the normal work of the *Comisión Mixta*: most hearings were held in front of it.

The two *ad hoc* reporting committees were the *Ponencia* on EMU and the *Ponencia* on Political Union. Their purpose was to contribute to the formulation of the Spanish position for the IGCs.[7] Although they began their work well in advance of the Conferences, they produced little information. The production of the EMU report involved only three hearings with ministers, 13 government officials and 25 other persons during 21 sessions between June 1990 and 30 May 1991. The document that was approved endorsed the main lines of the Delors Plan. The document produced by the sub-committee on Political Union was issued only after the Maastricht summit.[8] Both in terms of the information and documentation received, the record of this sub-committee was minimal: there were two hearings with ministers and the only available documents for discussion were the proposals tabled by the parliamentary groups themselves. Although the Government was asked to discuss the EPU document in a plenary session, the petition was rejected.

During the 5th legislature, two *ad hoc* reporting sub-committees were created; one was the *ponencia* for the study of the effects on Spain of EU enlargement and institutional reform, and the other was on EMU and the cohesion and structural funds.

PARLIAMENTARY ADAPTATION: THE CHANGES AFTER THE TEU

A second reform of the powers of the *Comisión Mixta* was undertaken in 1993–94,[9] with the aim of adapting the committee to the effects of the Maastricht Treaty. Apart from some cosmetic changes, such as formalising the arrangements for co-operation with similar organs in other parliaments and the EP, and joint meetings with Spanish MEPs, the main objective of the new bill – approved in May 1994[10] – was the reinforcement of the powers for acquiring information during the process of EC law-making. The changes that were introduced were as follows.

Government information to plenary sessions. The practice developed between 1986 and 1993 of the Government providing information in plenary sessions of the Congress after every ordinary or extraordinary European Council meeting has been institutionalised. The Government statement is then followed by a debate, with all the parliamentary groups taking part.

General information and control powers. The new bill forces the Government to send all available information on the activities of EU institutions. The Government has to provide information on the guidelines of its European policy and, before each ordinary European Council, it has to send a report on developments during the outgoing presidency. Control powers *a posteriori* have been particularly reinforced. The Government has to report on Council decisions and agreements, and the *Comisión Mixta* may call on the Government to explain the negotiation and results after approval by Council of a proposal.

Control over EC law making. The objective of the reform was to allow the *Comisión* to receive legislative proposals from the Commission (and not only those related to issues on which the Parliament had a reserve of law) with time enough to report, eventually, on them. Moreover, the Government has to add a brief report on the proposals and their potential effect for Spain. The Committee can ask for further information and it may ask other standing committees to report on a proposal or topic.

Finally, there is the possibility of debates on specific measures within the committee or in plenary session of either chamber with Government participation. The *Comisión*, for example, recently called a debate on the reform of the Wine Common Market Organisation.

ANALYSIS

The characteristic of the Cortes participation in EU affairs is the relative lack of interest in parallel to a very poor record of both qualitative and quantiative outcomes in its treatment of EU affairs. The explanation lies at the junction of the following variables.

Constitutional provisions

The Spanish Constitution empowers the Government to direct foreign policy. Relations between the executive and the Cortes in dealing with foreign affairs are framed in Article 93. This establishes that it is incumbent upon the Cortes Generales or the Government, as the case may be, to guarantee compliance with international treaties and with the resolutions emanating from international and supranational organisations in which the powers have been vested.

The legislative role permitted by the EC legal system is, as has already been emphasised in this volume, limited to the implementation of directives. Given the very technical nature of the matters usually dealt with in directives, they have seldom been dealt with by the Cortes. If the issue is not subject to a 'reserve of law' in Spain, the implementation may be carried out by the Government. If the matter is under 'reserve of law', then either the Cortes implements the Directive though a bill or the Government implements it through a delegation bill from the Cortes. Although the diminution of competences linked to EC membership affects Parliament more than the Government, there appears to be agreement that in Spain EC membership has not resulted in an excessive disequilibrium in the distribution of powers between them.[11]

The constitutional design is complicated by the quasi-federalist structure of the State. Since the case law of the Spanish Constitutional Court has established that there are not specific competences for the execution of Community law, the Comunidades Autónomas may be competent to implement EC legislation. Therefore, implementation depends on the topic dealt with. For this, some parliaments of the Comunidades Autónomas have passed delegation bills similar to the 1985 bill of the Cortes. Congress and Senate legislating committees are precluded from interfering with the competences of the Comunidades Autónomas.

The powers of information and control of the *Comisión Mixta* do not extend to the implementation undertaken by the Communidades Autónomas: it cannot scrutinise legislation enacted by the Communidades Autónomas to give effect to EC law, even though responsibility for dealing with non-compliance remains with the central Government. An amendment to provide for scrutiny was proposed during passage of the

1988 revision act, but it was dismissed on the grounds that the presence of senators (who, theoretically, are regional representatives) in the Committee rendered this unnecessary. Therefore, legislative involvement and control of the regional executives is reserved to the regional parliaments which, in some cases, have created specific bodies specialising in EC affairs. The *Comisión Mixta* is restricted (under Article 44 of the Rules of Procedure) to collecting information and, eventually, calling information hearings with officials from the regional governments. The only monitoring activity has been an attempt, during the 4th legislature, to assess the fulfilment by the Communidades Autónomas of the actions included in the EC Development Plan for Objective 1 regions. The precise character of this action was diluted when the scheduled hearings with the presidents of the regional governments were substituted by vague and general questionnaires asking about a wide range of issues, from a general evaluation of the integration process for Spain to suggestions on how to face the '1992' challenge.

Overall, though, there is no evidence that the territorial structure of the State has implied a significant diminution or erosions of parliamentary involvement in EU affairs.

Ideology

Spanish EC policy has traditionally been based on a consensus among political parties, supported by public opinion, with no constituency opposed to Spanish membership or further integration being found.[12] The consensus on the benefits of Spanish membership and the lack of conflict over the issue are exemplified by the approval of almost unanimous majorities of the Accession Act, the SEA, the ratification of the Maastricht Treaty and the constitutional reform to approve the TEU.[13] The consensus is translated into a consideration of EC affairs as an area where it is necessary to develop 'State policy' (as opposed to party policy), and the Government has a primary responsibility for this. This, in turn, leads to a lack of preoccupation with the subject by the Cortes: in 1990 it was the only Parliament that did not present any contribution to the Rome *Assises*. The attitude towards control of the Government on EC affairs is also informed by this consensus. Thus, the *ponencias* on EMU and Political Union merely reproduced the arguments of the Government. In fact, the document of the *Comisión Mixta* on Political Union recalled the 'spirit of consensus' that led to the 1978 Constitution as a basis for government and parliamentary action during the phase of negotiation and ratification of the forthcoming Treaty.

The moves towards increasing parliamentary involvement in EC affairs coincided with a change of mood in public opinion and a loosening of the consensus among political parties. With the loss of a parliamentary majority by the Socialist Party and the prospect of an alternative majority, the People's Party intensified its attempt to increase control over the Executive, at the same time that personalities with prestige and knowledge of European affairs (such as Mareclino Oreja) became members of the *Comisión Mixta*. The People's Party tabled a proposal for reform of the *Comisión* that would have secured a more important input from the Parliament in early stages of EC law-making: under the proposal, the Government was obliged to provide information about all legislative proposals and either the *Comisión Mixta* or either chamber meeting in plenary session could issue an opinion. This opinion would not be binding but it could be taken into account by the Government. This was completed with *a posteriori* control: if the matter was debated in a plenary session, the Government was obliged to report again after the conclusion of negotiations. The Government, however, presented an alternative proposal that was supported by all the parliamentary groups except the People's Party.

The consensus is evident also in the input from both chambers and committees in their dealings with the Government. The *ponencias* on EMU and Political Union endorsed the Government's stance. The resolutions on particular proposals, such as the reform of the Wine Common Market Organisation[15] or the decision to postpone the ratification of the enlargement treaties if full Spanish incorporation into the Common Fisheries Policy was not agreed by the Council,[16] have been unanimously supported by all parliamentary groups, reinforcing the Government's negotiating position. If Spain is moving towards a more assertive or sceptical attitude toward EU affairs, it is doing it in a consensual way.[17]

Parliamentary Culture

Spanish parliamentary culture, interrupted for 40 years, has been redeveloped in parallel to EU membership and it is therefore difficult to evaluate whether membership has affected parliamentary custom. The consensual character of Spanish politics during the transition stimulated parliamentary procedures addressed to create a consensual style of parliamentary practice. The unintended consequence has been a reinforcement of Government majorities *vis-à-vis* opposition. In this line, the Rules of Procedure of the Congress have been designed to maximise the instrument available to an Executive that is not supported by a majority of MEPs, as was the case of the UCD between 1979 and 1982. Obviously, the overwhelming PSOE majorities between 1982 and 1993 magnified this effect.

In EU affairs, the grip of Government is evidenced by its position to the *Comisión Mixta*. Whilst most of the Congress and Senate standing committees are created through the respective rules of procedure (a power that emphasises Parliament's discretionary power of self-regulation), the specific instrument of control, the *Comisión Mixta*, was created through a bill of Parliament; the 1985 *Ley de Bases de delegación al gobierno para la aplicación de derecho de las Communicades Europeas*.[18] The creation through a bill implies that any elimination or modification of the Committee cannot be undertaken without the implicit acquiescence of the Government. As has been argued by the chief of the Committee, this may guarantee the stability and permanence of the Committee, but it makes it difficult to achieve any reforms.[19] The 1994 reform dismissed the opportunity to change the statutory character of the Committee.

Institutional Arrangements

The involvement of the Cortes in EU affairs is based on the *Comisión Mixta*, of which two characteristics are especially relevant. First, it is a joint committee of Congress and Senate, underlining the equal status of both chambers. This seems to have been the source of some dissatisfaction because the resources are not provided equally by both chambers; in fact, staffing is provided by the Congress. More importantly, initial assessments questioned the capacity of the *Comisión* to control Government as a result of its joint character: Government is held responsible in each chamber, but not in front of both of them at the same time. It was argued that, as a result, other committees, such as the Foreign Affairs Committee in either chamber, might compete more successfully for the control over Government EU policy.[20] Although there is no evidence of any competition for control, some committees can more profitably exploit their treatment of EU affairs. This may have been the case with the Foreign Affairs Committee of the Congress, which deals with some of the most salient issues regarding the EU, such as the ratification of the enlargement treaties.

The second characteristic is the lack of legislative competence by the *Comisión Mixta*. This, as we have seen, is a non-legislating committee. It cannot become involved in preparing legislation. Secondary legislation enacted in pursuance of EC law has to be scrutinised by the legislative standing committees. And the reform of the *Comisión Mixta* itself has to be carried through by a legislating committee (the Foreign Affairs Committee). Certainly, the *Comisión* has the right to pass its conclusions on to the competent committee in either chamber, but its use of the power to do so is conditioned by the attitude of the bureaux of both chambers. In very few cases, the *Comisión* has stimulated the involvement of other committees that do not depend on it for the provision of information. Proposals are sent by the government departments to the Congress and the Senate and they are distributed to the relevant committees by the bureau of the chamber. Despite the provision that the *Comisión Mixta* should be informed of legislative proposals, the bureau does not send them directly the committee. Not surprisingly, there has been frequent conflict over the demarcation of the responsibilities of the legislative committees and the *Comisión Mixta*.[21] However, this is not deemed to be a serious issue. The absence of any serious issue is proof of the low political profile of the *Comisión* and the fact that it is not generally considered in either chamber to be an important body.

CONCLUSION

The position of the Spanish Cortes regarding European integration and EC/EU politics has to be set in the proper historical perspective. Initially, Parliament, parties and public opinion alike were more concerned with the transition process and achieving political stability than with accession negotiations. This kept at bay a debate on membership costs and benefits. Besides, an overarching consensus among political parties (as well as public opinion) on the positive effects of European integration reinforced Parliament's lack of concern. Finally, successive continuing government parliamentary majorities diminished the possibilities for and the salience of parliamentary struggle, especially in such a non-controversial issue as European integration. The preoccupation raised by the Maastricht Treaty, the effects of the economic crisis and a changing perception of membership costs among public opinion has reinforced a parallel tendency towards differentiation among parties. The first consequence has been a reform of procedures and a greater Cortes involvement with EU politics. The long-term effects remain to be seen.

NOTES

1. Ley 47/1985 de 27 de Diciembre. Ley de bases de delegación al gobierno para la aplicación del derecho de las Communidades Europeas. B.O.E. 30.XII.1985 *corrigendum* B.O.E. 26.II.1986.
2. J. Barrat i Esteve, *Los Parlamentos nacionales y la legitimidad democrática de la Unión Eurpea*, Madrid: Communication presented to the Congress of the Associación Española de Derecho Constitucional y Teoría del Estado, Dec. 1993.
3. This is the so-called Grupo Mixto to which are ascribed deputies who are not incorporated in any other group. Under Article 23 of the Rules of Procedure of the Congress, 15 deputies – or 5 or more deputies from one or more political parties if they obtain 15 per cent or more of the votes in their constituencies (or 5 per cent nationally) – may form a parliamentary group.

4. Barrat i Esteve, 1993.
5. P. Pérez Tremps, 'Il raforzamento dell'esecutivo come conseguenza della integrazione nella Communitá Europea', in G. Rolla (ed.), *Le forme di governo nei moderni ordinamenti policentri* (Milano: Giufré, 1991), p.108.
6. September 1988 ACD Sec. General Leg. 4426 No. 3.
7. Both *ponencias* were created following an informal agreement between the Prime Minister and the Speakers of the parliamentary groups. H. Boyra Amposta, 'El parlamento español y la cesión de soberanía a la Communidad Económica Europea', *Revista de las Cortes Generales*, 29 (1993), p.65.
8. DOGC Sec. Cortes Generales. Serie A. Actividades Parlamentarias Num. 28.
9. BOCG Congreso de los Diputados V Legislatura Serie B Proposiciones de Ley 24 Septiembre 1993, Num. 34-1.
10. Ley 8/1994, de 19 de mayo, por la que se regula la Comisión Mixta para la Unión Europea.
11. Pérez Tremps, pp.93–104.
12. See, on this, Berta Álvarez-Miranda Navarro, *Los partidos políticos en Grecia, Portugal y España ante la Comunidad Europea: explicación comparada del consenso europeísta español* (Madrid: Instituto Juan March de Estudios e Investigaciones, 1995).
13. Accession Act (Ley Orgánica 10/1985 de 10 de agosto); Ratification of the SEA (Ley Orgánica 4/1986 de 26 de Noviembre); Ratification of the TEU (Ley Orgánica 28 de Diciembre 1992).
14. BOCG Congreso de los Diputados. Serie B Proposiciones de Ley. V Legislatura Num. 21-1 30 de Julio de 1993.
15. The resolution of the *Comisión Mixta* called on the Government to use with maximum firmness all available negotiating procedures, including the Luxembourg Compromise.
16. BOCG Congreso de los Diputados V Legislatura Serie D: Actos de Control Num. 146, 10 Octubre 1994.
17. On the change of Spanish attitudes, see C. Closa, 'National Interest and Convergence of Preferences: A Changing Role for Spain in the EU?', in S. Mazey and C. Rhodes (eds.), *The State of the European Union* (Boulder CO: Lynne Reiner Publishers, 1995).
18. Ley 47/1985, 27 Diciembre 1985. BOE 312, 30 Diciembre 1985.
19. M. Daranas, 'La Comisión Mixa para las Communidades Europeas', *Noticias CEE* 4: 37 (1988), pp.19–45.
20. M. Medina, 'El parlamento y la recepción de derecho comunitario en le derecho español, *Revista de la Facultad de Derecho de la Universidad Complutense* 72 (1987), pp.403–8. Some have argued that the *Comisión* is more of a body for reflecting on European politics than a body of control. See Barrat i Esteve.
21. Pérez Tremps p.108.

The Portuguese Assembleia da República: Discovering Europe

JOSÉ M. MAGONE

During the past two decades Portugal has experienced a consolidation and institutionalisation of its very young democracy. The toppling of the authoritarian dictatorship by a military *coup d'état* on 25 April 1974 opened the way to this transition and consolidation. The prospects for a parliamentary democracy were not very good in the first year following the collapse of the authoritarian regime. The radicalisation of the political field almost threatened the development towards a west European democracy. The elections to the Constituent Assembly on 25 April 1975 marked the turning point from a radicalised revolutionary situation to a democratic process of transition.[1]

The role of the European Community in monitoring this process towards democracy cannot be underestimated. The EC was very interested in promoting democracy in the southern European fringe for security and political reasons, but would not help a country which was in revolutionary turmoil. This constraint led to the end of the revolutionary process at the end of 1975.[2] In 1976, a new constitution was adopted by the Constituent Assembly and the process of democratisation became the major concern of the Portuguese political elite.

The first constitutional Government led by the Socialist Mário Soares saw as its priority the application for membership of the EC. This was regarded as the crucial factor to consolidate Portuguese democracy.[3] Prime Minister Soares submitted the application on 28 March 1977. This was welcomed by the EC in its opinion on the Portuguese application on 19 May 1978. The Commission gave special emphasis to the structural economic problems that Portugal faced in the future and the role of the EC would have to play in helping to address these problems.[4] After seven years of negotiations, Portugal became a member of the EC on 1 January 1986.

José M. Magone is Lecturer in European Politics, University of Hull. I wish to thank the Department of Politics at the University of Hull for giving me a R.N. Berki Memorial Fund Grant for field research in Portugal during September 1994. Special thanks for the encouraging monitoring by Philip Norton during the whole research process. I also wish to thank the staff of the Parliamentary Library and the other services in the Assembly of the Republic for their kind help and patience in supplying me with the relevant material for my research, Prof. Manuel Braga da Cruz for indispensable orientation, and Cristina Leston Bandeira and Pedro Magalhaes for their insight and knowledge of the Assembly of the Republic.

The period leading up to membership was characterised by political instability. The Portuguese Parliament, due to its incipient institutionalisation, was only marginally interested in the process of European integration. Its primary focus was the very unstable domestic situation. Besides, political instability prevented a routinisation of parliamentary work. The first three legislatures (1976–85) did not run over the prescribed four years, but unstable governments had to call for early elections. The process of democratic consolidation was nonetheless linked to the wider process of European integration.[5] The accession to the EC was seen as the only way to consolidate the very young Portuguese democracy.[6]

PARLIAMENTARY ADAPTATION

The Pre-Accession Period (1978–85)

The process of establishing institutional links between the European Parliament and the Portuguese Assembly of the Republic was started as early as March 1978. The bureau of the EP set up a delegation of 18 MEPs to ensure permanent contacts with Portugal and suggested the creation of a corresponding delegation coming from the Portuguese Parliament composed of 18 national MPs. In April 1980 the Portuguese Parliament created a delegation of 17 MPs to participate in the first official meeting between delegations of the European Parliament and the Portuguese Parliament.

In 1980 the Assembly of the Republic created a new committee of European integration (*Comissão de Integraçao Europeia*) which was in charge of monitoring the process of negotiations between the Portuguese Government and the EC. Subsequently, the Committee had meetings with the EP delegation twice a year until 1985.

These meetings were attended too by representatives of the Portuguese Government and intended to gather the opinion of MPs and MEPs on the process of negotiations between the EC and Portugal. Some meetings were held outside Portugal and these provided an opportunity to get to know the position of other parliaments of the EC on matters related to the process of the European integration. This can be regarded as an important factor in helping consolidate the Portuguese Parliament and improve the quality of its activities. In this sense, the joint Assembly of the Republic/ European Parliament committee contributed to the routinisation of the parliamentary work in the Portuguese Parliament.

The Joint Committee set up three working groups covering the areas of economy and finances, agriculture and fisheries, and political affairs. It attempted successfully to play an influential role in this process of negotiations. In 1985 the Joint Committee was in charge of monitoring the appointments of Portuguese representatives to the Communities and the implementation of several pre-accession aspects.[7]

This phase initiated the Portuguese MPs into the EC institutional framework and contributed massively to a consolidation of democratic procedures in the Portuguese Parliament. This phase of political learning was invaluable in the period after accession which coincided with the implementation of the White Paper on the Single European Market and the introduction of the Maastricht Treaty in November 1993.

From Accession to the Introduction of the SEM (1986–93)

The accession to the EC did not significantly change the role of the Portuguese Parliament in the overall process of integration. The Committee on European Integration continued to be in charge of monitoring the integration of Portugal into the EC, but it took several years to adapt to the new situation. In a report of the Committee presented in the plenary session of the Assembly of the Republic on 20 June 1986 several adaptation problems were referred to by the rapporteur Silva Lopes. The Committee was very keen to clarify the position of the Assembly in scrutinising and monitoring the process by which EC legislation was introduced into national law. This was relevant because Portugal had not only to integrate the new legislation relating to the SEM, but also the legislation which had accumulated since the 1950s. The Committee suggested that the Assembly should be concerned with all the legislation which could be of national importance and have a considerable impact upon the political, social and economic system.

The Committee also felt that the information received from the Commission and other institutions of the EC came too late to them or not at all. The information channels were considered inefficient and directed towards the Government. The Committee was dependent on information provided by the government which prevented it from exercising its auditing role in the implementation of EC legislation.

Moreover, the Committee complained that some of the Portuguese MEPs coming from the liberal Social Democratic Party (Partido Social Democrata-PSD) and the conservative Democratic Social Centre (Centro Democrático Social-CDS) were not interested in participating in a joint committee of members of the Committee of European Integration and Portuguese MEPs. These two parliamentary groups referred to the fact that they were organised within supranational organisations and this prevented them from taking part in any nationally oriented committees. These problems of adjustment prevented a fast response by the Portuguese Parliament to the demands of the integration of Portugal into the EC.

Although the Single European Act was signed in February 1986 and came into force on 1 July of the following year, the Committee continued to refer to the lack of information and the democratic deficit of the decision-making process in the EC.[8]

The adoption of law 29/87 of 29 June 1987 and its subsequent revocation by law 111/88 of 15 December 1988 (Law on the monitoring of the Assembly of the Republic in matters related to the participation of Portugal in the European Communities) established the legal framework

TABLE 1

REFERENCES ON EUROPEAN AFFAIRS BY THE PORTUGUESE MPs IN THE
PLENARY SESSIONS OF THE PORTUGUESE PARLIAMENT (1976–94)

LEGISLATIVE SESSION	INTERVENTIONS
1ST LEGISLATURE (1976-80)	**12**
1976-77	7
1977-78	2
1978-79	1
1979-80	2
2ND LEGISLATURE (1980-83) no credible data available	
3RD LEGISLATURE (1983-85)	**21**
1983-84	3
1984-85	18
4TH LEGISLATURE(1985-87)	**18**
1985-86	10
1986-87	8
5TH LEGISLATURE(1987-91)	**18**
1987-88	5
1988-89	8
1989-90	5
1990-91	-
6TH LEGISLATURE(1991-)	**12**
1991-92	1
1992-93	9
1993-94	2

Source: These data were kindly supplied in raw form by the *Direcção-Geral de Informaçao Legislativa e Parlamentar*. These are calculations made by the author and therefore subject to error.

for the role of the Assembly in monitoring this process of European integration. The Committee on European Integration was renamed the Committee on European Affairs and was, at least, legally entitled to play an influential role in the decision-making process related to EC matters. The Government submitted annually a report on the impact of the EC on the different policy sectors of the Portuguese political system.[9] This required a subsequent evaluation by the Assembly of the Republic which in the period between 1987 and 1993 was not always fulfilled according to the law 111/88. Therefore, in this period the absolute majority government of the PSD was not effectively monitored by the Assembly of the Republic. This problem of institutional adjustment was even more evident due to the fact that the bulk of legislation relating to EC matters increased substantially between 1986 and 1991.

TABLE 2

LEGISLATION RELATED TO EC MATTERS (1985–91)

Legislatures	IV	V	VI	
			1 Legisl.	2 Legisl.
	1985–87	1987–91	1991–92	1992–93
Laws	3	21	–	–
Ratifications	3	–	–	–
Resolutions	2	17	1	5
Government Bills	3	–	6	6
Private Bills	1	–	7	7

Source: Actividade Legislativa da Assembleia da República na IV Legislatura 1985–87 (Lisboa: Assembleia da República, 1988), pp.119–30; Memória da V. Legislatura (Lisboa: Assembleia da República, 1993), pp.257–77; Diário da Assembleia da República, II-Série C, Número 8, 28 November 1992 and Diário da Assembleia da República, II-Série C, Número 4, 19 November 1993. Data compiled by the author.

Unfortunately, the new law was not able to improve legislative-executive relations in this field. On the contrary, the evaluation of the impact of law 111/88 by the Committee on European Affairs in June 1994 draws a quite negative balance by concluding that 'it was not able to establish "a regular process of exchange of information and consultation between the Assembly of the Republic and the Government" in these matters . . . . In this sense, it was not able to bring European Affairs closer to the Portuguese Parliament, as it is pretended in the Treaty of Maastricht'.[10]

The main bulk of legislation is enacted by the Government through governmental decree-laws. The annual report of the Government lists the translation of EC directives into national legislation.[11] In 1990 Portugal was regarded by the Commission as the most successful country in enacting legislation related to the Single European Market. It was able to increase its transposition rate of 34.4 per cent to 85 per cent. In early 1993 Portugal had already enacted 95 per cent of the whole single market-related EC legislation.[12]

TABLE 3

TRANSPORTATION OF COMMUNITY DIRECTIVES INTO NATIONAL
LEGISLATION BY THE PORTUGUESE GOVERNMENT (1986–93)

YEAR	1986	1987	1988	1989	1990	1991	1992	1993
Directives	-	-	-	184	261	86	79	96

Source: Portugal nas Comunidades Europeias 1986–1993 (Lisboa: Ministério dos Negócios Estrangeiros 1987–94). Annual reports of the Ministry of Foreign Affairs on the impact of the EC on sectoral policies.

In the 1990s the Portuguese Parliament improved its access to EC information by receiving documentation directly from the Commission and the European Parliament, and by the introduction of an information system in the library and direct links to the Portuguese representatives in the Committee of Permanent Representatives (COREPER).[13] This has led to a more active role of the Committee on European Affairs, led by the MP Helena Torres Marques and, later on, MP Leonor Beleza. Nevertheless, it is only after the Presidency of the Council in the first half of 1992, the Maastricht debate and and Danish referendum that the Assembly has begun to play a more assertive role in the process of European integration.

The Maastricht Treaty and the Assembly: The Awareness of the 'Democratic Deficit'

Although the Treaty on European Union was approved by an over-whelming majority of MPs (by 200 votes to 21) on 10 December 1992, this was preceded by an intensive discussion on a referendum. The major political parties were against a referendum. Only the conservative CDS and the Communists wanted one. They were supported by several associations in Portuguese civil society. Prominent leaders of the two major parties, the Socialists and the Social Democrats, were split over the referendum. The referendum in Denmark destabilised even more the political elite. The main protagonist of the pro-referendum movement was the CDS leader Manuel Monteiro, who was advocating rejection of the treaty in order to prevent the development of a political union. He transformed his Democratic Social Centre from a Christian-democratic-inspired party into a more nationally oriented political group.[14]

The Maastricht Treaty served as a reminder of the existing 'democratic deficit' in the process of democratic integration in Portugal. It showed that the process of European integration had, until then, been an enterprise led by political elites. The population had not been integrated into the process. Even the Socialist leader António Guterres changed his stance and, during the Euro-elections of June 1994, advocated a referendum to be conducted at least in 1996.

The emergence of civil society and the lukewarm acceptance of the TEU in some Member States had a spill-over effect on the Assembly of the Republic. After 1992 the Committee of European Affairs organised several conferences, invited people from different fields of social and economic life in the country and attempted to assess the impact of the TEU on the Portuguese political system.[15] Also other committees, such as the Committee on Foreign Affairs, Portuguese Communities and Cooperation, and the Committee on Economy, Finances and Planning, tried to assess the impact of the TEU in their policy fields.[16]

This dynamism and involvement have been due to personalities such as Helena Torres Marques, who has now become a MEP, and the present President of the Committee on European Affairs, Jorge Braga de Macedo, who was previously the Minister for Economy and Finances. Since he started his presidency in early 1994, he has achieved a revision of law 111/88 which ensured the right of the Assembly to monitor the process of European integration. The new law, 20/94 of 15 June 1994, concedes more competences to the Committee on European Affairs.

For the first time, under the leadership of Braga Macedo, the Committee is able to make a general evaluation of the annual report 'Portugal and the European Union', submitted by the State-Secretariat for European Affairs attached to the Ministry of Foreign Affairs. The Committee is able to gather specialised evaluations from the other committees and therefore play the role of auditor more efficiently. More than that, due to the fact that Braga de Macedo is well connected to the present Government, the flow of information coming from the individual ministries appears to function quite well. In this sense, it seems that the overall improvement in the access to information, the dynamism of Braga de Macedo and other members of the Committee such as the communist Luís Sá and the former Socialist MEP João Cravinho, will change the nature and role of the present Committee of European Affairs, and of the Assembly of the Republic.[17]

The previous diachronical comparison has shown that the Portuguese Parliament had difficulties in responding to the demands of membership and the introduction of the Single European Act after 1986. Quite different was the approach of the Assembly of the Republic after the adoption of the TEU in December 1992. In the post-Maastricht period the Parliament was able to play a crucial role in informing the population about the effects of the Treaty. The involvement of MPs in the discussion of the effects of the TEU received national coverage through the press and television. Moreover, civil society was woken up by the discussion that was conducted in other Member States. The European Union was an important factor in enhancing the democratisation process in Portugal. The institutionalisation of democracy in Portugal was, after the revolution, oriented towards European integration. The thickening of the institutional networks between the supranational and national levels reinforced even more the prospects of democratic consolidation and institutionalisation.[18]

This intertwined process of national democratisation and European integration can be shown in the fields of constitutional provisions, political attitudes and elite culture in relation to the European Union and the transformation of the institutional setting related to the European Union inside the Assembly of the Republic.

Constitutional Provisions

The Portuguese Constitution of 1976 was considered one of the most Marxist of western Europe. It underwent several revisions in 1982, 1989 and 1992. Although never explicitly expressed, the revisions were undertaken to bring the Portuguese Constitution closer to that of the other European Member States. The coinage of the revolutionary legacy remained until 1989, when all the major passages that included a Marxist content were removed. With the revision of 1989 the Constitution came to resemble that of the other Member States in its commitment to a liberal democratic form of government and representation.[19]

The constitutional law 1/92 of 25 November 1992 finalised this process. The third constitutional revision changed several articles to adapt the Constitution to the TEU. The TEU had already been adopted by the Assembly in early 1992 under the condition that the Constitution had to be adapted to it first. The constitutional adaptation to the demands of the EC/EU were never regarded as a problem. Only the Communists and, since the adoption of the TEU, the conservative CDS referred to the claim that national sovereignty was being eroded. Strangely, the Government of the unitary Portuguese state is a strong supporter of federalism in Europe. Its main concern is the 'Europe des Regions' which was regarded as a major threat to the unity of the country.[20]

The role of the Assembly was better defined after this third constitutional revision. In Article 200 it is stipulated that the Government has 'to present ... to the Assembly of the Republic information related to the process of the construction of the European Union'. In Article 166 it is assigned to the Assembly of the Republic 'the role to accompany and evaluate the participation of Portugal in the process of construction of the European Union'. These constitutional changes enhanced the role of the Portuguese Parliament in auditing the government and, as already emphasised above, this has led to an improvement of executive-legislative relations.

Mass and Elite Political Attitudes

The different Eurobarometer surveys show that the Portuguese population is quite pro-European. In general, it supports further European integration. About 70 per cent of the Portuguese respondents answered positively to the question as to whether the country has benefited from EU membership (against 24 per cent giving negative responses and eight per cent don't knows). In Portugal a majority (54 per cent) think that EU membership is a 'good thing' against 13 per cent who think that it is a bad thing. About 32 per cent think that it is neither a good nor a bad thing. A majority of respondents are also in favour of European Government being responsible to the European Parliament.[21]

The benefits of membership have been considerable. The flow of structural funds since 1986, and especially after the reform of the structural funds in 1988, transformed the country. Nevertheless, one cannot deny that the other face of this economic and social transformation has been the virtual collapse of the Portuguese agriculture and fisheries sectors. Farmers and fishermen are regarded as the losers of European integration. Most of the structural funds went to the industrialised regions of Portugal located on the Atlantic coast. The peripheral eastern areas were not able to attract enough funds to compensate the gap between the richer and poorer regions of Portugal.[22] Nevertheless, the European Union is regarded as a positive factor in changing the mentalities of the Portuguese political elite. The population assigns a modernising role to the EU. Although there are still no studies of the attitude of the population towards Parliament and parliamentarism it seems that the growing civil society in the urban centres is asking for a more active role of the Assembly of the Republic. Inside the Assembly it is a common belief that the better access of the population to parliamentary work will enhance the role of the MPs *vis-à-vis* the Government. In general, the degree of knowledge on the EU has increased in certain circles regarded as opinion leaders, but for the vast majority the EU continues to be far remote from their lives. The Portuguese respondents to the Eurobarometer survey in 1994 responded to the question 'Feeling informed about the European Union' as follows: very well one per cent; quite well 19 per cent; not very well 46 per cent; not at all well 30 per cent; don't know four per cent.[23] This can be assessed as rather problematic, because the European integration process is still a project of political elites.

The political elite was always very pro-European. All the acts of European integration since 1978 have been accepted without any problems.[24] The situation changed after the adoption of the TEU. The question of the referendum divided parties and continues to be present in domestic politics. The democratic deficit is seen first of all as a 'domestic problem' and then as a European one. This can be assessed as very positive, because the political elite has become more divided and aware of the necessity to include the population more in decision-making mechanisms. The spectre of the Danish referendum during the Portuguese Presidency of the Council still continues to dominate Portuguese domestic politics.

National and Parliamentary Culture

Before 1986 the Portuguese Parliament was not very professionalised and routinised. The information channels of the European Union run primarily to the Government. This prevented the development of an assertive role in the pre-accession period. Lack of information, lack of material and human resources and the non-coordination of activities prevented this professionalisation and routinisation. The EC, like the democratisation process, was an unknown field to Portuguese politicians. In the first decade of democracy the Portuguese political elite was absorbed by political problems.

These problems were gradually overcome after 1986. The election of Portuguese members to the European Parliament, the development of direct contacts between the Portuguese and the European Parliament and the role of conference of the bodies dealing with European affairs (COSAC) consolidated the positive perception of European integration by Portuguese MPs.

It seems that since the Portuguese presidency of the first half of 1992 we can observe a stronger more assertive presence of Portuguese MPs and the national political elite in the institutional setting of the European Union. The level of knowledge and professionalisation has increased substantially. Portuguese MPs seem to regard as very important the need to take part in the process of EU development.[25]

Institutional Arrangements: The Committee of European Affairs

As already stated above, the Portuguese Parliament achieved a higher level of professionalisation and routinisation after 1992. The most evident reason seems to be that the Social Democrats under the leadership of Anibal Cavaco Silva were able to achieve an absolute majority in the general elections of July 1987 and October 1991. The political and governmental stability had a spill-over effect on the stability of the parliamentary work. In the period after the TEU one can observe a stronger engagement of the Committee on European Affairs. Its main task has been to monitor and evaluate the proccess of construction of the European Union. This is legally defined by the constitutional provisions set up in 1992 and by a new law 20/94 of 15 June 1994. The new law consists of six articles and enhances the role of the Assembly of the Republic in the European integration process.

Article 1 stipulates that a continuous process of exchange of information and consultation between the Assembly and the Government has to exist. The Government is required to provide the Assembly with all the information related to agreements and conventions with other Member States, binding acts of law derived from the treaties which institute the European Communities, acts of complementary law, namely decisions approved in the Council of the European Union, non-binding acts of derived law considered important for Portugal, and documents referring to the general lines of economic and social orientation as well as sectorial orientations. It is also provided that in the first trimester of each year the Government has to submit to the Portuguese Parliament a report on the impact of implemented EU measures on Portugal. Furthermore, after each presidency of the Council by a Member State a debate with members of the Government has to be conducted. Last, but not least, the Assembly evaluates the impact of the structural and cohesion funds (Arts.2 and 3).

The new law specifically defines the Committee on European Affairs as the central organ to fulfil these functions of monitoring and evaluating European affairs. The Committee is likely to generate an even greater participation by the Assembly in the activity of the European institutions and particularly to increase the exchange of reciprocal facilities and regular meetings with interested MEPs, particularly Portuguese MEPs. Last but not least, the Committee appoints the Portuguese representatives to COSAC and evaluates its activity and the results of the conference (Art.4).

The new procedure of monitoring and evaluating the European integration process requires that the Committee co-ordinates the evaluation process with the other specialised committees and submits a report to the House Speaker and the Portuguese Government.[26]

This annual evaluation of the impact of the European Union on national policies was undertaken for the first time in 1994. The report of the Government, 'Portugal and the European Union – The 8th Year' was studied by all the relevant permanent specialised committees. The Committee on European Affairs then issued a report which gave special attention to the economic and social problems that the Union would face in the near future. Interestingly, the report followed the structure of the legislative programme 1993/94 set up by the European Commission, the Council and the European Parliament. The main critique of the Committee on the report of the Government was that it was very inconsistent in its approach.[27] The Committee report covers the rights of citizens, the promotion of balanced and sustainable economic and social developments, the assertiveness of the identity of the EU in international affairs, and the need to develop closer co-operation between the national governments in the field of justice and European affairs, and the functioning of the institutions and the community organs.[28] The whole procedure is very similar to that of the budgetary one. The report of the Government is studied in its various aspects by the specialised committees. The final report is submitted to the plenary where it is discussed and subsequently voted on. In the case of failing to be approved, the report is sent back to the Committee. The final report is then sent to the Government.[29]

It was due to the leadership of Jorge Braga de Macedo that the new procedure was successfully implemented in the Portuguese Parliament. The Committee on European Affairs was able to get the opinion of the other committees on time, prepare the report and submit it to the Assembly. It seems that the Committee is asserting itself within the Parliament. Since 1995 the Parliament has provided the Committee with two research assistants. This has contributed substantially to the work of the Committee and its dissemination of information.[30]

On the whole, one can argue that the parliamentary structures are increasing their capacity to adapt to the demands of the European integration process. In general, it can be observed that the Portuguese MPs are playing an important role in enhancing the influencing ability of its national Government. Executive-legislative relations have improved substantially since 1992. The European integration process seems to be a challenge to modernise and further democratise the present Portuguese political system.

CONCLUSIONS

We have started with a general hypothesis that in the case of Portugal we have two intertwined processes which seem to have a spill-over effect upon each other. The first process is the democratisation process that Portugal has undergone since its transition to democracy in the mid-1970s. The second one is that of European integration which was crucial for the consolidation of democracy due to the fact that the European Community played a monitoring role in the pre-accession period.

The first period was marked by the negotiations of Portugal and the European Community. Although the Parliament did take part in the decision-making process, it was not a very dominant actor. On the contrary, the inexperience of the MPs, the lack of information and governmental instability prevented a routinisation and professionalisation in European affairs.

The second phase after 1986, until the introduction of the SEM, gradually transformed the attitude of MPs. The lack of information, the non-coordination of activities between the Government and the Parliament and the instability of the political system was subsequently overcome and parliamentary work became more professionalised and routinised.

But it was only in 1992 that the parliamentary political elite began to be more active in the process of monitoring and evaluating the impact of European integration in Portugal. The socialisation of the MPs in COSAC, the contact with Portuguese MEPs and the better access to information has led to a more assertive engagement of Portuguese MPs. The processes of approving the TEU and the Presidency of the Council in the first half of 1992 were crucial factors in fostering a more active role in the decision-making process of the European Union.

Institutionally, the Portuguese Parliament has been able to develop a more efficient procedure for monitoring and evaluating the process of European integration. The Committee of European Affairs is now quite experienced and includes among its members very well-qualified Europeanists who know the institutional framework of the European Union.

All this seems to suggest that the political will to promote European integration is quite strong in the Portuguese Parliament. This has to do with the feeling that after the decolonisation process in the 1970s Portugal had to find a new role and perhaps a mission in the international field. The longevity of the authoritarian dictatorship until 1974 had deprived the Portuguese of the opportunity to be engaged on the European scene. This changed completely after 1974. The revolutionary process reinforced even more this positive attitude towards European integration. It is for a small country quite a matter of pride to have a voice in the European institutional setting. The role of the Portuguese Parliament is to assure that this voice can be heard in an atmosphere of co-operation and peace. This has always been the main aim of the European Union.[31]

NOTES

1. On the Portuguese Revolution and democratic transition see the classic José Medeiros Ferreira, *Ensaio Histórico Sobre a Revoluçao de 25 de Abril. O Perído Pre-Constitucional* (Lisboa: Casa da Moeda, 1981); Martin Kayman, *Revolution and Counter-Revolution in Portugal* (London: Merlin, 1987) and Lawrence S. Graham and Douglas L. Wheeler, *In Search of Modern Portugal* (Madison: The University of Wisconsin Press, 1983).
2. This was at least the declaration of Robert Kergorlay, assistant director-general of the DG for foreign relations on 20 October 1975 in Lisbon, *The Times*, 20 Oct. 1975.
3. See the great study of Bernd Rother, *Der verhinderte Uebergang zum Sozialismus. Der sozialistische Partei Portugals im Zentrum der Macht (1974–1978)* (Frankfurt a. M.: Materialis, 1978), pp.214–21, and the classic study by Rainer Eisfeld, *Sozialistischer Pluralismus in Europa. Ansaetze und Scheitern am Beispiel Portugal* (Koeln: Verlag Wissenschaft und Politik, 1984).
4. Opinion on the application for accession of Portugal (submitted from the Commission to the Council), *Bulletin of the European Communities*, Supplement 5/78.
5. This intertwined process of mutual institutional change of both the European Union and the national political systems has been addressed recently by Juliet Lodge, 'Preface: The Challenge of the Future', in J. Lodge (ed.), *The European Community and The Challenge of the Future* (London: Pinter, 1993), pp.xiii–xxv, particularly pp.xxiv–xxv and Simon Hix, 'The Study of the European Community: The Challenge to Comparative Politics', *West European Politics* 17, 1 (Jan. 1994), pp.1–30.
6. This is the thesis presented in my *The Impact of the European Community on the New Iberian Democracies (1974–1993). An Empirical Contribution Towards a Theory of Regional Monitoring of Democratic Transition and Consolidation Processes*, Centre for European Union Studies, CEUS, University of Hull, Working Paper, 1995.
7. Most of the information was supplied by the former research assistant of the Committee on European Integration Dr José Alberto Vasconcelos, who is now a senior officer in the Office for Parliamentary Support (Gabinete de Apoio Parlamentar): interview, 21 Sept. 1994. He supplied the following documentation which was used for this section: *Relatório da Comissao de Integraçao Europeia ao Plenário da Assembleia da República*, Assembleia da República, 11.1.1985, xerox, Assembleia da República, *Organizaçoes Parlamentares Internacionais* (Lisboa: Assembleia de República, 1991), pp.53–4.
8. *Diário de Assembleia da República* (DAR), I-Série-Número, 21 June 1986.
9. DAR, I-Série-Número 53, 11 Oct. 1987.
10. Assembleia da República, *Portugal na Uniao Europeia. Lei de Acompanhamento e Apreciaçao* (Lisboa: Assembleia da República 1994), p.9.
11. The reports were called *Portugal e as Comunidades Europeias 1°–7° Ano* (Lisboa: Secretariado de Estado de Integraçao Europeia/Assuntos Europeus 1987–93) and since 1994 *Portugal e a Uniao Europeia 8° Ano* (Lisboa: Secretariado de Estado de Assuntos Europeus, 1994).
12. Comissao de Assuntos Europeus, *Portugal na Uniao Europeia em 1993. Apreciaçao Parlamentar* (Lisboa: Assembleia da República, 1994), p.34.
13. Interview with Dra. Teresa Feles, Parliamentary Library, Assembleia da República, 22 Sept. 1994.
14. Expresso, 6 June 1992, p.A2, Expresso, 13 June 1992, p.A2, Expresso, 20 June 1992, p.A5.
15. Comissao de Assuntos Europeus, *A Assembleia da República e o Tratado da Uniao Europeia* (Lisboa: Assembleia da República, 1993).
16. Comissao dos Negócios Estrangeiros, Comunidades Portuguesas e Cooperaçao, *A Problemática do Tratado de Maastricht* (Lisboa: Assembleia da República, 1992) and Comissao de Economia e Finanças, *A Coesao Económica e Social: Da Convergência nominal à convergência real. Colnferência das Comissoes de Economia e Finanças dos Parlamentos da Uniao Europeia* (Lisboa: Assembleia da República, 1994).
17. Interview with Dr Ana Fraga and Dr Pedro Valente, Research Assistants in the

Committee on European Affairs, 21 Sept. 1994.
18. André Thomashausen, *Verfassung und Verfassungswirklichkeit in Portugal* (Koeln: Nomos, 1981); *Constituição da República Portuguesa* (Lisboa: Porto Editora, 1989); Rui Chancerelle de Machete, 'Os príncipios estruturais da Constituiçao de 1976 e a próxima revisao constitucional' (995–1018) and António de Almeida Santos, 'Os limites materiais de revisao constitucional à luz da doutrina e do bom senso' (1037–44) both in Coordenado Mário Baptista Coelho, *Portugal. O Sistema Político e Constitucional 1974–87* (Lisboa: Instituto de Ciências Sociais, 1987).
19. The concept of *democratic institutionalisation* was taken up from Giuseppe di Palma, 'Parliaments, Consolidation, Institutionalization: A Minimalist Approach', Ulrike Liebert and Maurizio Cotta (eds.), *Parliament and Democratic Consolidation in Southern Europe: Greece, Italy, Portugal, Spain and Turkey* (London: Pinter, 1990), pp.31–51, meaning essentially transforming democracy qualitatively. One has to contradict Giuseppe di Palma in his assertion that there are no external influences in the process of democratic consolidation and institutionalisation of parliaments (p.45). The Portuguese example clearly provides evidence to the contrary. See also the article by William Mishler and Richard Rose, 'Support for Parliaments and Regimes in the Transition Toward Democracy in Eastern Europe', *Legislative Studies Quarterly* XIX, 1 (Feb. 1994), pp.5–32, and Leonardo Morlino, 'Consolidamento Democratico: Alcuni Ipotesi Esplicative', *Rivista Italiana di Scienza Politica* XVI, 3 (Dec. 1986), pp.429–59. Last, but not least, Juan J. Linz has also emphasised the role of parliamentarianism in the consolidation and institutionalisation of democracy: sese 'The Perils of Presidentialism', *Journal of Democracy*, 1 (1990), pp.51–69; quoted pp.68–9.
20. *Público*, 30 July 1994.
21. Eurobarometer, 41, July 1994, p.A23 and A28. In the last Eurobarometer survey Greece has similar scores, but in Spain the assessment has been more negative (38 per cent positive, 42 per cent negative and 19 per cent don't know) Eurobarometer, p.A23.
22. A general assessment of Portugal's membership in the EC until 1993 is Silva Lopes (ed.), *Portugal and the EC Membership Evaluated* (London: Pinter, 1993). Also see note 18.
23. Eurobarometer, 41, July 1994, p.A22.
24. To my knowledge there are still no studies on the attitudes towards European integration of the Portuguese political elite. On the attitudes towards European Integration of the Portuguese and Spanish MEPs see my *The Iberian Members of the European Parliament and European Integration. Their background, their attitudes and the prospects for transforming elite cultures*. Centre for Mediterranean Studies, University of Bristol, no.7, June 1993.
25. On the role played by Portuguese MPs in the tenth Assis see *Comissao de Assuntos Europeus, Transparência, Alargamento, Emprego. Teses Portuguesas na X COSAC* (Lisboa: Assembleia da República, 1994).
26. Assembleia da República, *Portugal na União Europeia. Lei de Acompanhamento e Apreciação, pp.15–19*.
27. *Assembleia da República, Portugal na União Europeia em 1993*, pp.29–30.
28. Assembleia da República, pp.31–74.
29. Interview with Dra. Ana Fraga and Dr Pedro Valente, Committee on European Affairs, Assembly of the Republic, 21 Sept. 1994.
30. Interview with Dra Ana Fraga and Dr Pedro Valente.
31. On this see the recent article by Kevin Featherstone, 'Jean Monnet and the "Democratic Deficit" in the European Union', *Journal of Common Market Studies*, 32, 2 (June 1994), pp.150–70; particularly p.152.

The View From 'Brussels'

MARTIN WESTLAKE

'BRUSSELS'

'Brussels' is a convenient shorthand term used to describe a number of different institutions and actors. These include: the European Parliament, the Commission, the Council, and the European Council, but also individual parliamentarians, commissioners, and ministers. Thus, it would be wrong to assume that there is only one view from Brussels; there are many different views. However, this article will concentrate only on the main ones.

THE TURNING POINT OF THE SINGLE EUROPEAN ACT

Until 1987, the European Parliament was a relatively obscure and uninfluential body.[1] During the 1970s it gained significant budgetary powers, but it lacked the political will and legitimacy to use these until after the first direct elections in 1979. In theory it could censure the Commission, but the censure motion was considered too powerful and misdirected to be used. Above all, the EP played no part in the Community's legislative process; the Council of Ministers was the Community's sole legislature. Following an unexpected 1980 Court of Justice ruling, the EP wrested to itself the power to delay certain legislative processes, but this was never anything more than an ingenious use of its rules of procedure, a procedural *legerdemain* whose full extent has never been tested before the Court. Thus, until the mid-eighties, most normative debate within the Community about reforming its legislative processes tended to focus on how the European Parliament could become more fully involved. It was generally felt that national parliaments were already involved, through the clear lines of accountability running between them and the national ministers participating in the Brussels legislative process in the Council.

The implementation of the Single European Act in 1987 marked a

Martin Westlake is an Associate Member of the Centre for Legislative Studies at the University of Hull and principal administrator in the Secretariat General of the EC Commission. A first draft of this paper was delivered at the Workshop of Parliamentary Scholars and Parliamentarians, Berlin, 19–20 August 1994. Any views expressed are entirely the author's own.

constitutional turning point. Three factors were of particular importance. The first was the introduction of qualified majority decision-making in the Council. The Council is by its nature a consensual body. It is composed of the representatives of sovereign states, and great pains are taken by the Presidency-in-Office and its Secretariat General to ensure the broadest possible consensus on any particular decision. Such extra-Treaty arrangements as the 'Luxembourg compromise' (1966)[2] and the much more recent 'Ioannina agreement' (1994)[3] show the extent to which the Member States have been prepared to go to seek maximum consensus. For much of the Community's life, an absence of decision was preferred to a decision which did not enjoy the full support of all Member States. But, by explicitly introducing qualified majority decision-making in certain policy areas, and by simultaneously introducing three- or four-month deadlines in the second reading stage of the co-operation procedure, the SEA seemed to undermine the Council's consensuality. Although, in practice, the effects were dampened by the Council's continued search for maximum consensus wherever possible, qualified majority voting (QMV) had an important consequence for the Community's theoretical lines of accountability. Previously, with *de facto*, across-the-board unanimity the general rule, national ministers could be considered accountable to their respective national parliaments for all decisions emanating from 'Brussels'. (The word, 'theoretical', is used advisedly because, with the exceptions of the Danish Folketing and the UK House of Commons, few national parliaments consistently exerted anything like the full scope of their theoretical powers of accountability.) The SEA created the possibility for national ministers to be out-voted – the normative question then rose as to how, under those circumstances, such outvoted ministers could be considered accountable for such decisions before their national parliaments.

The second factor introduced by the SEA was a vast raft of legislation relating to the creation of the internal market, and a facultative deadline ('1992') by which it all had to be adopted. Previously, the Community's legislative processes had been painfully slow. Now, with the Council and the Parliament co-operating as the SEA's draftsmen had intended they should, legislation (much of it very technical) became rapid. The leisurely scrutiny processes national parliaments had established were suddenly inundated with large amounts of substantial legislation. This had two consequences. In the first place, the Community's legislative process was very much more evident to national parliaments. In the second, the scale of the legislation involved necessarily meant that national parliamentary scrutiny (in a majority of the Member States scrutiny mechanisms did not change substantially) became more perfunctory.

The third factor introduced by the SEA was the positive, if limited, involvement of the European Parliament in certain of the Community's legislative processes. The SEA's draftsmen saw the co-operation procedure very much as a quid pro quo for the introduction of QMV in the Council; democratic accountability (however theoretical) lost to national parliaments had to be reasserted at the 'Brussels' level, and this could only be done via the European Parliament, which had its own direct democratic legitimacy based on universal suffrage. The co-operation procedure substantially reinforced the EP's scrutiny powers and introduced new lines of accountability, both with regard to the Commission and with regard to the Council.

The overall effect of these changes was to put the constitutional boot on the other foot so that, by the time of the 1991 intergovernmental conference negotiations that preceded the Maastricht Treaty, the constitutional debate was not only about the role of the EP, but also about how national parliaments could be better involved in the 'Brussels' process (as evidenced by the Commission's contribution to the IGC[4]). No institution was more aware of this than the European Parliament itself.

THE EUROPEAN PARLIAMENT

The EP is the only Community institution that has expressed its views regularly on the subject of the role of the national parliaments. Historically, the Parliament has been engaged in a long and hard battle to win a substantial place for itself in the Community's institutional arrangement. Consequently, the Parliament is jealous of its hard-won prerogatives and wary of any reassertion of national sovereignty which, it feels, would necessarily lead to an erosion of its own role. Nevertheless, it has always recognised the existing role of national parliaments and encouraged them to assert fully their established powers. The EP has also sought, particularly through its standing committees, to create lines of communication and information.[5]

In addition to a tactical defence of its institutional prerogatives, the EP has a longer term view of the Community's constitutional evolution which colours its view on the role of national parliaments. The EP has consistently militated in favour of a federal Europe, and has devoted considerable energies to drafting constitutional blueprints of a future European Union.[6] These exercises have obliged the EP to reflect in detail on the ultimate role of all of the Community's political institutions, including the Member State parliaments, as well as on an appropriate distribution of powers and mechanisms to ensure such a distribution. (It was the EP, for example, that first introduced the concept of subsidiarity into the Community's political vocabulary, through its 1984 Draft Treaty Establishing the European Union.) The Parliament has consistently espoused a purist, bi-cameral constitutional vision of the European Union, which sees the Commission as an embryonic executive, the Council (made up of the representatives of the Member States) as an embryonic upper chamber, and the EP itself (made up of the representatives of the people), as an embryonic lower chamber. To a considerable extent, its point of reference has been the German Constitution, which has successfully preserved powerful regions (the *Länder*) and yet allowed for strong and effective central government. Having reflected on the matter for so long, the EP is deeply attached to its constitutional vision and wary of any development that might carry the vision further away.

The European Parliament is undertaking preparatory work for the 1996 IGC. Although it cannot take part in the work of the IGC itself (a right it has long demanded), it was represented in the preparatory working group established by the June 1994 Corfu European Council. The detail of the constitutional vision the EP will ultimately propound cannot be fully known, but it is safe to predict that the EP will not depart from the general vision of the EU's development that it has consistently espoused so far.

In conclusion, the EP's view about the role of national parliaments is coloured not only by tactical considerations about possible encroachments on its prerogatives, but also by its longer term vision of the evolution of the European Union. Both elements were apparent in its reaction to President Mitterrand's 1989 suggestion that a parliamentary *Assises*, involving both the European Parliament and the national parliaments, should be established.

THE COMMISSION

The Commission would not normally pronounce on the role of national parliaments, nor in the normal course of things would it presume to advise sovereign parliaments (including the European Parliament) as to what constitutional role it thinks they should play, but in its submission to the Maastricht intergovernmental conference, it set out its constitutional vision of the European Union, and in this it did not differ substantially from the view of the European Parliament. The Commission distinguished between, first, any transfers of sovereignty from the national parliaments to the European Parliament and, second, the possible involvement of Member State parliaments in the Community's legislative process. With regard to the former, the Commission pointed out that amendments to the treaties could only take place after ratification by the national parliaments and presumably with them being fully aware. With regard to the latter, the Commission recalled that, in the Community system, 'it is national governments, sitting in the Council, that take the major decisions. Since national governments are accountable to national parliaments, it is for them to involve elected representatives in Community affairs in a manner which respects national traditions'. The Commission listed as its two principal concerns democracy and efficiency, and argued that these had to be reconciled. In its opinion, the European Parliament is uniquely placed to render the Commission democratically accountable. Regarding efficiency, the Commission (which is the prime mover and arbiter of the legislative process) has repeatedly voiced concern about possible breakdowns in the Community's legislative machinery. As with the Parliament, these considerations coloured its views in relation to the proposals made at the time of the Maastricht intergovernmental process as to how national parliaments could be better involved in the Community process. For the Commission, reinforcing the powers of the European Parliament *and* ensuring better involvement of national parliaments were two sides of the same democratic coin. It suggested that new mechanisms might be created in order to inform the Member State parliaments about particularly important decisions, but concluded that, in the first place, it was up to the sovereign European Parliament to decide how best national parliaments could be involved.

THE EUROPEAN COUNCIL

The Council as such does not express views on constitutional matters, but during the Maastricht IGC the European Council considered the involvement of national parliaments at considerable length (the June 1990 Dublin European Council had already pointed out that 'a greater involvement of the national parliaments in the democratic process of the Union, in particular in areas where new competences will be transferred to the Union' should be considered). These deliberations ultimately resulted in two declarations appended to the Maastricht Treaty. A first considered 'that it is important to encourage greater involvement of national parliaments in the activities of the European Union'. It went on to suggest that the exchange of information and contacts between national parliaments and the European Parliament should be stepped up 'through the granting of appropriate reciprocal facilities and regular meetings between members of Parliament interested in the same issues'. The second declaration established a 'Conference of Parliaments'.

THE CONFERENCE OF PARLIAMENTS

The Conference of Parliaments as ultimately established by the Maastricht Treaty was the fruit of two very different sets of proposals, one concerning constitutional reform, and the other concerning democratic oversight of certain new decision-making processes.

The first proposal was made by President Mitterrand in an October 1989 address to the European Parliament. He asked the Parliament why it did not organise '*Assises* on the future of the Community in which, in addition to Parliament, delegations from the national parliaments and representatives of the Commission and the governments would also participate'.[7] It is important to remember the heady atmosphere in which this proposal was made. The Berlin Wall was about to fall. The idea of a European Economic Area had been launched. Austria had already applied for membership of the Community. The June 1989 Madrid European Council had already agreed that there should be an IGC on economic and monetary union. In short, Europe was on the move, and Mitterrand felt that national parliaments should be more closely involved in deliberations about future constitutional reform. For the reasons enunciated above, the EP was at first very wary of the French President's proposal. But others, particularly the speaker of the Belgian *chambre*, Charles-Ferdinand Nothomb, were enthusiastic, and the EP rapidly came to the opinion that, if it wished to lessen any 'threat' from national parliaments, it would be best advised to take in its charge the organisation of the *Assises*. This it did, and with great success, harnessing the *Assises* to its own agenda; a concluding, 32-point resolution called for the European Parliament to be granted the same ratification powers as the national parliaments over future treaty amendments (the Maastricht IGC ignored this call). But some national delegations, particularly the British, were less enamoured with the experience and the outcome of the *Assises*.

The second proposal was made by the French Government during the 1991 Maastricht IGC negotiations,[8] and was part of a broader debate about whether or not the 'Community method' should be extended to new areas of competence. The French Government favoured a 'tree' model with two new intergovernmental 'pillars' dealing with foreign and security policy and justice and home affairs. The French proposal was soon favoured by a majority of the Member States, and the question then arose as to how parliamentary involvement could best be assured. The French Government proposed the creation of a European 'Congress', which would be composed of national and European parliamentarians and would be consulted on the Union's major policy options, particularly those in areas lying outside the traditional Community method, and hence beyond the purview of the European Parliament. This idea met with opposition on various grounds and was gradually diluted down into a declaration establishing the Conference of the Parliaments. The declaration states:

> The conference invites the European Parliament and the national parliaments to meet as necessary as a Conference of the Parliaments (or 'assises'). The Conference of the Parliaments will be consulted on the main features of the European Union, without prejudice to the powers of the European Parliament and the rights of the national parliaments. The President of the European Council and the President of the Commission will report to each session of the Conference of the Parliaments on the state of the Union.

The declaration is ambiguous on several important points. The most important is the mechanism for the convocation of the Conference. The declaration invites it to meet 'as necessary', but until recently it has been assumed that this would require the agreement of all of the Member State parliaments and the European Parliament. Could such agreement be forthcoming, when the House of Commons Foreign Affairs Select Committee had already declared that 'We see greater merit in the development of a series of bilateral contacts between the European Parliament and each national parliament and the further development of national parliaments' pre-legislative role?'[9]

The 1996 IGC provides the first occasion since the implementation of the Maastricht Treaty (1 November 1993) when the Conference might be convoked. Latterly, the unanimity proposal has been questioned[10] and the European Parliament's President, Klaus Hänsch, has spoken out strongly in favour of convoking the Conference.[11] Whatever occurs, it seems clear that the Conference will not meet frequently, and may thus play only a relatively minor role in better involving national parliaments, even in considering 'the main features of the Union'. However, there has been a growing realisation among both national and European parliamentarians that, even if it were to meet on a fairly regular basis, the Conference could not meet one of the underlying concerns which led to its creation. This is what Jean-Louis Bourlanges, a French MEP, has described as the existence of 'grey zones' within the European Union's competences, where neither the European Parliament nor the national parliaments exercise any control. In the EP's opinion, these 'grey zones' include the mechanisms for the common foreign and security policy and even more so co-operation in the fields of Justice and Home Affairs (the second and third pillars respectively), but also those of the embryonic Economic and Monetary Union, particularly the excessive deficit procedure and overall economic policy formation.

INTERPARLIAMENTARY CO-OPERATION

Notwithstanding the indifferent experience of the original November 1990 *Assises*, bilateral and multilateral interparliamentary co-operation has developed apace,[12] and this in itself is partly a reflection of the growth of parliamentary committees specialised in Community affairs or legislation. But interparliamentary co-operation gives rise to a number of problems at both the prescriptive and more purely practical levels:

> Who is the chief interlocutor of the Community institutions in the parliamentary domain? If there is not to be a single interlocutor, then what should be the division of roles and competences? Can such a division be clear, or will competences necessarily overlap? Should mechanisms be developed to govern the division of competences?[13]

The fundamental problem is bound up in the diversity of the European Union's parliaments – no two are the same and, after all, why should they be? Thus, the 1996 IGC is likely to see a renewed debate about whether the current *ad hoc* arrangements should be allowed to continue to grow organically (the view of the House of Commons Foreign Affairs Committee, for example), or whether a formal, treaty-based framework should be created.

A 'SECOND CHAMBER'

In recent years a number of proposals have been made for the creation of a second chamber. In 1989, Michael Heseltine proposed the creation of a European Senate, which would be composed of delegated national parliamentarians.[14] In 1993, the European Policy Forum proposed a 'two-chamber parliamentary review process with delegates of national parliaments introduced as a formal element into procedures for legislative review'.[15] In 1994, Philippe Seguin (Speaker of the French National Assembly) proposed that the European Parliament should become a senate, and that a lower chamber, composed of delegated national parliamentarians, be created. Most recently, Sir Leon Brittan has proposed the creation of a Committee of Parliaments, also composed of national parliamentarians and charged with specific review tasks.[16] What all of these proposals have in common is the suggestion that national parliaments should be bound into some form of institutionalised mechanism for the review of Community legislation *in addition to the current powers entrusted to the national parliaments and the European Parliament*. Most of the criticisms of such proposals point to this element of duplication, and to the practical difficulties involved in organising such a chamber on a regular basis.

In July 1990, the European Parliament adopted a resolution on the subject drafted by one of its noted constitutionalists, Maurice Duverger.[17] Naturally, the Parliament could be expected to argue against the creation of a body which might be in competition with it, and Duverger duly considers that 'it would not be useful' to set up a new institution alongside the European Parliament. However, the three arguments he advanced remain objectively powerful.

The first is that the experience of the European Parliament prior to direct elections showed the limitations of any appointed or delegated body. It seems axiomatic that composite, delegated institutions (for example, the parliamentary assemblies of the Council of Europe and the Western European Union, or the North Atlantic Assembly) have only the weakest of consultative powers. If, Duverger argues, national parliaments wish to reassert their authority, they will not do so by sending appointed delegations to such a body (unless – an unlikely prospect – a second chamber were given substantial powers).

The second is the EP's traditional argument that the Community institutions already include a body representing Member States and a body representing the electorate directly. They also include a body representing the regions, and a body representing economic and social interests. Do the national parliaments need to represent themselves in a similar fashion and, if so, is a second chamber the most appropriate way?

Duverger's third argument, and perhaps the most compelling in an enlarging Community, is that 'decision-taking would become even more complex and, therefore, less transparent'. Yet the need for greater transparency was one of the clear conclusions drawn from the fraught experience of the ratification of the Maastricht Treaty.

THE CONSEQUENCES OF THE MAASTRICHT TREATY RATIFICATION
PROCESS

The negative result in the first, June 1992, Danish referendum provoked far-reaching reflection within the Community institutions as to what exactly had gone wrong. Ironically, in view of the Commission statement quoted above, the problem did not lie with the Danish parliament (the Folketing ratified the Maastricht Treaty on 17 March 1992 by 130 votes to 25) nor with the French Parliament (the French Congress – National Assembly and Senate in special joint session – approved the constitutional amendments needed for the Treaty by 592 votes to 73), but with the

Danish and French citizens. However, the outlines of a solution drawn up at the October 1992 Birmingham European Council and the solution ultimately agreed at the December 1992 Edinburgh European Council *did* involve national parliaments, as well as their citizens, particularly in attempting to render the Community's decision-making procedures more transparent. For example, the Council agreed to hold certain meetings in public (though not those where it takes decisions) and to publish its minutes where decisions were taken by qualified majority, although it has since qualified these undertakings considerably. The Commission promised to make information and its drafting processes more accessible to national parliaments, particularly through greater use of green and white papers. This it has done but, to take one example, the Commission's White Paper on Growth and Competitiveness[18] has not sparked off the debate in national parliaments that its principal author, Jacques Delors, would have liked to have seen.

Of all the Community institutions, it was perhaps the European Parliament that most took to heart the Maastricht Treaty ratification experience. With a view to the declaration on national parliaments, the EP had already established an administrative unit within its Secretariat General entirely devoted to relations with the Member State parliaments, and it had become a firm believer in the subsidiarity principle as a mechanism for determining the most appropriate level of decision-making on various issues. But the Danish and French referendums showed the EP that it alone could not, or could not yet, act as a prime explanatory, popularising agent *vis-à-vis* the European people. It remained distant from them, as the turnout levels in the 1994 European elections were to confirm. From this perspective, national parliaments remain vital intermediaries, but the Maastricht Treaty ratification process showed that they, as much as the European Parliament, were 'out of touch' with popular attitudes.

A PARADOX

'Brussels', in the shape of the European Parliament and the European Commission, finds itself in a paradoxical position. Both institutions recognise the importance of sovereign national parliaments and, by implication, both feel that national parliaments are not fully playing the role they might. But paradoxically, because those parliaments *are* sovereign nobody, least of all the EP or the Commission, could presume to do anything more than express encouragement and make suggestions. The experience of the Maastricht Treaty shows that even treaty-based declarations are ineffective if they do not coincide with the agreement of the institutions involved; to twist a phrase, you can take a parliament to water, but you cannot make it drink.

NOTES

1. See M. Westlake, *A Modern Guide to the European Parliament* (London: Pinter, 1994).
2. See A. Teasdale, 'The Life and Death of the Luxembourg Compromise', *Journal of Common Market Studies* XXXI, 4 (Dec. 1993).
3. Council Decision of 29 March 1994 concerning the taking of Decision by qualified majority, *Official Journal* C 105, 13.4.94, p.1.
4. Commission des Communautés européennes, 1991, 'Conférences intergouverne-mentales: contributions de la Commission', *Bulletin des Communautés européennes*, Supplément 2/91, Luxembourg.
5. For example, in the 1987–90 period, the EP committee responsible for a large part of the internal market legislation, the Committee on Economic and Monetary Affairs and Industrial Policy, invited its counterparts in all of the Member State parliaments to visit it separately in order to exchange views about the internal market legislative process. Most national parliaments accepted the invitation and sent delegations, but these were small, some were not particularly well-informed, and the level of most of the exchanges remained general.
6. European Parliament, Resolution on the Draft Treaty establishing the European Union, OJ C 77, 19.3.84, pp.53–4, and Resolution on the Constitution of the European Union, adopted 10.2.94.
7. European Parliamentary Debates, OJ 3-382, 25.10.89, p.163.
8. See R. Corbett, *The Treaty of Maastricht. From Conception to Ratification: A Comprehensive Reference Guide* (Harlow: Longman, 1993).
9. Cited in European Parliament, 1993, Information Note, 'The Second Report on "Europe after Maastricht" of the Foreign Affairs Committee of the House of Commons', Brussels (unpublished document).
10. See Charles-Ferdinand Nothomb, 'The Rôle of National Parliaments and the European Parliament in the Construction of Europe', *Brussels Review*, Autumn 1994, and Martin Westlake, 'The European Parliament, the National Parliaments and the 1996 Inter-governmental Conference', *Political Quarterly*, Spring 1995.
11. He argued that it should meet before the European Council decided on the scope and mandate of the Intergovernmental Conference. See *Agence Europe*, 6365, 26 Nov. 1994.
12. See P. Norton, 'National Parliaments and the European Union', Paper presented to The Workshop of Parliamentary Scholars and Parliamentarians, Berlin, 1994. See also Westlake, *A Modern Guide*.
13. Westlake, *A Modern Guide*.
14. M. Heseltine, *The Challenge of Europe: Can Britain Win?* (London: Weidenfeld and Nicolson, 1989).
15. European Policy Forum, *A European Constitutional Settlement*, London, 1993.
16. L. Brittan, *Europe: The Europe We Need* (London: Hamish Hamilton, 1994).
17. Resolution on the preparation of the meeting with the national parliaments to discuss the future of the Community (the 'Assises'), adopted 12.7.90, C 231, 17.9.90, p.165.
18. European Commission, *Growth, Competitiveness, Employment. The Challenges and Ways Forward into the 21st Century. White Paper* (Brussels: Office for Official Publications of the European Communities, 1994).

Conclusion: Addressing the Democratic Deficit

PHILIP NORTON

Our initial hypothesis was that national parliaments would respond to moves toward European integration by undertaking some institutional change. What is apparent from the papers in this volume is that the national parliaments of the Member States of the EU have undergone institutional change in response to the development of the European Community/Union. What is notable is the stage at which that adaptation has taken place. It constitutes a middle stage in the developing relationship between national parliaments and the moves towards European integration.

LIMITED INVOLVEMENT

The first stage was that essentially of limited or no involvement. Most chambers of the legislatures of the original six Member States did not modify significantly their structures or procedures in response to the moves towards European integration. The parliaments were accorded no formal role in the process of supranational law making and they had little inclination to seek such a role. Elite and mass opinion within the six countries favoured moves towards European integration and the concomitant transfer of powers to supranational institutions in order to achieve that integration. There appeared to be no strong orientation within the political culture of each country to the national Parliament and certainly none strong enough to disturb the moves towards integration. National interests remained protected through national governments. A policy inimical to the national interest could be killed off in the Council of Ministers. There appeared little reason for national parliaments to get involved. 'Europe' was essentially a matter for the Executive and an issue that rarely exercised public opinion.

Within the national parliaments, a committee to consider European affairs was established in only one lower chamber – the Belgian House of Representatives in 1962. As Lieven De Winter and Thierry Laurent show, that committee was neither particularly active nor effective and

---

Philip Norton is Professor of Government at the University of Hull.

was abolished in 1979. The remaining parliaments either established no such committee – treating such matters as within the remit of the committee(s) dealing with foreign affairs, paralleling the position in government where the ministry of foreign affairs was the lead department – or else (in the case of Holland, Italy and Germany) established committees in the upper chambers. The majority of legislative chambers lacked a dedicated European committee.

THE CHALLENGE OF THE SINGLE EUROPEAN ACT

The second stage was that of adapting to changing developments within the Community. Adaptation took place early in the case of the three countries that joined the EC in 1973. The United Kingdom and Danish parliaments adopted a stance very different to that of the parliaments of the original six. Both countries adopted an instrumental approach to membership and had parliaments that were jealous of their status within the national law-making process. The Danish Folketing established an advisory committee in advance of membership and the two Houses of the British Parliament established committees consequent to the UK's accession. The Irish Parliament, a marginal political actor within a culture that strongly favoured membership of the EC, established a joint committee of the Dail and Seanad, but – as Eunan O'Halpin has emphasised in this volume – the committee achieved little and was treated by most members as a 'complete backwater'.

Though the changes made within the Folketing and the British Parliament may have prompted some other legislatures to contemplate change, the principal spur to institutional change in the 1980s was the publication of the White Paper on the Completion of the Single Market and the enactment of the Single European Act. That is the clear conclusion to be drawn from the contributions to this volume. The White Paper and the SEA ensured that the reach of EC institutions extended into sectors that were previously the exclusive domain of national governments. To cope with the changed conditions, national governments adapted their procedures for dealing with EC affairs. So too did most of the national parliaments. There was a realisation not only that the policy competence of the EC was being extended but that a shift in the decision-making process was also taking place. As we noted in the Introduction, the SEA effected a shift in power relations between the institutions of the EC and the national institutions of the Member States and a shift in power relationships within the institutions of the EC. Policy-making power was flowing upwards to the supranational level and with a directly elected Parliament having a greater opportunity than before to be involved at that level.

From the perspective of national parliaments, the most significant consequences of the White Paper and the SEA were that there were more regulations and directives emanating from 'Brussels' and that such legislation impinged now on matters previously the exclusive concern of national governments. For national parliaments, there was the problem of how to respond to the changed conditions. It was at this stage that we witness the institutional change taking place that we hypothesised would occur. The national parliaments could not rely solely on the European Parliament to scrutinise EC documents and hold the Commission and Council of Ministers to account. The EP was accorded a greater role to play than before, but it was still not a fully fledged legislature. There was a need for national parliaments to get involved.

The result has been that, in the field of EC affairs, national parliaments have exhibited, from the mid-1980s onwards, three distinct characteristics: (i) greater specialisation, (ii) greater activity, and (iii) some attempts to integrate MEPs into their activities. In combination, these features suggest that national parliaments have adapted to moves towards greater European integration and are seeking to play a more active role in that process. However, those attempts are influenced significantly by country-specific factors. Those factors also complicate moves to create a more active role for national parliaments in the future.

(i) Greater Specialisation

The specialisation is to be found in the creation of committees devoted to European affairs. The 1980s became the decade of EC Committees, especially in lower chambers. The Belgian House of Representatives established its Advice Committee in 1985. It was followed by six other parliaments (see Table 1), including the two new Iberian Member States (though Portugal had established a committee prior to accession). In 1990, the Belgian Senate established an Advice Committee. In 1991, the German Bundestag appointed a Standing Committee on European Community Affairs, superseding the sub-committee of the Foreign Affairs Committee. By the 1990s, EC committees were the norm. Each national Parliament had one or more committee dealing with European affairs.

(ii) Greater Activity

The extension of the policy competence of the EC, and the drive towards achieving a single market by 1 January 1993, resulted in a significant growth in the volume of EC Regulations and Directives. National parliaments began devoting more and more time to scrutinising documents to be submitted to the Council and/or the implementation of Directives.

TABLE 1

DATE OF CREATION OF EC COMMITTEES IN NATIONAL PARLIAMENTS, 1957–88

Date of creation	Country, committee and chamber
December 1957	Germany: Ausschuss für Fragen der Europäischen Gemeinschaften (Bundesrat)
July 1968	Italy: Giunta per gli Affari Delle Communita Europee (Senato)
June 1970	Netherlands: Vaste Commissie voor Europese Samenwerkingsorganisaties (Eerste Kamer)
October 1972	Denmark: Markedsudvalget (Folketing)
August 1973	Ireland: Joint Committee of the Secondary Legislation of the European Communities (Oireachtas)
April 1974	United Kingdom: Select Committee of the European Communities (House of Lords)
May 1974	United Kingdom: Select Committee on European Legislation (House of Commons)
July 1979	France: Delegation de l'Assemblee Nationale (et du Senat) pour les Communautes Europeennes (National Assembly)
April 1985	Belgium: Comite d'Avis Charge de Questions Europeennes/ Adviescomite Voor Europese Aangelegenheden (Chambre des Représentants/Kamer van Volksvertegenwoordigers)
December 1985	Spain: Comision Mixta para las Communidades Europeas Cortes Generales)
October 1986	Netherlands: Vaste Commissie voor Eg-Zaken (Tweede Kamer)
June 1987	Germany: Unterausschuss des Auswärtigen Ausschusses für Fragen der Europäischen Gemeinschaften (Bundestag)
July 1987	Italy: Commissione Affari Esteri e Communitari (Camera dei Deputati)
October 1987	Portugal: Comissão de Assuntos Europeus (Assembleia da Republica)
June 1988	Germany: Kammer für Vorglagen der Europäischen Gemeinschaften (Bundesrat)

Source: Bodies within National Parliaments specialising in European Community Affairs, *European Parliament: Research and Documentation Papers, National Parliaments Series No. 3* Luxembourg: Office for Official Publications of the European Communities, 1989.

In many cases, the burden fell on the European Affairs Committee. In other cases, it was shared between committees, some additional committees being created to supplement the established committees. In 1988 the German Bundesrat set up a second committee, giving it specific responsibility for EC documents. In 1991 the British House of Commons established two European Standing Committees to consider EC Documents recommended for debate. Some of the burden has also passed to the plenary. In the case of the Dutch Parliament, for example, there has been a marked increase in the number of times a European item has been considered in plenary session and in committee (debates) and in the number of new European themes put on the parliament's agenda (dossiers). As Rinus Van Schendelen notes, there has been an increasing involvement of the Parliament in European affairs. 'The turning point is the session 1984–85'.

(iii) Integration of MEPs

As the papers in this volume record, various attempts have been made to integrate MEPs into the work of the national parliaments. These have taken different forms. In some cases, as we have seen, it involves MEPs serving as members of parliamentary committees. Irish MEPs were included as members of the Joint Committee of the Oireachtas when it was established in 1973. The Advice Committee of the Belgian House of Representatives has ten MEPs and ten MPs as members. The German Commission on European Affairs, in existence between 1983 and 1986, had 11 MEPs and 11 MPs as members. Eleven MEPs are given 'observer' status in the new German Standing Committee on European Affairs, though without the right to vote. A number of other chambers allow MEPs to attend committee meetings, either as of right or by invitation. In other cases, the relationship has developed – or is intended to be developed – through meetings between members of the national Parliament and the country's MEPs, as in the case of Spain and Portugal, or through inviting MEPs on occasion to provide information or give evidence to committees, as in the case of the committees of UK House of Lords and the Dutch Eerste Kamer. Some links may also be established through the medium of party: in the British House of Commons, for example, party committee meetings are open to the party's MEPs, and MEPs from the Labour Party now form part of the Parliamentary Labour Party (PLP) electorate in the election of the party leader.

These developments, taken together, indicate a substantial response by national parliaments to the 1985 White Paper and the passage of the Single European Act. There have also been further changes in response to the debate over, and the implementation of, the Maastricht Treaty.

Some countries have strengthened the position of their parliaments in determining whether treaty provisions should be implemented (Germany, for example, and the Netherlands). Article 88 of the French Constitution was amended in June 1992 to allow the National Assembly the right to intervene – through the submission of resolutions – in the conduct of European policy, previously treated as falling within the domain of foreign policy. Some countries, such as Portugal, have also extended the competence of their European affairs committees. Some parliamentary committees have also made some efforts to meet on occasion with their equivalent committees in the EP. There is also growing co-operation through COSAC, the conference of representatives of European Affairs committees in the national parliaments.

This may be deemed to constitute progress in enabling national parliaments to adapt to greater European integration and maintain, indeed extend, their capacity to influence the process of European law-making. The 1985 White Paper and the SEA – followed by the Maastricht Treaty – may be seen as having a salutary effect, forcing national parliaments to address the changing nature of EC law-making and to create the means for dealing with that change. On the face of it, they appear to have done a competent job.

Against this assessment must be set a number of variables which, taken together, demonstrate that national parliaments not only remain marginalised within EC/EU law-making but are increasingly marginalised. These variables are important also in informing the debate about the role of national parliaments as means for wiping out or reducing the democratic deficit within the Union. To many bodies involved in preparing proposals for the 1996 Inter-Governmental Conference (IGC) on the EU, national parliaments are part of the answer to the problem of the democratic deficit. However, there are two obstacles that stand in the way of national parliaments fulfilling that role. One is different interpretations as to the problem. The other comprises the country-specific variables that militate against a uniform response by national parliaments.

SOLVING THE DEMOCRATIC DEFICIT?

The third stage of development is one in which national parliaments are viewed as important means of addressing the democratic deficit within the Union. The 'democratic deficit' has been subject to different definitions,[2] but may be said to derive from the limited input into the law-making processes of the EC by directly elected representatives of the people. As we have seen, the European Parliament was not initially elected nor even formally styled a Parliament. The original treaties provided no role for national parliaments. The only control parliaments had over the law-making process at Community level was through ministers in the Council of Ministers, where negotiations could result in decisions that differed from the position taken originally by national parliaments and where the decision-making process could not always be integrated with the pace of deliberations of national parliaments.

Though there appears to be widespread recognition, both at the national and supranational level, of the need to tackle this perceived deficit, there are conflicting interpretations of how it should be tackled. On the face of it, there is general agreement that national parliaments should play a more active role. The view that they should be more actively involved found expression in two declarations appended to the Maastricht Treaty. It also finds expression in the proposals being prepared for the 1996 IGC. The British Government, the Commission, and the European Parliament each take the view that national parliaments should be more actively involved in EU affairs.

Yet there is a difference of opinion as to the nature of the role that national parliaments should play. The difference is over the level at which the parliaments should operate. One level is the individual level, which means essentially each national parliament becoming more active in relation to the national government, in essence scrutinising and acting as a potential constraint on government. The other is the collective level, which entails national parliaments collaborating in order to be more involved in scrutiny and, potentially, constraint at the supranational level.

The two roles are not mutually exclusive and both found expression in the two declarations appended to the Maastricht Treaty. The declaration on the role of national parliaments (reproduced in Figure 1) envisaged that national parliaments should receive Commission proposals in good time for examination and that there should be a greater exchange of information and reciprocal facilities between the national parliaments and the EP. This, in effect, gave voice to the first view. The declaration on the Conference of the Parliaments – establishing the Conference and stipulating that it should be consulted on the main features of the European Union (Figure 1) – gave expression to the second view.

The first view has been supported by the European Parliament. In a resolution adopted on 16 February 1989, the EP said that it considered it necessary 'for the national parliaments to monitor the proper application of the Single European Act by the relevant national representatives in the Council of Ministers and the European Council and to ensure the speedy incorporation of directives ... and for this reason will ensure to it that the national parliaments are kept informed ...'. It also welcomed the creation of EC affairs committees by national parliaments and recommended that

FIGURE 1

MAASTRICHT TREATY DECLARATIONS ON THE ROLE OF NATIONAL
PARLIAMENTS AND THE CONFERENCE OF THE PARLIAMENTS

National Parliaments

The Conference considers that it is important to encourage greater involvement of national
Parliaments in the activities of the European Union.

To this end, the exchange of information between national Parliaments and the European
Parliament should be stepped up. In this context, the government of Member States will
ensure, inter alia, the national Parliaments receive Commission proposals for legislation in
good time for information or possible examination.

Similarly, the Conference considers that it is important for contacts between the national
Parliament and the European Parliament to be stepped up, in particular through the granting of
appropriate reciprocal facilities and regular meetings between members of Parliament interested
in the same issues.

Conference of the Parliaments

The Conference invites the European Parliament and the national Parliaments to meet as
necessary as a Conference of the Parliaments (or 'Assises').

The Conference of the Parliaments will be consulted on the main features of the European
Union, without prejudice to the powers of the European Parliament and the rights of the
national parliaments. The President of the European Council and the President of the
Commission will report to each session of the Conference of the Parliaments on the state of the
Union.

each parliament appoint liaison officers in their committees to be
responsible for contact with the EP and its committees.

The second view found expression in the meeting of the Conference of
the Parliaments in 1990. The Conference, described already in Martin
Westlake's paper, involved more than 300 members of national parliaments and of the EP (in a ratio of roughly three to one). Members sat in
party groups and not by national delegation. The Conference endorsed
the position of the EP on European union and declared its support for
enhanced co-operation between national parliaments and the EP, as well
as for more meetings of such Conferences.

The second view on the collective role of national parliaments has also
been espoused by a number of politicians, not least British politicians. In
1989 a senior member of the British House of Commons, Michael
Heseltine, argued the case for 'creating an upper House of the European
Parliament *from within the membership of the national parliaments*'
(emphasis in original).[3] EC Commissioner Sir Leon Brittan made a
similar though not identical call in his campaign for the Commission

Presidency in 1994. He advocated a Committee of the Parliaments consisting of representatives from each national parliament and vested with limited powers in the law-making process. 'If voters felt their local MPs were lending a hand to the process of Euro-legislation', he wrote, 'it would greatly strengthen the EU's democracy and enhance its credibility.'[4] From a somewhat different but nonetheless collective perspective, as Thomas Saalfeld reports in his contribution to this volume, the German *Länder* want a Regional Chamber of the EU with significant powers.

The problem with the two approaches is not that they are logically incompatible but rather is to be found in a political incompatibility. Vested interests militate against a consensus being mobilised in support of both. The European Parliament believes that the way to meet the democratic deficit is to increase its own powers – thus strengthening it in relation to the Commission and Council of Ministers – and to strengthen national parliaments at the national level – that is, in relation to their own governments. Thus, for instance, the leader of the European Parliamentary Labour Party, Wayne David, has argued for the EP to be able to initiate legislation, to have greater control over the EU budget, to have the power to propose candidates for the Commission Presidency, and to have a full role in the legislative process through the co-decision procedure whenever decisions are taken by qualified majority voting.

> But as well as considering the democratisation of the EU at a European level, we should not lose sight of the fact that the democratic deficit also extends into the British Parliament . . . . Rather than seeing the European Parliament and the House of Commons as competitors, we ought to see both institutions as partners in the process of creating a more democratic Europe.[5]

However, this partnership does not extend to according national parliaments a collective role. The EP supports the first view, but not the second. Allowing national parliaments a collective role – through a second chamber or even through a Conference of the Parliaments – is seen as usurping the role of the EP itself. It takes the view that it represents electors at the supranational level. National parliaments represent voters at the national level and can feed in their views through the Council of Ministers and through contact with MEPs. The EP has therefore been an opponent of a second chamber and has taken a critical view of the Conference of the Parliaments. An additional chamber or regular meetings of the Conference would, according to EP President Klaus Hänsch, 'lead to confusion'. 'I am not against the whole idea of assises', he declared, 'but we should have them, if we have them, only on special issues and on a special agreement.'[6] As Martin Westlake records, when the EP found it could not prevent the meeting of the Conference of the Parliaments in Rome, it manoeuvred instead to ensure that it controlled the administration of it. Given that there is little incentive for national parliaments to press for it to meet regularly – it lacks powers, a fixed timetable and institutional leadership independent of the EP – the omens are not good for it to develop as a body of collective influence.

Though the British Government appears supportive of the second view, attempts to rally support for it in 1995 among other national governments in the run-up to the 1996 IGC apparently failed to make much headway.[7]

Some supporters of the second view – wanting a collective role for national parliaments – are also opponents of any extension of the powers of the European Parliament. They tend to view parliamentary power as a zero-sum game: any extension of power to the EP takes power away from national parliaments. Furthermore, any extension of the EP's powers would not, in their view, address the democratic deficit. The EP has not yet engaged the interest and enthusiasm of voters throughout Europe. Hence the emphasis on national parliaments and the potential for them to act collectively.

The problem with making progress on the first view is the stance taken by many if not most national governments. This view involves national parliaments having some impact on EU affairs through national governments. Hence they serve as potential constraints on national governments. Even the British Government, keen to see some role for national parliaments as potential brakes on the activities of EU institutions, is less keen to see British parliamentary committees act as brakes on *its* activities in relation to the EU. It has thus refused, for example, to approve a widening of the terms of reference of the EC Committee in the House of Commons.[8]

Though the idea of national parliaments playing a more active role in the EU attracts considerable support, perceptions of what that role should be clearly differ. That is the political problem. Even if agreement were to be reached on the role national parliaments should play, there are practical problems. Those problems affect both a greater input at the national level and the collective level. These problems are shown in the contributions to this volume. They derive from the variables identified in the introduction.

LIMITATIONS

To have some informed idea of what role national parliaments may be able to play in the moves towards European integration, it is essential to have an understanding of the role they have played already in that process. What emerges from the papers in this volume is a picture of institutions that have been marginal actors in the process. They have been unable and, in many respects, unwilling to play a significant role in European law making.

The inability to play a significant role is constitutional and, to a lesser extent, procedural. The unwillingness is essentially ideological and cultural.

Constitutional

As is clear from the papers in this volume, the disparate institutional response of national parliaments to moves toward European integration have been affected significantly by the different provisions and norms of national constitutions. Some have clearly facilitated the integration of the State into supranational processes, others – such as those of the United Kingdom and Germany – have created some difficulties, the UK from the time of accession and the German Basic Law more recently in relation to the position of the *Länder*.

However, more fundamental is the situation created for national parliaments by the European treaties. As we have seen, the original treaties accorded no formal role to national parliaments in EC law making. The declarations appended to the Maastricht Treaty still accord them no formal role in that process, and the declarations themselves pale into insignificance alongside the power shifts effected by the Single European Act and the Maastricht Treaty. The extension of qualified majority voting in the Council of Ministers limits the capacity for national parliaments to affect outcomes. Even if the role of national parliaments is strengthened in relation to national governments – the first level discussed above – national governments are themselves limited now in their capacity to prevent undesired outcomes.

Procedural

What I term procedural limitations derive from the existing structures, procedures and workloads of national parliaments, from the jealousies of parliamentarians, and from the fact that these features vary considerably from one parliament to another. What constitutes a European Affairs Committee in one parliament may display little resemblance to a European Affairs Committee in another.

In some parliaments, responsibility for consideration of EC documents lies with subject-specific committees, the European Affairs Committee acting as a co-ordinating body rather than as the lead committee for discussing such documents. This is the case, for example, in Ireland and the Netherlands. The French *délégations* report to the six permanent committees of the National Assembly. Some operate through sub-committees, as in the British House of Lords and the *Comisión Mixta* of the Spanish Cortes. Some are vested with considerable powers, notably the European Affairs Committee of the Danish Folketing and the committees of the Italian House, but most are not. The size and competence of the committees vary considerably. This is sometimes apparent within two chambers of the same parliament. The British House of Lords, as we have seen, is a very active committee, operating through sub-committees. The House of Commons has one committee on European Legislation, with more restricted terms of reference than its House of Lords counterpart, and making no use of sub-committees. Documents recommended for debate by the Commons committee stand referred to a European Standing Committee. Documents recommended for debate in the House of Lords are debated in the chamber.

These procedural differences mean that there is no standard 'European Affairs Committee' in the parliaments of the Member States. In some cases, as in the German Bundestag, there is some conflict between committees over responsibility for EU affairs. The specific arrangements can limit the impact of the Committee that has the 'European' designation. The failure in some cases to create an effective committee structure has led to calls for further change, such calls in the case of Ireland and the Netherlands actually calling into question the continued existence of the 'European' committees. Taken together, these differences limit the capacity for collective action and influence – that is, at the second level discussed above. To talk of European Affairs committees is to convey an impression of a uniformity that does not exist.

There is also a problem deriving from the workload of legislatures. Again, there is variation from parliament to parliament. However, it is clear from the contributions to this volume that dealing with an increasing volume of European documents places great pressures on the institutional capacity of a national parliament to deal with it. When the Procedure Committee of the British House of Commons, for example, recommended the creation of European Standing Committees, it initially proposed five such committees; the Government agreed to three but eventually announced the formation of only two on the grounds that not enough members could be recruited to serve on three. And, as noted in the UK chapter, the House of Lords voted in 1992 to reduce the number of EC Committee sub-committees, with some peers taking the view that the sub-committees absorbed the energies of too many peers and that more time should be devoted to other matters.

There is thus a practical problem in seeking to cope with the amount of material coming from Brussels. There is an allied problem, apparent from the preceding chapters. Even if parliamentarians are keen to maintain links with MEPs, there is the problem of finding the time to build those links. It is often not easy for MEPs to spend time visiting national parliaments. Even where MEPs serve as full or advisory members of committees of the national parliament, as in the case of Greece and Ireland, they are noted more for their failure to turn up than for assiduous attendance. Similarly, for members of national parliaments to spend time in Brussels and Strasbourg requires a commitment of time that may be difficult to achieve.

Attempts to achieve change within some legislatures have also fallen foul of the jealousies of existing committee members, not willing to see their remit limited. These jealousies exist not only between committees within a legislature but also, as we shall see, between parliaments and MEPs.

These practical problems have limited the capacity of national legislatures to give the time and attention to European affairs to the extent that they may wish and, in so far as national parliaments address European issues, have produced a patchwork quilt response. The existing workload of some parliaments means that it will be difficult for them to be more involved in EU affairs. The patchwork quilt of EC committees means that it will be difficult to co-ordinate a collective response in the future. This is apparent from meetings already of COSAC and the Conference of Presidents (the presiding officers of national parliaments): in the case of the former, there is the problem of selecting members who are representative of their committee and parliament, and in the case of the latter impartial presiding officers (notably those of the two Houses of the British Parliament) are thrown together with political figures who occupy leadership roles.

Constitutional and procedural variables combine, then, to limit the capacity of national parliaments to have a significant impact on EU affairs. There are then the variables that render some parliaments unwilling to be centrally involved.

Ideological

The ideological constraint refers to the position taken on the issue of European integration. In the case of many parliaments, there is a commitment to the principle of European integration and hence a recognition that the supranational level is the appropriate one for the formulation, debate and enactment of European law. The commitment to European integration has been shown by *Eurobarometer* survey data to exist at mass level in most Member States. This commitment has been reflected most notably at elite level in the stances taken by government and parliaments.

The commitment was apparent in the stance taken by the original Member States. That commitment remains strong in countries such as the Netherlands. As Rinus Van Schendelen notes in his paper, the emphasis there is very much on supranationalism. This view found expression in the Dutch proposals for European Political Union in 1991 and was also reflected in the stance taken by Dutch parliamentarians towards the Rome *Assises*. They took the view that the matters discussed were properly within the remit of the EP and not of national parliaments. It is a view shared by some of the more recent recruits to the EU, not least Spain and Portugal. As Carlos Closa observes in his paper, this ideological dimension has resulted in an absence of preoccupation with European affairs in the Cortes. It was, as he records, the only parliament that made no submission to the *Assises*.

Culture

Some observers place what I have termed the ideological limitation under the heading of culture. Where both parties take a similar view of European integration, then the issue ceases to be politically salient. There is therefore no incentive to focus on 'European' issues. This is reinforced in the case of Italy by the fact that the EU has little patronage effect and by a willingness to look to other institutions to do the jobs that national institutions have proved incapable of doing. There may also be a culture of parliamentary quiescence. In Ireland, as Eunan O'Halpin has shown, this culture is well established. There, the absence of a strong tradition of scrutiny and challenge of the domestic executive lends itself to a distinctly casual and unquestioning attitude towards European institutions.

However, by culture I refer also to what may be termed a culture of mistrust between national parliaments and the EP. Even though there may be a commitment at the ideological level to European integration, there may be a more specific hesitancy about the role to be played by the EP and by MEPs. Members of national parliaments have variously displayed a territorial instinct in their dealing with the EP and with MEPs. This might be explicable, even predictable, in the case of the UK Parliament given the longevity of the institution and the UK's ambivalent attitude at times towards European integration. However, it is to be found also in a number of parliaments with an ideological commitment to integration. A survey of 72 out of 81 German MEPs in 1987–88 found that almost half of them felt that Bundestag MPs had very little interest in contacts with them. Three-quarters of the MEPs believed that their relationship with national MPs was strained by feelings of rivalry on the part of the Bundestag MPs.[9]

This culture of mistrust may also be inferred from the unwillingness of national parliaments to integrate MEPs fully into their procedures. Even the most integrationist are generally unwilling or unable (by virtue of their rules) to go beyond conferring limited powers to attend and speak. Others, such as the Danish Foketing, accord MEPs no formal role at all in parliamentary deliberations. And, though the number of meetings between committees of national parliaments and the European Parliament has increased in number, the number remains small in absolute terms and few committees of national parliaments have shown much enthusiasm for regular or institutionalised contact. Even in the Spanish Cortes, with a strong ideological commitment to European integration, the relationship between the *Comisión Mixta* and the EP is best described as limited. Contact between Dutch MPs and MEPs has, as Rinus Van Schendelen notes, become 'scarce and exceptional'.

There is also some evidence to suggest that MEPs, for their part, dislike the fact that members of the national parliament still tend to attract more attention from constituents and the mass media than they do. This is brought out in the case of Ireland by Eunan O'Halpin's paper. A similar feature is notable in the United Kingdom. MEPs may therefore bear some resentment at the fact that they are members of a body with increasing political powers, but receive little acknowledgement of their growing role within a national context. The relationship has been well summed up by Dinan: 'National MPs generally resent their European counterparts' lifestyles and posturing, and MEPs resent not being taken seriously by their national counterparts. Restoring the dual mandate is neither practical nor desirable, but closer contacts between MPs and MEPs are urgently needed'.[10]

CONCLUSIONS

What conclusions can be drawn? Clearly, power has passed from national institutions to the institutions of the EU. That is a consequence of membership and has been exacerbated by the provisions of the Single European Act and the Maastricht Treaty. As policy-making power has passed to Brussels, so those seeking to influence policy outcomes have shifted their attention there as well. There are a mass of committees – over 1,000 in the orbit of the Commission – to serve as the focus for their activities.[11] Since the 1985 White Paper, lobbying of European-level institutions has become big business.[12] The Commission estimates that there are 5,000 permanent lobbyists in Brussels.[13] Of passes issued each day to individual visitors to the EP, it is estimated that about three-quarters go to lobbyists.[14] Many other organisations without representatives in Brussels also seek to influence policy, including through MEPs.

National parliaments have been left behind in the rush. They have no formal role in the process of policy making, other than indirectly through national governments or in a sporadic and advisory form through the Conference of Parliaments. Attempts to develop the means of exerting indirect influence – or even direct influence through links with the EP – have been limited, bearing relatively little reward for the effort expended. Many European committees have had difficulty coping with the burden of EC documents and some have fallen foul of demarcation disputes between committees.

There has thus been a major shift of political power upwards to the institutions of the European Union. That shift has not been matched by a shift in democratic accountability, either at the level of the EP or through national parliaments. The EP has increased its powers enormously, but could be described as still only on the edge of constituting a legislature. Furthermore, it is still not clear that popular perceptions of its role accord with the increase in power. In some countries, such as Ireland and the United Kingdom, service in the EP is still seen as secondary to service in the national legislature. Though there are signs of some shift in the other direction (UK Parliament to EP, rather than vice versa) the fact that service in the national parliament is the principal route to ministerial office may serve to deter seeking election instead to the EP where, in Martin Westlake's words, the 'only way up is out'.[15] Despite a commitment to the principle of integration, there is a perception of 'Brussels' as distant, with little popular involvement in elections to the European Parliament. In terms of voter turnout, national parliaments can still claim a greater popular mandate.

Until popular perceptions change and the EP acquires the status it seeks, the democratic deficit not only will remain but may, given the events surrounding and subsequent to debate on the Maastricht Treaty, become more – rather than less – pronounced. If national parliaments are to contribute to remedying the deficit – and, for reasons already discussed, that remains a very big and much contested if – then it is far from clear what they can do in order to achieve that. They lack any formal role in the process and there is no obvious means by which they can achieve that role, even if they want to. Both the EP and national parliaments recognise the need to co-operate with one another, but remain wary of the motives of the other.

The 1996 IGC has the task of reviewing the institutional framework of the Union. One of its biggest challenges wil be to address the democratic deficit. What is clear from our review is that its task will be far harder, and certainly more demanding, than some observers believe it to be. It has to square a circle that may not be amenable to such manipulation.

NOTES

1. Some sections of this conclusion draw substantially on, and develop, P. Norton, 'National Parliaments and the European Union', *Talking Politics*, 7, 3 (Spring 1995), pp.168–73.
2. K. Neunreither, 'The Democratic Deficit of the European Union: Towards Closer Cooperation between the European Parliament and the National Parliaments', *Government and Opposition* 29, 3 (1994), pp.299–300.
3. M. Heseltine, *The Challenge of Europe: Can Britain Win?* (London: Weidenfeld and Nicolson, 1989), p.35.
4. L. Brittan, *Europe: The Europe We Need* (London: Hamish Hamilton, 1994), p.226. See also L. Brittan, 'Making Law in the European Union', *The Journal of Legislative Studies*, 1, 1 (Spring 1995), pp.23–5.
5. W. David, 'Foundations for an Open Union', *The House Magazine*, 24 April 1995, p.6.
6. K. Hänsch, 'Europe's Parallel Parliaments', *The House Magazine*, 22 May 1995, p.19.
7. *The Times*, 29 March 1995.
8. See J. Garrett, *Westminster: Does Parliament Work?* (London: Victor Gollancz, 1992), p.220.
9. Survey by Hrbek and Schweitzer, cited in T. Saalfeld, 'Previous Research on the Bundestag and its Links with the EC', note prepared for the Research Group on National Parliaments and the European Union, Centre for Legislative Studies, University of Hull, 1993.
10. D. Dinan, *Ever Closer Union?* (London: Macmillan, 1994), p.290.
11. G.J. Buitendijk and M.P.C.M. Van Schendelen, 'Brussels Advisory Committees: A Channel for Influence?', *European Law Review* 20, 1 (Feb. 1995), pp.37–56.
12. See, e.g. S.P. Mazey and J.J. Richardson, 'British Pressure Groups in the European Community: The Challenge of Brussels', *Parliamentary Affairs* 45, 1 (Jan. 1992), pp.92–107, and S.P. Mazey and J.J. Richardson (eds.), *Lobbying in the European Community* (Oxford: Oxford University Press, 1993).
13. G. Ford, 'Racism stays on Europe's Agenda', *The House Magazine*, 10 April 1995, p.5.
14. F. Jacobs and R. Corbett, *The European Parliament* (Harlow: Longman, 1990), p.235.
15. M. Westlake, *Britain's Emerging Euro-Elite?* (Aldershot: Dartmouth, 1994), p.6. And, as the author goes on to note, 'the Maastricht Treaty's provisions will not change this stark fact'.

Index